The New Local Government Series
No. 18

———◆———

LOCAL GOVERNMENT IN BRITAIN AND FRANCE

The New Local Government Series
Series Editor: Professor Peter G. Richards

LOCAL GOVERNMENT IN BRITAIN AND FRANCE

Problems and Prospects

Edited by

JACQUES LAGROYE
Institut d'Etudes Politiques, Bordeaux

and

VINCENT WRIGHT
Nuffield College, Oxford

London
GEORGE ALLEN & UNWIN
Boston   Sydney

First published in 1979

GEORGE ALLEN & UNWIN LTD
40 Museum Street, London WC1A 1LU

© George Allen & Unwin (Publishers) Ltd. 1979

British Library Cataloguing in Publication Data

Local government in Britain and France. – (The new
local government series; no. 18).
1. Local government – Great Britain 2. Local
government – France
I. Lagroye, Jacques II. Wright. Vincent
III. Series
352.041   JS3095   78-41236

ISBN 0-04-352081-2

Typeset in 10 on 11 point Times by Watford Typesetters
and printed in Great Britain
by Billing & Sons Limited, Guildford. London and Worcester

PREFACE

The present volume of essays on the problems and prospects of local government in Britain and France is the work of a group of scholars from both sides of the Channel, representing a wide spread of universities. The group first met at the Institut d'Etudes Politiques in Bordeaux in May 1975 when the subjects were chosen, and met again in Paris in April 1977 when the papers were completed.

The choice of subjects was not easy: the real problem was not what to include but what to exclude. After some debate, it was decided to deal with the following subjects:

(1) *a descriptive account of the emergence of the present systems;*
(2) *the impact of change on traditional institutions;*
(3) *local elites;*
(4) *the attempts to order urban change;*
(5) *local finance;*
(6) *the problem of decentralisation and devolution.*

The group was fully aware of the gaps involving important areas of local government. These gaps include:

(*a*) *the outputs of local government* which are touched upon in several essays but nowhere comprehensively analysed. An analysis of the social, economic and cultural policies of local authorities would have been interesting, especially as it might throw light on the question of local autonomy;

(*b*) *the growing problem of participation* at local level is alluded to in several places but is not a topic of separate study;

(*c*) *the place and power of pressure groups at local level*, a subject which is now just being explored. In France, for example, recent studies of towns such as Poitiers, Caen, Le Havre, Grenoble, Rennes and Bordeaux have added greatly to our knowledge of the nature of social and economic forces in local decision making;

(*d*) *the optique Marxiste* – the Marxist approach to the study of local power which has been so influential in France. This is regrettable, but the problems of finding a common approach were already formidable. Readers will note, however, that many of the French contributions are imbued with Marxist assumptions and marked by Marxist terminology;

(*e*) *the problems of the capital cities* are not dealt with, but it was felt that they were so vast and so complex that they warranted a separate study.

The aim of the authors was not to present the fruit of common research, or even to write research papers. Rather they wished to present essays which were general in scope and which would incorporate recent research. Readers will find no neat uniformity in these essays, either in content or in approach. But the editors felt that imposing rigid limits on the discretion of the authors would have been artificial and would have hidden the revealing fact that different approaches to apparently similar subjects betray the differing preoccupations and priorities of France and Britain.

The editors would like to thank the Franco-British Council, the Social Science Research Council and the Centre National de la Recherche Scientifique for their financial aid, and Professors Monica Charlot, Jack Hayward and Albert Mabileau for their assistance and encouragement. Finally they would like to express their gratitude to Connie Ostmann who translated the French papers into English.

CONTENTS

LIST OF CONTRIBUTORS

Birnbaum, P.	University of Paris I
Cathelineau, J.	University of Limoges
Croisat, M.	*Institut d'Etudes Politiques*, Grenoble
Goldsmith, M.	University of Salford
Jones, G. W.	London School of Economics
Lagroye, J.	*Institut d'Etudes Politiques*, Bordeaux
Machin, H.	London School of Economics
Newton, K.	Nuffield College, Oxford
Rhodes, R. A. W.	University of Strathclyde
Sharpe, L. J.	Nuffield College, Oxford
Sorbets, C.	*Centre d'Etude et de Recherche sur la Vie Locale*, Bordeaux
Souchon, M.-F.	*Institut d'Etudes Politiques*, Grenoble
Stanyer, J.	University of Exeter
Thoenig, J.-C.	*Centre d'Etude et de Recherche sur la Vie Locale*, Bordeaux
Wright, V.	Nuffield College, Oxford

1. Service provision.
2. Eases overload of c.g.
3. Scapegoat
4. Urbanisatⁿ
5. Nationalism
6. Centralisatⁿ

Democracy
1. Rep/ness
2. Officials v bureaucrats (part/n).
3. Internal dem. (part/n).
4. Turnout.

Residual   v conceded domain.

French - Centralized - but can resist
reforms far more effectively than
GB is it able to.

Chapter I

INTRODUCTION: LOCAL GOVERNMENT IN BRITAIN AND IN FRANCE – THE PROBLEMS OF COMPARISONS AND CONTRASTS

How valid are comparisons between the local government systems of Britain and France? And how useful is it to compare them? Without raising the general questions involved in comparative political and institutional analysis it might be considered on the basis of the following essays that, in spite of the enormous difficulties involved, it is useful to compare the two systems of local government, since even a comparison illuminates aspects of each system. After all, it is interesting to know not only what a system is, but also what it is not, and why it is not.

Several areas of valid comparison spring to mind. The first relates to the basic functions which are performed by both systems. Both are the providers of services, either directly or indirectly. In the direct provision of services the local authorities of both countries are democratic agencies for the ordering of local priorities and the implementation of local demands. Both are essential mechanisms for relieving overloaded central government of some of the many services it is expected to provide, and help to legitimise decisions made at central level. In both countries, it should be noted, central governments heap mandatory services upon local government which is then pilloried for financial profligacy when it raises and spends the money necessary to carry them out. The local government systems in both countries are massive spenders: in Britain, for example, between 1962 and 1974, local government expenditure rose from 9·2 per cent to 12·4 per cent of the gross domestic product. Both systems also act as the recruiting agencies for the local political elites (and in the case of France for the national political elite) and both serve to sensitise central government to local exigences. In short, both are, in principle, agencies for the efficient and democratic provision of services.

The second area of valid comparison lies in the pressures and problems confronting both systems. Both have been put under severe strain as the result of sweeping demographical changes, population mobility and occupational upheavals. France, in particular, has undergone almost revolutionary changes in those respects. It should be noted, however, that whilst Britain has been concerned in the last generation with the experience of *suburbanisation* (the city spread and decaying city centres), France has had to come to grips with the problem of rapid *urbanisation* (with the unprecedented move from rural to urban areas), and only recently has suburbanisation emerged as a major problem. Both countries, however, have been forced to think about the rational use of geographical space.

Another major problem of the systems in both countries is provided by the nationalists or neo-nationalists. The movements in Scotland and Wales have their counterparts in Brittany, Corsica and, to a lesser extent, in the Basque country. In Britain and France nationalist protest mingles complaints about economic deprivation and cultural impoverishment with demands for greater self-expression and participation. In Britain the nationalist challenge has taken an electoral form, and the Scottish Nationalist Party now represents a major political force. In France, on the other hand, nationalist movements are a minority phenomenon, small, elitist, frustrated and frequently violent. The responses of central government to the nationalist challenge have differed considerably; Westminster is poised to concede important powers to Scotland and Wales whilst Paris has indulged in timorous regionalism.

The erosion of autonomy is the third major problem facing local government in both countries. The impact of successive wars and increasing State interventionism, the growth of national planning objectives and agencies, and the secular egalitarian trend involving apparently insatiable – and costly – demands for minimum standards in housing, health, education and other welfare services are amongst the many pressures pushing in a centralist direction. The imposition of minimum standards has led to widespread fears that the control of central government over local government will grow even tighter. Certainly that control is real, and is manifested in the flood of circulars and advice that inundates the offices of local authorities. Central control takes many forms – political, technical and financial. It is the latter which causes most resentment, since local government dependence is more than evident: in Britain, for instance, grant now finances two-thirds of local government fund expenditure. The autonomy of local government is threatened in another direction. In both countries local elections are becoming increasingly sensitive to national political trends: they are used to pass judgement on – or rather to express dissatisfaction with – the party or coalition in office. Local elites, often with distinguished records, are rejected not because of their own performance but because of that of their national leaders. This has been translated at a local level in Britain by political upheavals and in France by the steadily mounting supremacy of the Left. For a number of reasons, therefore, observers have pointed with alarm to the process of the increasing 'nationalisation' of local government in France and its 'delocalisation' in Britain.

Another major problem facing both local government systems concerns their efficiency – and at two levels: both in their relations with the centre and within local government structures real problems of duplication and co-ordination have emerged. The French have been obsessed with improving centre–periphery co-ordination whilst the British have been more preoccupied with internal managerial efficiency. Both have also been faced with the increasing problem of geographical rationalisation or what the French call 'harmonisation', for in both countries a tangled web of bodies of a regional and local nature has been constructed in somewhat haphazard fashion.

The final problem facing both systems is that of democracy at local level. This relates less to the low level of voting in local elections (in France turn-out is normally very high) than to three other phenonema. The first relates to the representativity of local elites, for (as the papers of Newton and Birnbaum indicate) locally elected elites are drawn disproportionately from better educated, middle-class, ageing or aged men. The second relates to the control exercised by the locally elected official over the bureaucracy. And the third involves the degree of internal democracy within the local authorities, their sensitivity to local demands and their institutional responses to the challenge of participation.

To the functions and the problems common to local government systems may be added a further point of similarity which is their obsession with the need to reform local government. In the last generation both countries have indulged in an orgy of such reform. With the help of Redcliffe-Maud, Bains and Layfield the British have peered into almost every area of local government. The results of their work are examined throughout this collection of essays. The French have been less radical than the British, and have proceeded in much more gradual and piecemeal fashion, but it is worth recording that since the foundation of the Fifth Republic they have created the twenty-two regions with their councils, rationalised administrative services within those regions, established administrative *missions* with the task of co-ordinating administrative functions in difficult policy areas, enacted various measures designed to weaken prefectoral supervision (*tutelle*) of the local authorities. They have also created new towns and have attempted by a variety of means to encourage intercommunal co-operation. Finally, they have reorganised the Paris region and profoundly modified the government of the capital itself. It is true that some of the reforms merely recognised the established practice whilst others (notably those related to the regions) were limited in intention or impact. Nevertheless, there are very few areas of local government which have not been affected.

Comparisons may, therefore, be drawn between the two systems of local government at the level of their functions, their problems and predicaments, and their indulgence in constant and often far-reaching reform. But there are differences between the two systems which are perhaps more striking and more profound than their similarities. These differences are rooted in the social environment, in the historical traditions and conventions which underpin each system, in the political and economic setting, and in the institutional arrangements of each country.

The social and economic underpinning of the British system differs considerably from that of France. Britain modernised economically long before France, and the reforms of the last twenty years have taken place within the context of a complex, urbanised and rapidly suburbanising community, in which the distinction between town and country has rapidly been losing any real meaning. Moreover, many of the problems are related to industrial and urban decline. The French, on the other hand, have been faced until the 1974 energy crisis with the consequences of a booming and dynamic economy, as well as immense demographical and occupational upheavals. The France of 1978 is barely recognisable by the observers of 1945. The traditional local government system has been confronted with an explosion of demands, the impact of urban construction and the arrival of urban elites who contest the dominance of the traditional rural elites. Amongst the other consequences of the very rapidity of the industrial and urban explosion in France has been the lack of preparation of local elites, until recently, in dealing with the power of certain groups such as the *promoteurs* – the now much disparaged property developers whose attachment to profitable destruction was always more apparent than their sensitivity to costly preservation. The result was that Gaullist Frenchmen emulated the Victorian British in destroying much of their architectural heritage.

A second major difference between the two systems lies in their geographical and historical settings. France is a far bigger country than Britain (even though its population size is roughly the same) and is characterised by sharper geographical diversity: the differences between, for instance, Lille and Marseilles or Rouen and Perpignan are far greater than between any two British cities. Greater geographical differentiation may help to explain the French obsession with the need for strong and centralised State authority, for national unity is thought to be less than secure. Two other factors feed the obsession. First, parts of France have been invaded and occupied by enemy forces no fewer than three times in the last hundred years or so – in 1870–1, 1914–18 and 1940–5. Secondly, certain areas of France are comparatively recent acquisitions: Savoy and the area around Nice were attached to France in 1860, whilst Alsace was absorbed into Germany between 1871 and 1918, and again between 1940 and 1944. Certain historians, such as Eugen Weber, even argue that France became truly united only in the last generation before the outbreak of the First World War – when 'peasants became Frenchmen'. In contrast, until very recently when the full impact of Scottish and Welsh nationalism became so sharply felt, the question of British national unity was never really posed. And whilst the endemic demands of the Corsicans, the Bretons and the Basques for greater autonomy have rarely been a really serious threat to French unity, they have always been perceived as such. Furthermore, it was always felt by French politicians that centralisation was the only means of holding together a people so prone to social, political and religious strife – what General de Gaulle called the 'perpetual effervescence' of the French. The historical experiences of the two countries have a bearing on the spheres of competence of their local authorities. It has been argued, for example, that the powers of the local authorities in Britain belong to a *residual domain* – to areas where the local authorities have managed to repulse the encroachment on their legitimate and traditional powers by a marauding and malevolent Westminster. In contrast, it is argued, the powers of French local authorities belong to a *conceded domain* – to areas traditionally belonging to Paris but resentfully transferred to the localities. From this flows an important psychological fact: in Britain, the centre has to justify any impingement upon the powers of the periphery, whereas in France the periphery has to justify to the centre any plea for increased autonomy. It might further be argued that the boldness of the British devolution proposals compared with the neurotic timidity of the French regional reforms may spring ultimately from the underlying certainty of the British about their national unity and the French uneasiness about theirs.

A third significant set of differences between the two systems relates to their institutional arrangements. The differences may be summarised as follows:

(*a*) *The number and size of local government units.* In Britain, as the result of the 1972 Act the number of local authorities was reduced from about 1,500 to 400. In France, in spite of a spate of measures to encourage the merging of communes, the number remains very high: there are still over 36,000 local government units – more than the total of all her Common Market partners. It has been calculated that at the present rate of disappearance of communes France will have as many local government units as Britain in the year 2230! It also seems certain that no radical diminution in the number will take place: the Guichard Report of 1976 advocates the maintenance of the present number, but recommends that their powers be drastically reduced, arguing that most of those powers should be transferred by 1985 to 750 urban communities and 3,600 communal communities (in the rural areas). The size of local authority units has important consequences for local autonomy, since very small units are unlikely to enjoy the same technical and financial resources as bigger units.

(*b*) *The absence in Britain of an overall supervisory role which is exercised, in France, by the prefect.* In each *département* of France there is a prefect who, aided by the local sub-prefects, enjoys the power of *tutelle* – of tutelage over the local authorities – and the duty of co-ordinating the local administrative agencies. The prefect is the physical embodiment of the State, the representative of the government as a whole and of the Ministry of the Interior in particular. He is given a vast array of functions and powers which, in principle, enables him to control the local authorities. In practice, for a number of complex reasons analysed by Howard Machin, the power of the prefect has been steadily eroded, and he is no longer (if he ever was) the undisputed master of his *département*. Yet a skilful and experienced prefect may still exert considerable influence.

(*c*) *The presence in France of a hierarchised and centralised bureaucracy, appointed in Paris,* which carries out many of the tasks that are implemented by locally appointed bureaucrats in Britain. There are, of course, in Britain field service officials (social security and employment officers are two examples) who administer central services directly, and others who have a general supervisory role over areas of local government. But they are many fewer than in France, supervise many fewer areas, and they do not belong to the powerful and centrally organised corps. In practice, many of these French bureaucrats are often enmeshed in local forces for which they become the spokesmen, but their links with and loyalties to Paris remain intact. As a corollary of the above, there is an absence in all but the biggest French towns of an extensive, educationally qualified and technically equipped and powerful local bureaucracy. The power of the locally appointed bureaucracy and of certain local bureaucrats in Britain has no equivalent in France. One of the results of this state of affairs is that the kind of managerial problems discussed in the Bains Report have not loomed large in France.

(*d*) *The absence of a powerful locally elected executive officer in Britain.* Local political leadership is rare in Britain: that exercised by Herbert Morrison in London, by Joseph Chamberlain in Birmingham or, more recently, by Dan Smith in Newcastle, provide the well-publicised exceptions. Neither the leader of the majority group in a local council nor the chairman of the Central Policy and Resources Committee in the new structures enjoys or is likely to enjoy the same power, authority and prestige of the French mayor. Most French studies emphasise his importance as the key figure in local government. He is frequently mayor for a very long time (he is elected for six years by his local council and is eligible for re-election). Many are the sons of mayors and enjoy considerable social prestige. The French mayor is the commune's troubleshooter, father-figure, priest and policeman, and as such he exerts a degree of personal leadership that is virtually unknown in British local government. His strength lies in his control over local finances, in his privileged relationship with the prefect, in his social standing, in his administrative longevity and, in some cases, in his belonging to a Paris-based political or administrative elite.

The fourth major set of differences between the two systems relates to their political arrangements and conventions. In the first place, political parties are much more powerful at the local level in Britain than in France, in spite of the sweeping gains in the March 1978 French elections by the more structured and more disciplined parties of the Left. Several consequences flow from that phenomenon. In Britain, the power of local political personalities is curbed, local authorities are perhaps better protected against the bureaucrats and certain pressure groups, a greater element of social mobility amongst the locally elected elite is ensured, and the participation of people who might not otherwise be tempted by local office is encouraged. Those who decry the role of the parties in British local politics could do well to ponder on the democratic support they give to the system.

The existence in France of the phenomenon of *cumul des mandats* – the accumulation of offices – is a good example of the different political conventions of Britain and France. In Britain, very few national politicians hold local office. In France, however, such practice is common. President Giscard d'Estaing is still a local councillor at Chamalières, a wealthy suburb of Clermont-Ferrand. Since the foundation of the Fifth Republic, of the six predecessors of Barre as Prime Minister, five held local office either as mayor or as members of a town or departmental council. All Deputies are *ex officio* members of a regional council, and a large majority are mayors. The interpenetration of national and local elites in France has important consequences for the functioning of the local government system. It completely distorts the relationship between officials who, in theory, are empowered to control local authorities and certain local office holders who enjoy national notoriety and position.

For instance, the theoretical relationship between a prefect and a mayor is bound to be upset if the latter happens to be the Minister of the Interior who is the hierarchical head of the prefectoral corps and the man who is responsible for prefectoral appointments, transfers and dismissals. The phenomenon of *cumul des mandats* also ensures that Paris is constantly informed about, and sensitised to, the demands of the local authorities, and thus helps to attenuate the rigours of centralisation.

A second important political convention which is present in France and absent in Britain is that top-ranking civil servants may stand for local office, often on highly partisan lists. Amongst the departmental and town councillors of France may be found representatives of the central bureaucracies, the influential ministerial private staffs (*cabinets*), the technical corps and the prestigious *grands corps* such as the Court of Accounts, the Financial Inspectorate, the Council of State and even the Diplomatic Corps. Members of the *grand corps* and the technical corps colonise the important posts of the administration, the nationalised industries, the State-owned banking and insurance sectors and the semi-public corporations. Those who hold local office not only act as brokers of local interests (they were elected to do precisely that) but also help to sensitise the State machinery to local feelings and exigencies.

The fifth major difference between the two systems involves their integrative linkages – the means and mechanisms by which local government is linked with national governments. Of course, in both countries such linkages are provided by a battery of financial regulations, by legal stipulations, by the instructions and circulars that flow in ever-increasing numbers from the capital to the provinces, and by the pressure groups which have both national and local organisations and aims. But there are differences between the two countries. Professional bodies of local bureaucrats and, as already noted, the political parties, are much more powerful in Britain than in France. In the latter country, important links are provided by the prefectoral administration, by the nationally appointed local field services, by Paris-based politicians and civil servants who hold local office, and also by influential bodies such as the *Association des Maires de France* which have constant access to key points in the administration.

The final major difference between the two systems relates to the facility with which local government structures may be reformed. There is, in fact, an interesting paradox which is explored by Jim Sharpe in his paper. Why has the powerful and highly centralised French system proved so ineffective in imposing radical reforms on the local authorities? And how has the reportedly much more decentralised British system managed to impose its far-reaching modernisation proposals on local government?

Given the dissimilarities which exist between the two systems it is easy to point to the dangers of attempting comparison. Such comparison, it should be emphasised, is rendered even more difficult by the existence of a variety of local government systems within each of the two countries. That variety results from the interplay of a large number of factors which include the legal sphere of competence of the local authorities, their size and proximity to the capital, their political relationship with the centre, their internal party structure, the personality and power of their leaders, the extent and nature of their linkages with the centre, the quality and efficiency of their locally appointed bureaucrats, their tax base and their financial dependence on the centre. There may be more in common between Lille and Manchester than between Lille and one of the many very small French communes.

Pointing out these very real difficulties of comparison should induce caution not despair. The exercise of comparison may prove fruitful if ambitions are limited, for the ultimate value of comparison lies less in the spurious generalisations it might provoke than in the intellectual curiosity that triggered off the comparison, and in the insights it might provide about the basic premises, mechanisms, functioning and ends of each of the systems compared.

Chapter II

————◆————

THE CHANGING SYSTEM OF
ENGLISH LOCAL GOVERNMENT

To understand the present English local government system, it is necessary to know something both of its nineteenth-century changes and of the normative theoretical underpinnings on which the system has been based since the early 1830s. In terms of the latter, two themes are apparent – at least implicitly if not always explicitly – in nearly all the writings about English local government, although it is still true to say, with Mackenzie,[1] that 'there *is* no theory of local government'. Rather are there many theories,[2] even though most are variations on the two themes. The first of these is simply that local government is in some sense democratic: that is, *local* government promotes democracy, be it in terms of representation, participation or some other sense.[3] Undoubtedly, the major concern here has been to reflect a commitment to *representative* democracy as an ideal, tempered occasionally by a recognition of the virtues of consultative democracy, and, more recently, even tacit acceptance that wider public participation, particularly in planning,[4] might not necessarily be considered as undesirable.

The second theme reflects a concern with efficiency. Local government can be justified as an efficient provider of public goods and services in ways which central government cannot match. Thus, it is argued that locally elected authorities will know and understand local needs and wants far better than central government and can also respond to changes in these far more effectively than could the centre. This is a theme which runs through the English local government literature in various forms from the 1835 Report on Municipal Corporations to the 1969 Redcliffe-Maud Royal Commission Report. Most of the changes in the structure of English local government can be understood in terms of these two normative theoretical criteria, the constant competition between them, and attempts to achieve a satisfactory balance between them.[5]

But we also need a theoretical framework which will allow us to interpret the changing structure of English local government. Here my perspective, like that of many other writers on urban politics, is predominantly shaped by the systems analytic perspective associated with the writings of David Easton,[6] latterly tempered by the need to accommodate some of the criticisms of the systems approach, namely, that it is a form of environmental determinism which severely limits the importance of political explanations of events, policies and outcomes.[7]

Despite these criticisms, systems analysis still provides a useful conceptual framework with which to organise thoughts about local government, and particularly in terms of the changing structure of local government. The perspective allows local government to be defined as a system residing in an environment and responding to changes in that environment. Thus the changing structure of local government can be seen as a series of *system responses* to changes in the environment, responses which are partly regime changes (e.g. the spread of partisan local government); partly authority changes (e.g. the rise of public persons as local political leaders), and partly system changes (e.g. reform in organisation and function).

But, as we shall see, these changes cannot be simply interpreted as responses to the forces of social, economic and political changes in the local government environment, for to do so is to ignore the fact that such structural changes require action which is taken by men as political animals (*homo politicus* in Dahl's terms),[8] and that these actions will be determined by the way such men perceive environmental changes and their environment. As such, changes in the structure of English local government must be seen as changes determined by perceptions of the environment and environmental changes, perceptions which depend on the political ideology,[9] dispositions,[10] or assumptive world[11] of *homo politicus,* and which adapt only slowly to the process of environmental change.

In order to understand the changing structure of English local government, the recent history of English local government will be briefly described, then an examination will be made of the major environmental and system changes in the structure before the recent reforms, and finally the process of local government reorganisation during the last twenty years will be briefly considered.

English Local Government in the Victorian Age
In many ways, the nineteenth century was the 'golden age of reform' as far as English local government is concerned. Certainly it was during Victoria's reign that local government emerged from the control of appointed Justices to the elected form which is familiar today, and during the same period, local government acquired many of the functions it has today, albeit in embryo form. Furthermore, much of the pattern of central–local government relationships today have their roots in nineteenth-century developments.

It is convenient to consider the Victorian reforms in two groups: those between 1830 and 1880, and those after the latter date. The period between 1830 and 1880 was essentially one of *innovation* and *development*: the high period of the single purpose *ad hoc* local government unit. Beginning with the Poor Law Reform of 1834, designed to deal with the problem of destitution, these reforms include the greater public health reforms of 1848 and 1875, the first town improvement act (1847), and the introduction of public education (Forster's Education Act 1870). Each Act provided for the creation of a separately elected administrative authority (e.g. Poor Law Guardians/Sanitary Districts), each able to levy their own tax to finance their activities, and each subject to control by central government in some way or other.

The exception to this general pattern of *ad hoc* measures and responses was the Municipal Corporations Act 1835, since this Act provided for the creation of (albeit limited) elected most purpose authorities – a form of restricted local self-government. Essentially a form of urban government, the Act was essentially a response to the changing political environment, following as it does on the extension of the franchise to the new urban middle classes by the Reform Act of 1832, giving the towns and cities limited responsibilities for their own government following their incorporation as municipal boroughs.[12] This pattern of responding to suffrage extension and a changing political environment was to be repeated again, as we shall see. Not for the only time either, local government reform reflected a struggle for power between urban and rural interests, this time with urban interests to the fore in Parliament with its Whig or Liberal majority.

But apart from these relatively orderly urban areas, the result of this early period of reform was almost total chaos by 1870, as boundaries, functions, taxes and elections overlapped throughout the country, so that a further period of reform was needed. This second period was to be very much one of consolidation. The early reforms, themselves partly a response to changes in political environment, were very much more a response to the great social, economic and physical changes in the nineteenth-century environment, for it was during the first half of that century that Britain (and that meant overwhelmingly England) became an *urban* nation, reflecting the changes brought about by the process of an almost totally unfettered industrial capitalism. The free market forces of the industrial revolution created industrial, urban Britain – particularly in the northern half of the country, where great cities such as Liverpool, Manchester and Leeds developed apace.

One last theme is relevant in this early period of reform, namely, the pattern of central–local relationships. Two factors, then as now, determined that the centre would seek to become involved in the affairs of the locality. First, having required that the locality undertake to provide a particular service, such as Poor Law or Public

Health, central government needed to see that such a service was provided, at least to some uniform minimum standard. Second, and almost inevitably, having required the provision of a service, it was reasonable to expect central government to finance that service at least in part, and the period between 1830 and 1880 saw a number of struggles between the local and national tax-paying roles of the citizen. As a result of these early *ad hoc* reforms, a number of central government departments were established to oversee the work of the numerous local agencies.

By 1880, however, the local government system was in chaos, ripe for reform. In particular, important changes in suffrage had taken place. The 1867 Reform Act had extended the vote to the new industrial working class, whilst the 1884 Act gave the vote to the agricultural working class. These changes in the political environment, themselves reflections of further social, economic and physical environmental changes, were to lead to further reforms in the structure of English local government. This second period of reform was essentially one of *consolidation* and established a structure of local government which, outside London, was to remain largely unchanged until the early 1970s. This time, however, it was more a victory for rural over urban interests, the early reforms being introduced by Conservative governments.

The essential pieces of legislation in this period were the Acts of 1888, 1894 and 1929. As a result of the first two, the structure of local government was unitary or single tier in the larger towns, and two or even three tier in the rest of the country. The 1888 Act created the county councils, whilst that of 1894 produced the urban and rural district councils which were to be the second tier in the county areas.[13] But as Smellie has suggested, these structural reforms were largely uninspired by any general principles, unlike their predecessors. This is why these Acts should be interpreted as a consolidation, as Conservative legislation designed to protect the rural areas against further intrusions by the towns, and lastly as an attempt to introduce some vestige of local self-government along the lines suggested by John Stuart Mill. As such, the system would only cope with piecemeal alterations, even though it was intended to be flexible, and no real attempt at a general reorganisation was made until 1929.

Yet the system did reflect the political, social and economic realities of the late nineteenth century. At that time, it was still meaningful to distinguish between town and country, and it was created before it was possible to foresee the many stresses and strains that twentieth-century strains would bring; the 1888 local government system was created before the invention of the motor car; the introduction of universal suffrage in Britain (1928), and the creation of the welfare state and the rise of a social democratic party essentially concerned with representing (at least organised) working-class interests. Yet the 1888 system was to survive all these changes, remaining largely unchanged until the early 1970s.

Some idea of the rapid changes which overtook the new local government system shortly after its introduction and before its main revisions in 1929 can be seen from the following data. The population of England and Wales rose from 29 million in 1891 to 38 million by 1921, and this increase was essentially an urban one. Furthermore, the movement of population from the rural to urban areas continued, as the urban percentage of the population rose from 57 per cent in 1891 to 67 per cent in 1921. Unknown at the time of the 1888 Act, there were over a million road vehicles licensed by 1930. Also unknown in 1888 was the Labour Party: by 1929 it was in its second period of office, and its concern with social welfare was beginning to make itself felt, perhaps more strongly in the housing and planning fields.

However, the reforms involved in the 1929 Local Government Act were brought about not so much by these changes as by a crisis in another area, namely, the finance of local government. The 1888 Act had attempted a separation between local and national finance, but the ever-increasing scope of local government activity in the twentieth century ensured that such a separation could not be achieved.[14] Central government found it necessary to give ever-increasing grants to finance the new services, whilst on the other hand, local authorities found that local taxes (rates) provided an ever-diminishing part of the revenue they required. Financial reforms were necessary to achieve three objectives: to meet part of the cost of the new and expanding services provided by local government; to enable the centre to supervise services expected to reach a certain minimum standard everywhere; and to correct inequalities in the burden of local taxes between different individuals and areas. To a certain extent, it was felt at the time that all these goals could be achieved by replacing the many individual grants in aid by a block grant, and by the exclusion of agricultural and industrial land from local taxes.[15] This the 1929 Act sought to achieve, together with some general tidying up of functions. As a result, however, the new grants generally increased the already apparent tendency for the central departments to exercise a general control over the work of local government.

Between 1929 and 1972, there were innumerable Acts of Parliament which, together with government committees, boundary commissioners and even Royal Commissions,[16] sought to ensure that the structure of local government could continue both to cope with the problems with which it was faced, as well as providing the various services required and demanded of it. Examples of important legislation include the Education Act of 1944; the Town and Country Planning Act of 1947, as well as the many Housing Acts. All of these increased the scope of local government activity considerably, whilst by contrast, the nationalisation legislation for gas and electricity and the introduction of the National Health Service in 1947 took functions away from local government. The basis of local government finance was also altered from time to time by such Acts as the Local Government Act of 1958, all of which generally increased the central contribution towards the cost of local services.[17] All of this legislation took effect with no fundamental review and change in the organisational and areal basis of local government until the late 1960s and early 1970s.

Nevertheless, local government underwent a number of important changes during this time, changes which fundamentally altered its nature and operation. It is to an examination of these that we now turn, for an understanding of them is essential to an understanding of why reform of local government was not only necessary, but possible.

Put succinctly, what has happened to English local government since 1888 is that it has become *delocalised*. In other words, a number of changes have posed problems for the structure of local *self*-government laid down by the 1888 Act, causing adaptations which have fundamentally shifted the emphasis away from democratic criteria and the locality, towards efficiency ones and the centre. These changes have been both national and local, as well as reflecting political, social and economic changes in the country.

It is convenient analytically to distinguish each of these categories of change and to consider them separately. One might want to argue that each has been sufficient in itself to have called into question the validity of the old structure: taken collectively, the ability with which that structure coped with the demands placed upon it and its ability to last as long as it did remains amazing.

Environmental changes
The old 1888 system's major premise was that town and country were separate and required a separate structure to deal with the differing problems they faced. Since then, the process of continuing urbanisation and industrialisation has made that separation meaningless as the process of increasing social and economic interdependence overwhelmed the existing local boundaries. Despite governmental attempts at containing urban England, nothing could stop the process of suburbanisation and the flight of industry out of the city.

We can gain some idea of the scale of these changes by referring again to some of the indicators referred to earlier. For example, population has continued to grow, reaching 60 million by the early 1970s. But the important factor here has been the increase in the urban proportions (now 77 per cent) of the population, particularly in towns betwen 50,000 and 200,000 people. In 1901 there were 61 of these, housing 22 per cent of the population. By 1961 the figures were 162 and 38 per cent respectively. Forty per cent of the population live in the six major metropolitan areas, though this proportion continues to decline as people continue to leave the major cities.

Car ownership had reached 12 million by 1970, compared with the 1 million of 1930. Owner occupation reached over 50 per cent in the early 1970s, whilst the supply of privately rented accommodation had dwindled to some 15 per cent: as a consequence the rental market is supplied by municipal housing, with over a third of the total housing stock falling into this category.

Changes such as these, many common to most of the developed countries, have brought considerable change to the environment to which local government must adapt. There were industrial changes as well: the motor industry provides a good example of the way in which heavy industry has located itself away from the city centre, with Ford at Dagenham and Halewood, British Leyland at Longbridge and Leyland, and Vauxhall at Luton and Ellesmere Port all providing examples. The development of the car and the subsequent spread of car ownership has meant that long-distance commuting (up to 30 miles each way) is relatively common around most cities outside London, whilst the development of suburban rail and underground services around the latter has meant commuting journeys of up to 50 miles and more. This has given rise to what Pahl has called 'a dispersed city' around London: between 1951 and 1971 the outer metropolitan area of London has grown from 3,500,000 to 5,300,000.[18]

One of the most important consequences of the growth of the dispersed city has been the impact of the old core cities, which generally have lost population and jobs. For example, Liverpool lost almost a quarter of its population between 1951 and 1971, many of them the younger and more skilled members. The much higher proportions of the semi-skilled and unskilled, of the elderly and of those who, for whatever reasons, are unable to leave the inner city, mean that the old core cities face a much higher demand for services, but also have a lower tax base on which to finance such services.

All of these changes, some of them aggravated by the public policies adopted by central and local governments, placed considerable pressure upon the structure of English local government to adapt.[19] Ultimately, of course, the pressure was such that the system changes associated with the 1972 Local Government Act became necessary. A system of local government devised to distinguish town and country and treat their problems separately would no longer cope with the industrial and residential changes associated with suburbanisation: decline of the city centre and pressure at the suburban fringe meant a new structure of local government was necessary to handle the problems of the post-industrial society.

Political changes

The socio-economic environmental changes described in the preceding section brought with them a number of political changes, that is to say, changes in the process of local politics. Despite their interdependence, it is convenient to consider these changes in terms of those which are essentially local in nature and those which operate in a national context.

The twentieth century has seen three important changes in the nature of local politics. First, there has been the extension of *formal party* politics into local government. As Bulpitt and a number of urban historians have shown,[20] party politics has certainly been present in English local government since at least the 1830s. Liberals and Conservatives often fought bitter contests at local elections,[21] particularly in urban areas, even if the number of contests in any one year were limited.[22] What has happened in the twentieth century is that a *working class* based (or at least orientated) party has emerged to challenge the domination of the other middle class orientated parties. This challenge was particularly successful in the urban industrial areas,[23] even though the success was often a long time coming in many parts of the country. Thus, despite the Labour Party's appeal to the working class in the 1920s and 1930s, rearguard actions by (Conservative-dominated) anti-socialist coalitions often kept Labour out of power for longer than might have been expected.[24] Nevertheless, by 1945 Labour had become the natural majority party in the cities and towns, as well as beginning to challenge (ineffectively) in the more rural parts of the country.

The rise of the Labour Party brought with it two important changes. First, it widened the spectrum of local debate, because of its emphasis on a wider provision of services than its opponents: municipal socialism meant interpreting council housing as a social service and a basic human right rather than as something for those in need. In other words, Labour widened the scope of local government, as a result of which it was to acquire many new functions, such as town and country planning, which would previously not have been seen as legitimately within the purview of local authorities.

Second, Labour changed the rules of the party game by its emphasis on a campaign programme, its introduction of the pre-council caucus meeting, and its sense of party discipline. As Bulpitt has shown, there is little uniformity in party politics in English local government, which run from rigid one-party states to loose multi-party ones. Nevertheless, one of the consequences of these Labour-associated changes was to force similar changes on the other parties, so that Conservative and Liberal local parties now have their own caucus meetings, select as candidates people who by and large have some *party* connection, fight local elections on a programmatic basis, and expect their representatives to support the party line.[25]

The rise of party in local government has produced another associated change, namely, in the nature of political leadership. Gone are the 'fit and proper persons', the urban squirearchy, the social leaders who dominated town and country government in the nineteenth century. No longer is social, economic and political power concentrated in the hands of an economic elite. As authors such as Lee and Jones have shown,[26] their place has been taken by public or party persons, that is to say, by people whose position in the political and social hierarchy of the community depends ultimately on their political skills and particularly on their party status and label. Now, more than ever, a candidate needs a *party* label to be elected at local elections, and truly independent elected members are becoming increasingly a rare breed.

As a consequence of the rise of the party man, there has also been a change in the way formal political leaders perceive the changes, issues and policies with which they deal. As Dearlove has shown,[27] the ideology of the local councillor is an important determinant of the kinds of policies he will favour or the way in which he perceives problems. The rise of party men has meant that party ideology has tended to become much more important as a determinant of policies: Labour councils will not sell council houses, for example, and Conservative ones are reluctant to create their own construction services.[28]

One important facet of this change has been the emergence of local political leaders who as leaders of their party or as major committee chairmen occupy influential positions in the formal local decision-making arena. Such men often have long records of unbroken municipal service, and often have local knowledge and expertise at least equal to that of their professional officers. Such men, however, depend on their party position and the continuing support of the electorate if they are to retain their influence. As both local government reorganisation and recent elections have shown, however, neither can be taken for granted.[29]

The third and in some ways most important change in twentieth-century English local government has been the emergence of the professional officer as an important factor in local politics. Given the social and economic changes discussed above, inevitably local government has become more and more complex, and (equally inevitably, given the part-time nature of elected members)[30] thus there has been an increasing need for professional expert advice to help provide solutions and policies. As examples of the rise of professionalism in English local government in the twentieth century we might simply note the emergence of such occupations as planner, social worker and housing manager, as well as the change from public to environmental health inspector. Each of these professionals is expected to obtain the qualification of his professional association, without which job, salary or promotion prospects are exceedingly limited.

The result, as people like Lee, Dennis and Davies have shown,[31] is that these professionals have risen to positions of enormous influence, if not dominance, in the local decision-making arena. Their position is one which many councillors find it difficult to challenge. Councillors argue that the expertise is expensive to hire, so that they must trust the advice they are given by their officials, or alternatively, if they had the same expertise as their officials, the latter would not be needed.[32] Alternatively, it may be argued that since the officials largely control the information on which decisions are based, councillors are unable to challenge officials' policy recommendations.

These professionals are very much specialists in their area of activity, rather than generalists as are their Whitehall counterparts, and as such their perceptions of change, their ideology in Dearlove's sense, is very much determined by the standards of their profession: such service areas as education and planning provide good examples. But, as Davies and others[33] have argued, for the planning field, such a professional ideology may well be little more than a facade beyond which middle-class values consciously or unconsciously predominate and in which the political consequences (in the distributive sense) of their proposals are largely ignored.[34]

All of these sets of changes, which were categorised at the outset as being of essentially local nature, are local only in their impact. The changes themselves have contributed considerably to what might be called the *delocalisation* of local government: it is in this sense that they are interdependent with the national changes. The strong involvement of national parties in *local* politics clearly has a *national* dimension,[35] which is clearly seen by local electors. Now more than ever, local electors use local elections as a means of passing judgement on the performance of parties at Westminster and in Whitehall, and national politicians use local election results as indicators of likely general/national election outcomes.

Similarly, the fact that local political leaders are likely to be *party* men means that they will use their position to implement the local dimensions of their party's national policies: the sale or non-sale of council houses is a good example. Many local leaders may be prominent within the ranks of the national party, even if they have no ambitions to rise further up the political ladder. In this way, national and local politics become entwined, and local politics become delocalised.

But local government has also been delocalised by the rise of the professional official with his ties with a national professional institution. The professional institutes are often very important influences on the form and content of legislation and its implementation: planning again provides a very good example with the 1968 Town and Country Planning Act.[36] Nevertheless, this remains an area about which little is known. Similarly the world of the local authority associations is under-researched. These *national* associations, such as the Association of County Councils and the Association of Municipal Corporations, have tremendous influence on all legislation affecting the work of local authorities; twenty years ago, one local government minister described them as 'part of the constitution of the country', and there is no evidence to suggest their influence has declined. In their own way, these *national* representatives of local authority interests have all contributed to the delocalisation of local government in England.

There have also been changes taking place at national level which have affected the structure of English local government. Twentieth-century British politics has been characterised by a massive centralisation of governmental and political activity focused on Whitehall and Westminster. In large part this centralisation has reflected the greatly increased scope of governmental activity with the growth of the welfare state since its inception in 1908.[37] These changes have had two consequences for the operation of local government. First, given the extended range of governmental activity, central government has been increasingly concerned with overseeing the work of local authorities, who are generally expected to provide the services reaching certain minimum standards. Second, the increased activity has greatly increased the extent of central government finance for local authorities. Just as it would have been unreasonable for central government to expect local authorities to finance these extra services out of local revenues, so it would have been unreasonable for local authorities not to expect central government to increase its oversight of the locality if it was responsible for providing the finance. But the growth of public sector expenditure (particularly the local authority part of it) and the increasing responsibility of government for the state of the national economy inevitably also meant increased central involvement in the affairs of the locality. Failure to control public sector economic activity is likely to have dire consequences for economic management generally, as recent British experiences will testify.

Constitutionally, as would be expected in a unitary system, local authorities are subordinate to central government, the relationship determined by the doctrine of *ultra vires* under which everything a local authority does must be permitted by Act of Parliament. Nevertheless, given the close involvement between the centre and the locality, it is important to realise that, as Griffith has noted[38] ultimately the relationship is one between two sets of permanent, salaried officials, each of whom has a different outlook or perspective on his role. We have already commented upon the professional, expert, specialist nature of the local bureaucracy. By contrast, that of the centre has remained generalist and amateur. Despite attempts to produce a change in the character of the Whitehall bureaucracy, professionals remain of secondary importance and status, and the top British civil servants continue to be largely general administrators.[39]

As a consequence, both groups of administrators are likely to bring different perspectives, ideology and assumptions to the policy-making process and to the relationship between centre and the locality. Again this remains a largely under-researched area, but clearly it is a relationship which has extensively influenced the organisation and structure of English local government.

This administrative relationship may be of prime importance, but that between politicians cannot pass without comment, if only because of the increasing importance of local elections as a *national* phenomenon. This has become more important since reorganisation. The enlarged metropolitan counties and districts, as well as the shire counties, represent important political prizes for the national parties, and they can each count on a number of MPs at Westminster to press their case.[40]

These kinds of national political changes have been part of the whole centralisation process in British politics referred to earlier. As a consequence, the centre became particularly involved in questions of local detail. Central government also felt the need to change the system of English local government, and by the end of the 1960s the environmental and political changes outlined above had created sufficient pressure to bring about systematic change. It is to the recent reform of the structure of English local government that we now turn in the concluding section of this essay.

Since the process of reform in England is both relatively recent and well documented elsewhere in this book,[41] only a brief summary of the story is presented here. At the outset, a number of general points may be made. First, the process of local government reform is a lengthy one: twenty years elapsed in Britain between the creation of the Royal Commission in London to the implementation of reform in Scotland in 1975.[42] Second, the idea of reform is itself unusual: most countries have systems of local government more appropriate to a rural society rather than an urban one. Third, the barriers to extensive or radical reform are considerable: for some, the British reforms may be considered only moderate, yet they are radical when compared with reform elsewhere.

Reform in Britain, as Jim Sharpe emphasises in his chapter,[43] was possible only because all the interested parties considered it necessary. In other words, the environmental and political changes discussed above were perceived as inevitably leading to a change in the structure of local government if the problems the changes had led to were to be tackled. That change was necessary was evidenced by the Royal Commission (Redcliffe-Maud) Report of 1969[44] whose criticisms are examined elsewhere in this book.

It is not necessary here to detail the changes made by successive governments to the Commission's original proposals.[45] Suffice it to say that the Labour government by and large favoured the original unitary proposals. This was to be expected, since they more closely approximated to what the main government departments wanted and were more favourable politically to the Labour Party. By contrast, the Conservative Party, not unnaturally, preferred to follow the advice of the many opponents of the Commission and Labour government's proposals, eventually producing the two-tier system, which respected old boundaries more faithfully and also tightly enclosed the new metropolitan areas. In this way, the Conservatives could preserve their rural/suburban political power base whilst claiming to produce a system which not only more accurately reflected what public opinion appeared to want, but also appeared to make the new system more democratic without (apparently) causing a considerable reduction in efficiency.

As a result, the new system for England and Wales which came into operation in 1974 contained more units (400+) of local government than originally proposed by Redcliffe-Maud (81), but in itself was a considerable reduction on the number previously in existence (1,500+).[46] Nevertheless, there is at least one important difference between the system as it operates in the shire counties and as it works in the metropolitan areas, reflecting the division of functions between the two tiers. Basically, the shire counties resemble strong federal systems, with the upper tier being politically and functionally the stronger. By contrast, the metropolitan areas approximate to weak federal systems, with the lower tier being more powerful. This reflects the experience of London, the Conservative government of 1972 reproducing its 1963 solution for London's government when it came to finding a solution for the country's other urban areas. If the experience of other countries is any guide,[47] then further reform is likely to be necessary within the not too distant future.

Having said that, it is still too early to provide a real assessment of the new system, which at the time of writing has only just experienced the second round of elections. Suffice it to say that there have been a number of calls for further reform, which after initially meeting stern opposition from the central government in the form of the Department of the Environment, have recently been receiving limited support in that direction. The whole question of local government finance has been examined by the Layfield Committee,[48] whose recommendations are analysed below by George Jones. By far the most important change has been brought about by the depressed state of the economy, where successive cutbacks in public expenditure are now leading to both reductions in the level of local service provision and redundancy amongst local authority staff. The new system was created to deal with the pressures of growth: it faces its severest test at present by the fact that declining population and industrial activity are the reality, though not for all authorities.[49]

Two other changes, however, pose demands to which the new system is in the process of reacting. The first is an internal one posed by successive attempts[50] to change the internal management and decision-making structure of local authorities. Detailed discussion of the movement to corporate management occurs elsewhere[51] and suffice it to say that these changes have probably greatly increased the power of the official whilst reducing that of the elected member.

The second change is perhaps more important. If the movement towards corporatism represents a shift towards efficiency, then the introduction of public participation into local government, albeit to a limited degree,[52] represents a move towards the democratic criteria. Though public participation in local decision making is at an early stage, it seems unlikely that central and/or local government in Britain will be able to go back on this commitment. Clearly, as the experience of public participation in structure planning shows, the commitment presents problems with which representative local government in Britain has yet to come to terms.[53] To date, it would also appear that only the articulate, well-organised, middle class have grasped the opportunities for participation afforded under the new planning system, and it remains to be seen whether the traditionally non-participant groups can be encouraged to follow suit. One possible result of this change is that British local government may become more open, more accessible, and may even produce a shift in the distribution of power within local communities. In turn this might make the local system more responsive to local needs, local demands, and changes in its environment generally: British local government might thus become both more democratic and more efficient! Whether or not this happens, however, will depend very much on the ways in which local and national decision makers perceive these changes and how they react to them: the evidence to date suggests the opposite is more likely.[54]

This paper has argued that the structure of English local government has changed over the last hundred years in response to a number of social, economic and political changes. As Britain became first an industrial and then a post-industrial society, the system of local government had to respond to the changes associated with these urbanisation and suburbanisation processes. As a result of a number of political changes, such as the rise of party politics and public persons, the increased role of the professional expert and the growing importance of national associations of local authorities and professionals, the locality and the centre have become closely entwined. Ultimately this has meant that English local government has become delocalised, so that efficient service provision has become the main criteria underlying the organisation of local government rather than the earlier stress on local autonomy.

NOTES

1 W. J. M. Mackenzie, *Theories of Local Government*, Greater London Papers No. 2 (London: LSE, 1961).

2 A good recent discussion is to be found in L. Feldman and M. Goldrick, *Politics and Government of Urban Canada*, 2nd edn (Agincourt, Ont.: Methuen, 1973).

3 See, for example, L. J. Sharpe, 'Theories of local government', *Political Studies*, June 1970, pp. 153–74.

4 Public participation in planning was introduced as a legal requirement under the Town and Country Planning Act. For a review of some experience in structure planning see DOE Linked Research Project, Interim Research Series, Dept of Extramural Studies, University of Sheffield, Nos. 1–12.

5 In this sense, debates about the structure of English local government have nearly always taken place within the theoretical framework suggested by the Western liberal democratic paradigm, rather than within a Marxist or class-based one. Thus, for example, even social democratic writers such as the Webbs or G. D. H. Cole write about local government within the liberal democratic framework rather than from a perspective which might see local government reform as a means by which a fundamental redistribution of power within the political system might be achieved. See for example, A. Sancton, 'British socialist theory of the division of power by area', *Political Studies*, June 1976, pp. 158–71 for a discussion.

6   D. Easton, *A Framework for Political Analysis* (Englewood Cliffs, NJ: Prentice Hall, 1965), and *Systems Analysis of Political Life* (New York: Wiley, 1965).

7   See, for example, J. D. Dearlove, *The Politics of Policy in English Local Government* (Cambridge: CUP, 1973), particularly pp. 61–71.

8   R. Dahl, *Who Governs: Democracy and Power in an American City* (New Haven: Yale University Press, 1961), pp. 223–8.

9   Dearlove, *Politics of Policy*, pp. 206–26.

10   N. Boaden, *Urban Policy Making* (Cambridge: CUP, 1971) pp. 24–6.

11   K. Young, 'Values in the policy process', *Policy and Politics*, March 1977, pp. 1–22.

12   Particularly important throughout this period, however, were the private Acts of Parliament promoted by (primarily urban) local authorities, which often gave them considerable powers in a number of areas. Housing, libraries, workingmen's technical institutes, parks etc. all provide examples.

13   There was a further Act (1894) which introduced parish councils below the rural districts. Also under the administrative counties were the non-county boroughs – towns, often previously with some independent status, now not large enough to be given county borough status. For a discussion see K. B. Smellie, *History of English Local Government* (London: Allen & Unwin, 1973), pp. 38–41, and pp. 71–2.

14   For a review of this question see *Report of the (Layfield) Committee of Inquiry on Local Government Finance*, Cmnd 6453 (London: HMSO, 1976) and the contribution by G. W. Jones, below, pp. 165–82.

15   These were excluded basically for economic reasons, as part of measures taken to resolve the problems posed by the Depression years of the late 1920s and 1930s.

16   For example, Housing Acts appeared almost annually in the late 1950s and early 1960s.

17   For example, the 1958 Act introduced the idea of a general grant *not* tied to a specific service, but related to a number of local indicators (e.g. population size), as well as a rate support grant, designed to help poorer authorities.

18   R. Pahl, *Readings in Urban Sociology* (Oxford: Pergamon, 1968), p. 263.

19   It can be argued, for example, that some of the land use planning policies adopted by central and local government had this effect, as did the various twists and turns in housing policy. For a discussion see P. Hall *et al.*, *The Containment of Urban England*, 2 Vols (London: Allen & Unwin/Sage, 1973) and A. Murie, P. Niner and C. Watson, *Housing Policy and the Housing System* (London: Allen & Unwin, 1976).

20   J. G. Bulpitt, *Party Politics in English Local Government* (London: Longman, 1968); G. W. Jones, *Borough Politics* (London: Macmillan, 1970); E. P. Hancock, *Fit and Proper Persons* (London: Arnold, 1973).

21   In Salford, for example, the Liberals won a majority at elections to the new Borough in 1844, taking all the aldermanic seats appointed as a reward. 'To the victor the spoils' is a theme which has dominated Salford politics from that day on.

22   See, for example, Jones, *Borough Politics*.

23   Given the origins of the Labour Party this is what one would expect.

24   Again, Salford provides an example: in 1929, when Labour almost had a majority of councillors, the mayor used his casting vote to keep the anti-socialist majority in power through the retention of their aldermanic seats.

25   Though, as Bulpitt, *Party Politics* shows, the extent to which parties enforce discipline on councillors is very limited.

26 Jones, *op. cit.*, and J. M. Lee, *Social Leaders and Public Persons* (London: OUP, 1963).

27 Dearlove, *Politics of Policy*, pp. 206–26.

28 For a discussion of party politics and local government in practice see H. V. Wiseman, *Local Government at Work* (London: Routledge & Kegan Paul, 1967).

29 In the May 1977 elections, such distinguished local party leaders as Sir Stanley Yapp, Labour leader of the West Midlands County Council, were defeated, whilst even the Labour leader of the GLC, Sir Reginald Goodwin, only kept his seat with difficulty. In these elections Labour lost control of the Greater London, West Midlands, Greater Manchester and West Yorkshire Metropolitan Counties, all of which would previously be regarded as Labour strongholds.

30 Increasingly many councillors now refer to themselves as full-time. Another Committee of Inquiry (the Robinson Committee) is currently investigating the question of councillors' allowances (payments) for their work.

31 J. M. Lee *et al.*, *The Scope of Local Initiative* (London: Martin Robertson, 1974); N. Dennis, *Public Participation and Planner's Blight* (London: Faber, 1972); J. G. Davies, *The Evangelistic Bureaucrat* (London: Tavistock, 1972).

32 One or two authorities have apparently considered this point to be valid: Rother District Council recently dispensed with the services of its Chief Executive on the grounds that he was unnecessary, despite the protestations of the Society of Chief Executives to the contrary.

33 Davies, *The Evangelistic Bureaucrat*; Dennis, *Public Participation*.

34 Transportation and land-use planning would be two areas where such a situation predominated until recently. Indeed, most professionals in these areas would still see them as apolitical.

35 Thus, London and the other metropolitan areas are very much political prizes to be won.

36 This Act was introduced following on the Report of the Planning Advisory Group in 1965, a group very much dominated by professionals.

37 The year which saw the introduction of both old age pensions and unemployment benefits.

38 J. A. G. Griffith, *Central Departments and Local Authorities* (London: Allen & Unwin, 1966).

39 For a series of articles on this question see the *Guardian*, April 1977.

40 Following reorganisation in 1973, local politics have very much polarised, with the urban areas solidly Labour and the rural/suburban areas Conservative. This year's elections have produced considerable change.

41 See, for example, B. Wood *The Process of Local Government Reform, 1966–74* (London: Allen & Unwin, 1976), and below, the contribution by L. J. Sharpe, pp. 42–73.

42 The process of local government reform is similarly long elsewhere: Ontario in Canada, for example, has been occupied with reform since 1953 (Toronto).

43 See below, pp. 42–73.

44 For a discussion of this Report see J. Stanyer in R. Chapman (ed.), *The Role of Commissions in Policy Making* (London: Allen & Unwin, 1973), pp. 105–43.

45 See Wood, *Process of Local Government Reform* for details.

46 The situation is markedly different in Scotland.

47 Toronto was reformed again in 1966, thirteen years after its original change, and Winnipeg in 1971 – some ten years after the first reforms.

48 *Report of the Committee of Inquiry on Local Government Finance* (op. cit.) and G. W. Jones, below. pp. 165–82.

49 Cheshire, for example, is an area attractive to much 'white' industrial activity. Compare this with the situation in many inner city areas.

50 For example, *Maud Committee on Management in Local Government*, 1967 and the similar Baines Report of 1972.

51 See the discussion in R. A. W. Rhodes, below, pp. 127–49.

52 The planning field is the only area of local government activity where public participation is statutorily required, though it is slowly creeping into other areas.

53 See W. H. Hampton, N. Boaden, M. Goldsmith and P. Stringer, 'Public participation in planning within a representative democracy', paper presented to the Annual Meeting of the Political Studies Association, Liverpool, April 1977.

54 ibid.

Chapter III

TRADITIONAL PATTERNS OF
FRENCH LOCAL GOVERNMENT

The French system of local government has long been based upon an uneasy alliance of elected officials, technical specialists in the field services of ministries, and the representatives of the central government, the prefects. Traditionally, in terms of formal authority, the prefects were the dominant actors, as they were theoretically empowered to supervise the actions of both elected local councils and ministry field services. In practice, however, power was essentially dispersed. The relationship between the three elements was complex and very often confused: they were usually in competition, occasionally in conflict, and not infrequently in collusion. Such collusion was generally aimed at obtaining concessions from the very ministries in Paris, on whose behalf and in whose name, prefects and field services alike were supposed to act. In practice, though not in theory, there was no clear-cut systematic distribution of power – neither between Paris and the periphery, nor even between the actors at the periphery. Certainly, in provincial France, the influence of any individual, be he prefect, mayor, councillor, Member of Parliament or head of a field service, depended little on his formal powers. Intelligence, hard work and common sense, knowledge of the area, its problems and potential, political and administrative weight in Paris, and diplomatic skills in contracts with local rivals, these were the qualities which determined the real influence of politicians and administrators alike.

Why was the traditional system of local government, whilst in theory so legalistic and uniform, in practice so personalised and localised? One answer to this question is that France had not one, but four systems of local government, based on four different ideas of legitimacy:

(1) the prefectoral system;
(2) the parliamentary system;
(3) the system of locally elected councils;
(4) the local field services of the public ministries.

The superimposition of these four systems and the co-existence of their conflicting theories are the subjects of this inquiry.

Departements.
Arrondisements
Cantons
Communes

THE PREFECTORAL SYSTEM

Created in 1800 by Napoleon, the prefectoral administration was a rational, hierarchical, bureaucratic system of central control. Underpinning this system were the beliefs in France as a nation-State, with one national interest, and, hence, needing a strong central government to interpret this national interest in laws and policies, and an efficient administration to ensure the uniform application of the government's decisions throughout the country. Hence, politics should be decided only in Paris and administered efficiently in the provinces.

The prefectoral system incorporated and adapted the national system of standardised units of local government created after the Revolution. These units had been created as equal divisions of 'the one and indivisible Republic' to replace a patchwork of national units – provinces, duchies, counties, and 'countries' – which had been the framework for local government under the *ancien régime*. It was thus intended to break down existing provincial loyalties and identities and thereby to reinforce national unity. Hence, the units of the top tier of local administration, all of similar territorial dimensions, were called simply *départements*. Individual names were taken from local geographical features such as rivers or mountains (Loir-et-Cher, the Lot, the Puy-de-Dôme and the Hautes-Alpes are good examples). Within each *département* an administrative capital (*chef-lieu*) was chosen – the location of the prefecture, the offices and residence of the State's representative, the prefect. The *départements* were subdivided into *arrondissements,* usually two to five in number in each *département*. They were named after their administrative capitals where the sub-prefectures (of the sub-prefects) were located. Each *arrondissement* was divided into a number of *cantons,* which themselves were subdivided into *communes,* the smallest units at the lowest level of the system. The boundaries of the *communes* coincided with those of the numerous small towns and villages in which most French people then lived.

One notable feature of this system of local government units was its extreme fragmentation. France was divided into 90 *départements,* nearly 500 *arrondissements,* over 2,000 *cantons* and 38,000 *communes*. It certainly cut across boundaries of the *ancien régime*: the former province of Brittany, for example, was replaced by five *départements,* whilst the French Basque countries and Béarn were grouped together in the Basses-Pyrénées *département*. The system had clear advantages when France was a rural society, with few demands for State intervention and only horses and stage-coaches for transport. It was, however, to produce problems in an urban France with cars, telephones and televisions and great expectations of State services. For a second noteworthy feature of this system was its permanence. The boundaries and names of almost all the units at all levels have remained largely unchanged since 1800. The number of *départements* is now 96, as five new *départements* were created in the Paris region in 1966 and Corsica was divided into two *départements* in 1975. Apart from the Haute-Loire and the Var, all are still administered from their original 'capitals', be they towns as 'uncapital' in size and facilities as Mende, Rodez or Guéret. The number of *arrondissements* was modified slightly by mergers in the 1920s and 1930s and the creation of new urban *arrondissements* in the 1960s. The *cantons* were increased in number by about 300 in 1973, once again by the establishment of new ones in the big towns. Finally, the *communes,* whilst given considerable encouragement to reduce their numbers through mergers by the 1971 Local Government Act, none the less still totalled 36,435 in 1976. In short, even in the 1970s, the local government units remained very largely the same as in 1800.

In the original Napoleonic system, all local responsibilities were given to a hierarchy of officials. To each unit at the *département, arrondissement* and *commune* levels one official was appointed to run the administration. In the *département,* global responsibility for executing government policy was allocated to the 'representative of the State', the prefect. Within his *département,* the subordinates of the prefect, the sub-prefects (one in every *arrondissement*), were to carry out his instructions or pass orders to their subordinates, the mayors of the *communes.* Thus a pyramid of command was established by which laws and decrees could be rapidly communicated from Paris to prefects, sub-prefects and mayors for uniform application in every part of France.

The original prefectoral system was not only for hierarchical central control from Paris, but also served as a channel of communication between periphery and centre. Mayors were given responsibility for registration of births, marriages, deaths and electoral eligibility. They were also instructed to inform their sub-prefects about any noteworthy events, whether social, economic, political or criminal, in their *communes.* The sub-prefects drafted regular reports on their *arrondissements* to the prefects, who in turn wrote monthly reports to the Minister of the Interior about all aspects of life in their *départements.* In the absence of any real parliamentary representation, the prefectoral pyramid was a major filter of information to the government about the needs and wishes of the people and their reactions to government policies. Up to the present time, mayors are still responsible for registration, and prefectoral reports continue to provide the minister with information, although in an age of parliamentary representation, telephones, opinion polls, pressure groups, economic planning and the statistical reports of INSEE, prefectoral reports seem increasingly unnecessary.

Two other features of the hierarchical structure of the original prefectoral system should also be noted: the importance of individual responsibilities and the predominance of generalists over specialists. At every level, authority was highly personalised: decision-making powers were delegated only to prefects, sub-prefects and mayors who were responsible for all deeds performed by their own local services. Article 3 of the law establishing the system stated simply that 'The prefect alone is responsible for the administration of the *département*.' One result was that prefects, sub-prefects and mayors were inevitably generalists. Whilst in 1800 three field services at the departmental level were placed outside the direct control of the prefect, they were subordinate to his general 'leadership' and his all-embracing emergency powers. All other special services in the *département* (the roads and bridges corps – *corps des ponts et chaussées* – was one such service) were subordinated to him. Hence, just as the Ministry of the Interior in Paris had competence for all 'internal' policies, so the prefects' offices in the prefectures had very wide responsibilities: public works, conscription, police, education, charities, religion, elections and agriculture all came within the sphere of competence of Napoleon's prefects. Since 1800, the responsibilities of the Ministry of the Interior have diminished. 'Specialist' ministries have been created with their own field services in the *départements*. Nevertheless, the 'generalist' prefects, the 'representatives of the whole government', are still responsible for supervising and co-ordinating the work of the specialist services, and the prefects formally still wield almost all administrative powers delegated from Paris (although not those delegated by the Defence, Justice, Finance and Labour Ministries). As recently as 1953, 1964 and 1970, governments attempted to restore the 'unity of state action' at the local level by increasing the effective supervision of the prefects.

The predominant role given to appointed officials was another remarkable element of the 1800 prefectoral system. Napoleon replaced the elected local councils of the Directory with powerless advisory bodies. These were to meet rarely and even their members were government appointees. Prefects, sub-prefects and mayors were all government-appointed agents of the State. The mayors of *communes* with over 5,000 inhabitants were chosen by the government in Paris, whilst to the smaller *communes* appointments were decided by the prefects. Ever since the Third Republic, when mayors became the elected executive officers of elected municipal councils, they have also retained their original role as State agents. The prefects became the executive officers of the general councils of the *départements,* but they have remained government-appointed civil servants. It is thus in no way surprising that whilst English talks of 'local government', French, in law and common usage, employs 'local administration'. The common French term *'l'administré'* – literally one who is subject to administration – has no English equivalent.

Although the first prefects, sub-prefects and mayors were appointed officials and had many purely administrative tasks (organising administrative services, deploying police forces, ensuring taxes were paid and conscripts did enlist are good examples), it would be misleading to describe them as bureaucrats. They also performed important political duties. In one sense, their information reports were political. More important, however, were their tasks of repressing opposition to and creating support for Napoleon and his policies. Citizens of hostile views were watched, excluded from State jobs and arrested at the slightest fault. The government's officers also sought to 'rally' to the Empire the most wealthy and influential families (the French term is *notables*) of every *commune, arrondissement* and *département*. To this end the prefects were given huge salaries and expected to entertain lavishly, making their prefectures the centres of departmental social life. Prefects also used their power of appointing all minor officials, to gain the loyalty, and reinforce the influence, of local elites: the creation of legitimacy by simple clientelism was the basic Napoleonic approach. These activities of repression and propaganda, practised actively in support of parliamentary candidates in the July Monarchy (1830–48), the Second Republic (1848–52) and the Second Empire (1852–70), were to gain for prefects and sub-prefects the hatred of the opposition parties. They have also led to the widely held current belief that prefects deploy their influence in support of the parliamentary candidates of the government of the day. The protests from the opposition in 1967 and 1973 bear witness that this belief still persists. Whether or not this view is accurate, prefects and sub-prefects are still seen – and see themselves – as the most 'political' administrators in France.

The counterpart to the freedom from local supervision of Napoleon's local government officers was their complete dependence on the central government. The officers at each level were required to make detailed reports on the work of their subordinates. None of the officers was given security of tenure. Mayors could be suspended or dismissed. No man was appointed prefect to a *département* where he had property, relatives or close friends. Periodic inspections of prefectoral accomplishments were made by members of the council of state. Loyalty was also encouraged by high salaries and enormous social prestige. All local officers were given impressive uniforms and expected to play leading roles in all public ceremonies. The prefects held the top rank in the order of precedence at all official occasions, and only Napoleon's generals were better rewarded with honours and titles.

Many of these methods of central control remain in operation to the present day. Mayors, elected since the Third Republic, are still legally under the 'tutellage' of the prefects, both as State officials and executives of their councils. The prefectures and sub-prefectures are still subject to inspection, and, since 1958, to visits by the Head of State himself. Prefects and sub-prefects are still well paid, lodged in luxury, chauffeur-driven in official cars – and subjected to instant transfers and dismissals. In a career as precarious as a post in the Chicago mafia in the 1930s, prefectoral loyalty is still enforced by a mixture of bribery and brutality.

THE PARLIAMENTARY SYSTEM

In the regimes which followed the Empire, parliamentary democracy was gradually introduced, bringing with it profound changes in local government. Governments, wishing to secure the re-election of the members of their parliamentary majorities, encouraged their prefects to use their control of all local administrative services in support of the pro-majority deputies. Members of Parliament, if in theory representatives of the nation and servants of the national interest, in practice became delegates of their constituencies and protectors of their local interests. Hence Deputies, whether in favour of or hostile to the government, increasingly sought to influence all decisions offering their constituencies, whether these were made in Paris or in the prefectures, and to take credit for all popular decisons. Thus the Deputies became competitors of prefects and sub-prefects both as channels of information to Paris and as decision makers at the local level. As long as strong executives dominated the legislature, cohesive majorities existed in the Chamber, and the suffrage was restricted, it was possible for both governments and their prefects to resist the pretensions of the individual Deputies and to use local administrative interventions, both repressive and clientelistic, solely in support of government majorities. When majority fragmentation and governmental stability gave additional influence to every single Deputy, and when all Deputies could claim the legitimacy of universal suffrage, there was little prefects or governments could do to prevent the development of a system of parliamentary clientelism.

Under the Restoration Monarchy (1815–30), suffrage was limited, majorities were fairly stable in support of relatively strong governments, and the prefects were allowed to stand for election. Many prefects used their control of appointments and administrative influence in their *départements* to assist their own election. There was little evidence of competition between prefects and Members of Parliament. During the July Monarchy (1830–48), the suffrage was marginally widened, the prefects prohibited from standing for election, and the governments' majorities far less cohesive. Individual Deputies were soon demanding a price for their loyalty – that the Minister of the Interior instruct the prefects and sub-prefects in their *départements* to assist their election campaigns. Later they came to demand that they, the Deputies, should decide the choice of prefect for their *départements*. In turn, prefects and sub-prefects saw that their promotion prospects – and indeed their tenure in their posts – depended on their electoral efforts. Prefectoral electioneering activities reached their summit during the early years of the Second Empire (1852–70), when the government was based – for the only time before 1958 – upon both a strong executive and universal suffrage. After the *coup d'état* of December 1851, an attempt was made to destroy parliamentary influence over the prefectoral system; it was the prefects who chose the candidates to represent the government, who led the repression of its political opponents and who used their administrative machines to 'encourage' the election of these candidates. Once elected, however, the Deputies soon adopted the old parliamentary habits. By the time the Empire fell once again Deputies were frequently intervening in Paris for favours for their constituencies, and to influence the choice of prefects, sub-prefects and mayors. They then obliged these local officials to campaign on their behalf. Paradoxically, many prefects became aware of the inefficiency of their local clientelism either for winning elections or for furthering their own careers.

The first seven years of the Third Republic (1870–1940) were a period of considerable political uncertainty. In 1877, the conservative President of the Republic, Marshall MacMahon, attempted to use the prefectoral administration once again – as in the early days of the Second Empire – to win the election of a majority favourable in the Chamber. With his failure and the triumph of the Republicans, the systematic use of the prefectoral electioneering activities (official posters, pressure on minor civil servants are examples) came to an end. Throughout the Third Republic and even during the Fourth Republic (1945–58) many Deputies – and Senators – still demanded, and obtained, electoral help from their prefects and favours for their constituencies from ministers in Paris. Governments were subordinated to the Deputies and Senators, and it was impossible that governments' representatives should not experience similar subjugation. In practice, Members of Parliament controlled both appointments to prefectures (formally the government's power) and local state jobs and favours (formally the prefect's power). Even a strong Minister of the Interior such as Georges Mandel admitted this was natural: 'Parliament is a fact; I have to take it into consideration. The Deputy is a representative of the nation: if he expresses a wish I must give him satisfaction if I can.'[1] Unfortunately, the multiplicity of parties and the lack of discipline within parties meant that both favours from Paris and election assistance from prefects were unsystematic or even highly individualised and localised: they did not have the effect of promoting stability of government.

It should also be noted that during the Third and Fourth Republics, as during the Fifth, many Deputies were also mayors or members of municipal or general councils. This accumulation of offices increased the tendency for direct appeals to Paris by the Deputies. Demands for favours – often subsidies or loans – for their local councils were made directly by the Members of Parliament to the relevant offices of the Parisian ministries, thus ignoring or completely bypassing the prefectoral system through which such demands should have been made. Governmental instability meant that many Deputies were also past, present or future ministers. They might also be mayors of very big towns (Herriot at Lyons, Defferre at Marseilles and Chaban-Delmas at Bordeaux are good examples). In either case it became very difficult, or even impossible for either the prefect to protest or the ministry to resist.

It does not appear that the powers of Members of Parliament in local government have been totally destroyed by the governments of the Fifth Republic: certainly their pretensions have not diminished. It may be, as opponents of the Gaullist alliance have claimed, that only the government's supporters now enjoy the ministerial respect for constituency claims and the influence in the prefectures formerly shared by all. The two public protests by pro-government Deputies Mondon and Edgar Faure when new prefects were appointed to their *départements* without their prior approval were noteworthy because they were the only such protests. Advance consultation with pro-government Deputies would appear to be the rule rather than the exception even today. Furthermore, governments of the Fifth Republic have made no attempt to sever the direct contacts between ministries and individual Deputies looking after the interests of their home towns.

THE SYSTEM OF LOCALLY ELECTED COUNCILS

After the local government laws of 1871 and 1884, the general councils of the *départements* and municipal councils of the communes became freely elected bodies with independent powers for local action. Even before this time, however, the membership of almost every general, and of a few municipal councils, had included men of considerable importance either in national politics or in key administrative bodies such as the Council of State. This gave these councils significant local influence despite their theoretical weakness and domination by the prefects. The reforms of the Third Republic institutionalised the power of the general councils and restricted prefectoral interference in communal affairs to a simple 'tutelage' – a check on the legality of actions by mayors and municipal councils.

General councillors are elected from single member constituencies, the cantons, for six-year periods of office, half the seats being contested every three years. The general council meets for two 'ordinary' sessions each year, and elects its own officers which include a president and a permanent committee. This committee meets once a month to supervise the work of the prefect. For the prefect is now the executive officer of the council – in addition to all his State functions. He takes part in council meetings, drafts the annual budget and is responsible for carrying out all council decisions.

The responsibilities of the general councils have always been many and varied. These include the building and maintenance of departmental roads, rural police centres for the *gendarmerie,* teacher training colleges, and the prefectures. Personal social services, public assistance and aid to communes are other important areas of council spending. In association with the government and the *communes,* the councils run public housing offices (*OHLM*), and economic development corporations. Amongst the numerous other activities of departmental interest in which the councils intervene are the organisation of school bussing, the provision of tourist facilities and the building of psychiatric hospitals. Normally many of the policies of the councils are carried out by State employees in the prefectures and field services.

The municipal councils have between nine and thirty-seven members according to the population of the *communes,* and are elected every six years by a complicated list system. Each council elects its mayor and, in the larger communes, a number of assistant mayors. After his election, the mayor wields most of the powers of the council. Only at the annual budget meetings can the ordinary councillors influence the policies of their mayor.

All mayors, although elected, remain officers of the State for certain functions. All are responsible to the prefects for the registration of births, marriages and deaths, the revision of electoral lists, the preparation of army conscription lists and the supervision of voting arrangements for elections. All mayors are also, in theory, responsible for the maintenance of public order. In practice, however, towns of over 10,000 people have State police forces directly under the control of the prefects, whilst small rural communes are policed by the *gendarmerie* which is also answerable to the prefect. Only in communes with between 5,000 and 10,000 people are there policemen employed by the mayors – but even these officers are commanded by a *commissaire* from the State police forces of the prefect.

The *communes* have the responsibility for constructing and maintaining all communal roads (these include most streets in towns and minor country roads). For this task most small *communes* hire the technical services of field services (either the roads and bridges or agriculture services), whilst big towns have their own services. Refuse disposal, another communal duty, is also differently administered according to the size of the *commune*: the towns provide professional collection services, whereas rural villages just purchase dumping grounds. Every *commune* also has to provide graveyards and gravediggers according to its needs. Throughout the Third Republic, it was the duty of each *commune* to construct and maintain school buildings, and this is still performed by the towns (although most *lycées* are built by the State). During the Fourth Republic, however, rural depopulation and the specialisation of secondary education led to the closure of some village schools and the introduction of bussing to schools serving groups of *communes*. This trend has continued and accelerated since 1958.

These examples of the provision of mandatory functions illustrate the vast practical differences between the potential roles of big and small *communes*. In the provision of discretionary services, whilst all *communes* in theory have the same unlimited powers, these differences are even greater. Towns with several thousand inhabitants can and do provide numerous and large-scale services such as markets, parks, public transport, theatres, sports grounds, libraries, public housing offices (in towns of over 20,000 people), tourist offices and abattoirs. The larger cities such as Lyons, Marseilles and Bordeaux have hundreds of municipal employees and enormous annual budgets. Many smaller *communes,* however, have only hundreds, or even scores, of inhabitants. For these villages basic services such as water supply or sewage disposal are only feasible through joint schemes with other *communes*.

The mayor of a big town is, as he always has been, influential, important and independent, even when he is not a Member of Parliament or a political ally of the government. The mayor deals directly with ministries in Paris for funding and support, and the ministries deal directly with the mayor to save time and duplication of actions. These direct dealings with ministries are also possible, as we have seen, for the small minority of mayors of small *com-*

munes who have national importance as Deputies, Senators or top civil servants. Most French mayors, however, do not have such access or influence, and must rely on sub-prefects, prefecture staffs and field services for advice and assistance.

THE FIELD SERVICES

When Napoleon established the prefectoral administration, he specifically exempted the field services of three ministries – those of war, justice and finances – from control by the prefects. Ever since that time, the armed forces, the law courts and the local tax-collecting services and departmental treasuries have retained their independence. Their officials have jealously guarded their prerogatives and resisted all attempts at intervention from the prefects. These services set an example of the legitimacy of specialists to administer at the local level without 'generalist' prefectoral control. It was an example others were keen to follow.

As we have already noted, a number of administrative *corps* inherited from the *ancien régime* were placed by Napoleon under the orders of the prefects (the 'roads and bridges' and 'waters and forests' *corps* are good examples). Many members of these bodies, however, resented this official subordination to the prefects and obstructed attempts at prefectoral intervention in their affairs. As the role of the State expanded during the nineteenth century, several sections of the Ministry of the Interior were hived off and established as separate ministries. In some cases, these 'technical' ministries took over these *corps* as their own field services. Hence the 'waters and forests' *corps,* for example, became a field service of the Ministry of Agriculture. Other technical ministries, in contrast, established their own new field services in the *départements.*

The result of this proliferation of ministries and services was that by 1950 the administrative capitals of most *départements* contained at least forty different field services, dealing with policy areas as varied as taxation and public health, archives and employment, agriculture and construction. In theory, almost all these specialist services remained subject to the guidance of the generalist prefects. In reality, however, the sheer number of the services, the technicality of much of their work, their unwillingness to communicate information about their activities and the numerous delegations of decision-making powers to heads of services instead of to the prefects, all resulted in the virtual independence of the services. By 1958, as one observer noted, 'if it is true that the prefect represents the minister, it is apparent every day that it is the heads of [field] services who represent the ministries'.[2]

During the Third and Fourth Republics, a number of ministries organised certain of their field services into regional groups – often for purposes of inspection or co-ordination. In some cases entire field services were regionally organised: education, mines and customs and excise are three examples of this. Unfortunately, whilst all these regional services administered to groups of *départements,* very few used the same regional groupings. It was often the case, for example, that the area served by a regional customs office was not co-terminous with that of the *rectorat* (regional education office). This most uncartesian administrative organisation continued into the Fifth Republic, although it was considerably changed by the reforms of the 1960s.

Traditionally, the attitudes of heads of field services towards their duties have reflected their specialist knowledge, their professional career structures and their close contacts in the areas where they work. Members of field services may work in districts where they have relations or property. They also often remain for long periods of time in the same posts. Hence it frequently happens that they become very familiar with the needs and problems of their areas and establish close links with mayors and local councillors. Field service members are normally recruited by competitive entry examinations and trained in professional schools; their subsequent careers depend on competence, experience and seniority – and not on the wishes of a government or an electorate. Finally, as specialists, many field service members become advocates – or even lobbyists – for both their services and their areas. Thus, for example, the departmental infrastructure director, in theory the local representative of the central Ministry of Infrastructure (*Equipement*), in practice frequently acts as a representative of his *département* to his ministry; he voices its needs for State construction and its claims to subsidies for local authority building. At the local level, however, many field service directors act towards prefects, mayors and councillors as spokesmen or salesmen for the types of administrative action which they represent.

LOCAL POWER AND CENTRAL CONTROL

Since the time of Richelieu, few rulers of France have trusted the people in the provinces. Local identities have remained strong, local languages and cultures have maintained their vitality, and the unity of France, a State created by dynastic marriage and military conquest, constantly has seemed fragile. Hence governments of France have wished to centralise, to ensure all policies are made in Paris and applied uniformly throughout the country. The prefectoral system, the field services and the limits on powers and financial dependency of local councils are all different mechanisms for the maintenance of this central control.

In the provinces, distrust of the rulers in Paris has been equally widespread, and the mechanisms of centralisation have been subject to frequent attacks and constant subversion. In general, subversion has proved the easiest and most profitable approach. The 'sale' of support in Parliament by Deputies and Senators in exchange for favours for their constituencies and power over local civil servants is one such means of subversive local influence. More frequently, mayors and councillors have won over the directors of field services and even those symbols of centralisation, the sub-prefects and prefects – to the defence of their interests against the Parisian ministries. Furthermore, the continued existence of the institutions of centralisation have become a positive asset to local politicians: all blame for unpopular policies is placed on Paris or its local representatives, whilst all credit for popular measures is claimed by the local councillors, mayors, Deputies and Senators.

The coexistence of different systems at the local level has not made local government in France more clear, more democratic or more efficient. Complicity and collusion are common, but there is also keen competition; all of these may prevent or delay much-needed actions. But it would be inaccurate to conclude that competition for power at the periphery is solely or indeed mainly responsible for the traditional slowness and unresponsiveness of local government. In practice, many local policy decisions have remained dependent on funds or authorisations from different ministries in Paris. And competition and conflict have been more typical of relations between ministries in Paris than of those between their representatives and local political leaders in the *départements* and *communes*. Power has traditionally been distributed between ministries in Paris, between Paris and the periphery, and between actors and groups at the periphery in such a complex way that any systemic model of local government is inevitably more misleading than revealing as a guide to what happens at any given moment in any particular local area.[3]

NOTES

1 J. M. Sherwood, *Georges Mandel and the Third Republic* (Stanford, Calif.: Stanford University Press, 1970), p. 155.
2 J. Bremas, 'La fonction préfectorale', *Promotions*, 1959, No. 49, p. 7.
3 Many facts and ideas in this article were taken from: B. Le Clère and V. Wright, *Les Préfets du Second Empire* (Paris: Fondation Nationale des Sciences Politiques, 1973); B. Chapman, *An Introduction to French Local Government* (London: Allen & Unwin, 1953); L. Wylie, *Village in the Vaucluse* (Cambridge, Mass.: Harvard University Press, 1957); F. F.

Ridley and J. Blondel, *Public Administration in France* (London: Routledge & Kegan Paul, 1964); P. Grémion, *La Structuration du pouvoir au niveau départemental* (Paris: Copédith, 1969); P. Grémion, *Le Pouvoir périphérique* (Paris: Editions du Seuil, 1976); J.-C. Thoenig, *L'Ere des téchnocrates* (Paris: Editions d'Organisation, 1973); E. N. Suleiman, *Politics, Power and Bureaucracy in France* (Princeton, NJ: Princeton University Press, 1974); J. Hayward, *The One and Indivisible French Republic* (London: Weidenfeld & Nicholson, 1973); S. Tarrow, *Between Centre and Periphery* (London: Yale University Press, 1977); unpublished ms. by J.-C. Thoenig.

Chapter IV

MODERNISING THE LOCALITIES: LOCAL GOVERNMENT IN BRITAIN AND SOME COMPARISONS WITH FRANCE

The modernisation of local government has been a feature common to most Western democracies over the past ten years or so[1] and to some extent in Eastern Europe as well.[2] This paper is principally concerned with the modernisation in the United Kingdom, and especially in England and Wales, that began with the creation of the Greater London Council and the London boroughs in 1964 and was broadly completed by the passing of the Scottish Local Government Act of 1973. By modernisation is meant, first, the alteration of the basic structure of local government so as to bring it more into line with the changed population settlement patterns and mobility of modern society and the scale requirements of local public services. Secondly, by modernisation is also meant changes in the internal decision-making processes of local authorities designed to make the system more efficient and coherent. The modernisation process may be summarised as an attempt to refashion the local government system on rational, politically neutral premises to meet what are claimed to be the radically changed circumstances of the postwar era. These are the terms in which it is almost always discussed both officially and otherwise; it is the formal public language of local government 'reform'. But there are other, perhaps equally valid, languages for describing the objectives and the causes of the modernisation process. In the first place, the rational-efficiency explanation for modernisation leaves out of account questions of party advantage. Yet almost all the urban local authorities are run on strict party lines that closely mirror the pattern at the national level so that any change in the status or boundaries of existing local units is bound to have implications that no national party can afford to ignore, least of all the party in power, that initiates the changes. Secondly, and much less obviously, the net effect of modernisation – as we shall see – is almost always likely to mean larger (territorial and population) units of local government; and larger units mean fewer units. Given the massive growth of government over the last half-century or so, the reduction in the number of organisations with whom a central government has to deal is an important objective of all governments whether these organisations are 'private' pressure groups or 'public' local authorities. In this sense, all central governments have a very strong interest in the aggregation of groups and interests within the State and a particularly strong desire to aggregate the units of local government. The growing public pressure for equality, central government's increasing financial contribution to local government and the increasing political sensitivity of a number of public services that are the responsibility of local government, all tend to increase central government's involvement with local government, and engender at the central level a corresponding desire to lighten its increasing management load by reducing the number of local authorities. Important though they undoubtedly are, with one exception[3] neither of the two motives just outlined for the modernisation of local government figure very prominently in the existing accounts of the reform process.[4]

DISTINCTIVE CHARACTERISTICS OF THE BRITISH SYSTEM

Absence of a Prefectoral System

Before discussing the modernisation process proper it is necessary to sketch in some of the principal characteristics of the British political system that are particularly relevant to the process – particularly those which sharply distinguish it from the French system. The first characteristic of the British political system that must be noted is that although like France it is a unitary State, it does not have an intermediate level between centre and locality of representatives of central government exercising *general* supervisory responsibilities for all State functions at the local level. In a word, it does not have a prefectoral system. There are various outstationed central officials that administer central services directly (for example, social security and employment officers) and other outstationed officials that exercise various supervisory and inspectoral powers in relation to local government, but there is no centrally appointed common general superior supervising and co-ordinating these activities as in a prefectoral system. Local authorities' relations with central government are instead mainly conducted directly on a departmental basis, function by function.[5] There is, therefore, no Ministry of the Interior which surmounts the common general superior system in the localities. The relationship between central and local government in Britain is governed by the legal doctrine of *ultra vires*.[6] That is to say, both local government and central government can only exercise powers specifically granted by Parliament under the appropriate statute, and usually in relation to specified services. If either wishes to go beyond these powers it must obtain parliamentary sanction.

This simple picture needs some modification, however, in the sense that there exist special arrangements for Northern Ireland, Scotland and Wales. In Northern Ireland, until the recent suspension of the constitution, there was a directly elected bicameral legislature (Stormont) which legislated for and administered most of the 'home' functions, but did not have a separate taxation system and in practice was heavily dependent on financial subvention from the central government in London.

Non-Executant Role of Central Government

The second peculiarity of the British political, or rather, administrative, system that must be noted is related to the first: for all 'home' functions (i.e. all those entirely related to State activities internal to the State) with the exception of the Health Service and certain social welfare functions mainly involving monetary transfer payments, British central government does not concern itself directly with executant activities. Central government confines itself to the roles of policy making, of regulation, of inspecting, of guiding, advising and controlling and in the main leaves operational responsibility to an executant agency of which there are three broad types. These are, first, the national public corporations[7] which are responsible for television and radio, the airlines, airports, atomic energy, railways, buses, ports and harbours, posts and telegraphs, coal, steel, gas and electricity supply and new towns. The second are *ad hoc*, quasi-governmental and quasi-non-governmental agencies sometimes national in scope, sometimes regional. These agencies cover a wide range of activities including water resources, arts and culture, sport, scientific research, the universities, national parks, historic buildings, race relations and consumer protection.[8] The third type of executant agency and the one which is the principal concern of this paper is local government. Local government in Britain is responsible for a very wide range of public services from institutions of higher education to refuse collection, and it absorbs about a third of public sector expenditure.

The significance of the non-executant tradition of central government is that the professional expertise needed for the effective execution of the activities undertaken by local government is employed and controlled by local government and not by central government. This means, first, that whatever the legal and financial controls exercised over local government by central government, there remains an irreducible element of autonomy exercised by local government because it recruits, pays and controls its own professional staff. The corollary of this arrangement is that the sense of corporate identity of these professional staffs is possibly weaker in Britain than in France and the autonomy they enjoy may also be less than under the French system where, despite the existence of the prefect, professional cohesion is enhanced by the existence of unified, functionally specialised command structures reaching down from the centre to the locality. The coal-face levels of those French hierarchies are often strongly susceptible to local influence and opinion. Moreover, each hierarchy itself is more loosely knit vertically than its ostensibly pyramidal structure would suggest,[9] and in the larger towns experts are employed who are largely independent of the national system.[10] None the less, the bulk of the expertise at the local level in France is rooted in one or other of the different professional hierarchies and as such have a relatively strong sense of separate identity. In Britain, by contrast, there is no hierarchy, and functionally compendious local authorities that employ the executant professionals tend to weaken the cohesion of the national professional communities by requiring each professional group to confront and bargain with competing professional groups at the local level, literally across the table. Employment by local government also provides them with another, non-professional, focus of loyalty – the local authority itself.

This characteristic of the British local government system is highly professionalised, each profession having its own national organisation which usually controls conditions of entry. Also, the career structure for the local professional specialist is the local government system itself, each specialist moving up the career ladder by moving from one local authority to another. This, too, tends to strengthen professional loyalties. Nevertheless, the fact that the civil servants at the directing and policy-making levels in the central departments are cut off from the operational 'coal-face', and in any case are generalists rather than technical specialists, means that the professional specialist working at the local level in Britain is in a weaker position in relation to the local politician and a stronger one in relation to the central government than his counterpart in France.

The Dominance of Functionalism

The third characteristic of the British political system that must be noted is linked to the two previous aspects in the sense that the non-executant tradition of the central departments as compared with France strengthens the growing tendency – which seems to be common to all advanced industrial democracies – to regard local authorities as primarily functional agencies; in the British case as being not essentially different from the other two types of decentralised functional agency, the public corporation and the quasi-governmental body. This tendency weakens the sense in which local government reflects the fact that the nation-State is made up of identifiable sub-communities which, because they evoke a sense of loyalty among their citizens, ought to be allowed to govern themselves within defined limits irrespective of their functional capacity. Secondly, the absence of an intermediate level between centre and locality has the same effect in the sense that it puts much greater pressure on local government to be functionally appropriate. The combined effect of these two tendencies is, paradoxically, both to give local government greater operational autonomy over and above its formal legal powers and at the same time to make it much more vulnerable than French local government to structural change. It is less able to defend itself from the charge of inadequacy precisely because it has become more and more cast in the role of a functional agency rather than a community government. We will return to this very important distinction between the two systems in a moment.

The functional character of British central–local linkages has also to be seen in terms of its much more confined and regularised character as compared with French central-local relations. This is partly derived from the fact that the actual point of contact is usually solely betwen two strictly functional agencies – the central department and the local authority department. Equally, those making the contact are predominantly civil servants who, not being part of a hierarchy, do not shun informal, sometimes face-to-face, relationships, with each other. The fact that they are civil servants further secularises the relationship, for if 'the line between politics and administration in France is singularly blurred'[11] nowhere in the Western world is the line less blurred than in Britain. Indeed, not only is there no institutionalised overlap between politics and administration either in the form of a politicised bureaucrat (city manager) or bureaucratised politician (French mayor) as there is in other countries, the British civil servant never crosses the line in his daily work or during his career. Dominated by such secular bureaucracies, the essence of the relationship between centre and locality in Britain in both theory and practice is order, regularity and harmony. Political considerations may be dominant in the relationship but they are never, or very seldom, made explicit; given the power and dominance of the two major parties at both levels that is the only way the system could work.

This secularised functionalism strongly affects the way the local authority defends its interests. In the first place it renders parallelism – i.e. bypassing the formal processes between centre and locality – largely pointless except in terms of open delegations to Whitehall, or hopeful buttonholing of MPs or peers. Certainly there is nothing comparable to the French practice of parallelism. This is partly because the tradition of the hyper-neutral civil servants insulates them from parliamentary influence. Also, no minister *ever* retains an active locally elected office or feels the necessity to do so; and the same applies to the vast bulk of MPs whose feelings towards the local authority in their constituency are, if anything, likely to range from the indifferent to the strongly hostile. Even those MPs who begin their political careers in local government seem to cut their links with it as soon as they reach the Commons.

The effect of this secularised functional system is to leave the local authority by French standards somewhat beleaguered when under threat from modernisation. Especially so, since the local bureaucrats also take part in the modernisation debates both via their professional associations and within the local authority associations. Their ultimate interests are, after all, better salaries and career structures and not any particular pattern of local government, and modernisation will at least mean that for those who find a place in the new system both will be improved.

Benign Central Government
The fourth characteristic of the British political system that bears upon the modernisation process is the somewhat different status of central government in British society as compared with France. It would be quite misleading to claim that central government is actively liked in a positive sense in Britain, and clearly one of the sources of the upsurge of Scottish and Welsh nationalism over the past ten years has been anti-centralism. On the other hand, there does not seem to be the almost automatic public attitude prevalent in France that sees central government as oppressive; as an alien force bearing down upon the localities from the imperium of Paris.[12] In Britain, where the central government has not seen itself as having the task of maintaining the unity of the State as it has in France,[13] central government *per se* is seldom viewed as oppressive and is often cast in the role of the beneficent umpire defending citizens' rights against the depredations of local authorities. It is thus released from the task of itself ensuring unity, with all that such a task entails in what, to British eyes at least, looks like an almost neurotic fear of disintegration shared apparently by all shades of opinion within the French political class.[14] British central government, unlike its French counterpart can, in short, play off the electorate against their own local government. And as politics has got increasingly turbulent over the past decade, the centre has seldom squandered the opportunity of so doing. A recent example of this tactic was the centre's attempt to identify local government profligacy as the cause of the steep rise in local taxes during the so-called 'rates crisis' in 1974. Quite apart from the immediate political gains of such ploys, they also have the useful effect of enhancing central government's standing with the electorate if not with local authorities.

It must be remembered that such tactics are able to capitalise on the assumption of an underlying unity within society which is itself based on a prior assumption (which also sharply distinguishes Britain from France), namely, that society is prior, and even superior, to the State. Such unarticulated premises raise no problems when such unity does in fact exist, but when it does not – which seems to be the case in Scotland and to a lesser degree in Wales – then the process of adjustment is both bewildering and painful. Bereft of any theory of the State, how do you defend it? Here lies the origin of the air of tentativeness, the sense of improvisation and the sheer unreality of the current process of devolution.

The more favourable standing of British central government as compared with French central government that these cultural traits produce is probably reinforced because, lacking a prefectoral system, it is detached from the grass roots, or is dispersed in separate functional outposts. This means that the State in Britain is not seen as being separate from society in quite the same way as it is in countries like France where the central apparatus reaches down to the localities in a uniform hierarchical command structure. It is of some interest that where the central government has taken on a direct operational role for a service which is vulnerable to public displeasure – the national motorway system and national airports are good examples – attitudes have been changing and central government is beginning to be viewed as unfavourably as it is in France.[15]

The significance of the relatively better public standing of central government in Britain in this context is that the possibility of local government modernisation is probably greater, since central government intentions in promoting a modernisation scheme are not automatically suspect as they seem to have been in France,[16] and it can draw upon a certain amount of public goodwill, at least initially.

Other Factors Facilitating Modernisation in Britain as compared with France
The central government has been further strengthened in its capacity to effect the modernisation of local government by another peculiarity of the British political system and this is the absence of any institutionalised leadership at the local level. It is true that from time to time local leaders do emerge onto the national stage, but they are very rare and their ascendancy is entirely due to personal circumstances, since the machinery of British local government is probably unique, in that it does not provide any executive office. This is because it does not recognise the necessity for distinguishing between the executive and deliberative (or legislative) functions. Power resides solely in the elected council, and although

there is a mayor he holds a purely ceremonial office (usually a single year's duration) other than presiding at council meetings. There is no equivalent of the French mayor, or indeed of any other form of executive that all other comparable systems of local government seem to find essential, whether it be the city manager, the municipal board or the Burgomeister.[17] The consequences of this lack of local leaders with a formal power base are manifold, not least as it affects the balance of power between centre and locality within the political parties themselves. In relation to local government modernisation, it has meant that on the national stage the localities are collectively relatively weak. They do have national associations which watch over their collective interests but at the time of the reorganisation there were no less than five of them, each representing a different type of local authority (county, county borough, urban district, rural district and parish). Consequently each association had a different interest at stake, often in direct conflict with another association. The degree of cohesion and continuity, and consequently the power, of a single association of local political leaders such as the Association of French Mayors can generate was therefore totally lacking.[18] The consequences of this weakness in relation to local government reorganisation are obvious and again we see that the possibility of modernisation was probably much greater in Britain than in France.

The British local authority pressure groups, like the local government system as a whole, also lack the defensive advantage of the French system in having direct links, via overlapping membership, with the two houses of the legislature; and perhaps of even greater importance, links with the ministerial cadres of the major parties.[19] As we have already noted, the number of MPs who maintain their seats on local councils are very few and far between. To do so indeed is itself a questionable act for an MP. Herbert Morrison who did retain his links with London local government was constantly taunted with the Tammany Hall jibe, and his constancy to his local power base probably cost him his chance of the leadership of the Labour Party.[20] Moreover, the parties in Britain, being fewer, are on the whole stronger than their French counterparts and dominate urban local government. When the party in power nationally also dominates the key urban local authority association – as it did during the period when the local government reform bills were going through Parliament – even the relatively limited power of the localities to resist is emasculated. In this last respect the contrast with France is particularly striking, since whereas the Gaullists completely dominated national politics from 1958 until the election of Giscard d'Estaing, the localities remained firmly in the hands of the anti-Gaullists who, when the occasion demanded it, could always effectively resist Paris on the local government modernisation issue.[21]

Perhaps, finally, we may permit ourselves the conjecture that, unlike its British counterpart, the French central government's heart was never really in the local government modernisation business simply because, for the reasons discussed earlier, the perceived need for such modernisation was less urgent. The small size of communes is of much less consequence if the bulk of them are functionally unimportant, the more so if enlarging them runs the risk of rendering the prefectoral structure obsolete. We shall return to this theme in a moment.

All things considered, we may conclude that the case for change in Britain was, or rather was felt to be, more urgent than in France and, moreover, the possibility of effecting it significantly greater. For these reasons we may expect that the French approach to modernisation would be less drastic, more hesitant and less successful than the British, and that, broadly speaking, is what we find. It is, therefore, difficult to see how this difference between the experience of the two countries[22] implies any great mystery, paradox, or even much surprise. Still less ought we to be tempted into translating the difference into some general hypothesis about the distribution of power between centre and locality in the two countries.[23] It may very well be that a great deal of commentary and discussion of central–local relations in France has perhaps failed to appreciate its subtlety and ambiguity and particularly its reciprocity.[24] It may have especially failed to give due weight to the dependence of the prefect on the mayor and the *notables* he is ostensibly supposed to be governing, and their capacity to bypass him.[25]

All this may be admitted, but the relatively muted French experience in local government reform as compared with the British does not permit us to go on to argue that 'the British system may in fact operate in a more highly centralized fashion than the French', and that each function of local government 'has in effect been nationalized and policies for each function rest unequivocally with the central administration'.[26] The French local modernisation experience does not, as has been claimed,[27] rest solely on the *power* of the commune but also in most parts of France on its functional (but not, of course, political) irrelevance. Or, to revert to the earlier discussion, where there already exists concentrated executive power at the centre (as in both France and Britain), the price of functional autonomy in local government is vulnerability to modernisation. It ought not to be forgotten in any discussion of centre–periphery relations that the role of the centre and the structure of local government are interdependent. That is to say, the integrated prefectoral model is not merely a product of French adhesion to the notion of the one and indivisible republic, but is also functional to a society where until the last couple of decades a very large proportion of its population, and a far larger proportion than in Britain, lived in small largely rural communities. As Thoenig has pointed out,[28] where this population pattern has changed to one of more concentrated and large urban centres the prefectoral system has broken down. In fact the prefectoral system has probably never really worked in its pristine form in the larger towns in any case.[29]

It is the exceptionally small scale of the average French commune as compared with the average local government unit in Britain during the 1960s that has also affected the very different *techniques* for effecting the modernisation of local government in the two countries. Getting two communes in, say, the Massif Central of two hundred souls apiece to amalgamate is a somewhat different exercise from joining up, say, Portsmouth and Southampton, each of over 200,000 population, with Hampshire. The first may be done by the simple expedient of extra cash, to refurbish the *mairie* perhaps or the water supply system; the other requires not financial incentives but statutes – sticks rather than carrots. This difference in technique tells us very little about whether the French have relinquished their alleged allegiance to Cartesian logic or indeed the one and indivisible republic; or, for that matter, whether the British have given up their alleged predilection for pragmatism.[30]

Finally, as Crozier pointed out many years ago, the French administrative system, like all strongly centralised systems, tends to be resistant to change. In the French case, as he also pointed out, there is the additional obstacle to change derived from the insulation of the horizontal layers of the hierarchy one from the other:

'People on top theoretically have a great deal of power and often much more power than they would have in other, more authoritarian societies. But these powers are not very useful, since people on top can act only in an impersonal way and can in no way interfere with the subordinate strata. They cannot therefore provide real leadership on a daily basis. If they want to introduce change, they must go through the long and difficult ordeal of a crisis. Thus, although they are all-powerful because they are at the apex of the whole centralized system, they are made so weak by the pattern of resistance of the different isolated strata that they can use their power only in truly exceptional circumstances.'[31]

THE CASE FOR MODERNISATION

The conditions for the modernisation of local government in Britain were particularly propitious, as we have just seen, but favourable conditions alone do not explain the fact of modernisation; there has to be a public case made out that is both persuasive and, since the actual structure of government itself is involved, ostensibly politically neutral as well. This is the rational-efficiency case noted at the outset, and this section of the paper will be devoted to spelling it out. In order to do so in a systematic fashion it is necessary to set out at the start what may be called the main *desiderata* of an effective local government system in an advanced industrial democracy.

Broadly speaking, there are four *desiderata* for an effective local government system, which in rough order of importance are that:

(1) it should be as democratic as possible; and this may be described as the democratic criterion;
(2) its structure should reflect as far as possible the population settlement pattern within the State; this is the socio-geographic criterion;
(3) its units should be capable of providing the major services to currently acceptable standards – the functional criterion; and
(4) it should have the right to raise some of its own expenditure by taxation; the tax-raising criterion.

These are necessarily very vague conditions; nevertheless they do provide a convenient framework within which we may discuss what were alleged to be the main defects of the British local government system and one, moreover, that may also be applicable to other comparable countries. The arguments discussed in this section are derived from the various investigations into the deficiencies of the local government system, the most important of which were the Reports of the Royal Commissions on Local Government in England[32] and Scotland[33] and the Local Government Commission's Report for Wales,[34] together with the various government White Papers.[35] Let us begin with socio-geographic criterion on the link between settlement pattern and structure because this is probably the one where the case for modernisation was at its strongest.

The Socio-Geographic Criterion

The pre-1974 structure had its origins in legislation passed in 1888 and 1894, and, so the argument ran, since then there had been a transformation of the pattern of population settlement in Britain. This is what may be called the urban revolution, which in its earlier phases was still partly attributable to population movement from rural to urban areas, but by the 1920s was predominantly the outward expansion of existing urban areas. That is to say, the expansion of urban areas was mainly the result of the centrifugal movement of existing urban dwellers. This trend is graphically illustrated by the incidence of population growth; in the intercensal period 1931–51 the rate of growth of population outside the old boundaries of the cities and towns was six times that of population growth within them. During the intercensal period 1951–61 virtually all population growth occurred outside the old urban boundaries. This process has continued since 1961 so that, today, Britain is probably the most urbanised, or rather, suburbanised, of all the advanced industrial democracies. Barely 3 per cent of its workforce is engaged in agriculture and that proportion includes fishery and forestry workers. This urbanisation process has been heavily concentrated in what has been called ironically by planners 'the coffin'. This is a broad tract of England that runs north-west to south-east, beginning with the twin urban concentrations of Liverpool and Manchester at the western corner of the northern end of the tract, with the West Riding of Yorkshire at the eastern corner, and ends at the southern end by embracing the whole of the south-eastern region around London, including Greater Birmingham and the Black Country on the way. About 70 per cent of the British population live in 'the coffin', and such was the centrifugal movement of the urban population out in the rural and semi-rural hinterlands of the urban centres in the bulk of this area that it was no longer meaningful to talk about a distinctly rural or a distinctly urban way of life, but, rather, of differing degrees of urban-ness – if not urbanity!

The structure of local government, however, was based on the assumption that there was a clear distinction between town and country such that it assumed that the built-up area of cities required a separate form of unitary government (the county borough) whereas the rest of the country, including the city's contiguous suburbs, was governed under a two-tier structure of county and district. Yet in 'the coffin' at least such a distinction no longer bore much relation to reality. In this area most people, so it was argued, were dependent on an urban centre for their jobs, shopping and services although some of them may be living in a rural or quasi-rural environment. The advent, first of cheap public transport and later of the cheap motor car, and rising disposable incomes, meant that the modern city has extended itself well beyond the continuously built-up area to include a penumbra of satellite settlements surrounding it. This is the so-called 'spread city' and, it was claimed, the local government structure, because it is charged with the responsibility for providing services that are closely linked with the underlying socio-economic structure (planning, public transport and traffic management), ought to reflect its existence by the creation of a new unit of government that embraced town and country.

In other words, the old system was said to be irrational and inefficient because many local authorities were no longer self-contained in service terms. In consequence the public goods they provided – further education, shopping centres, parking facilities, traffic management, new roads – had increasing externalities, so that not only was it impossible to control many of the causes of policy problems, but the core of the democratic political process at the local level – the allocation of resources – had become increasingly unreal. Some authorities were providing public goods services a large part of which were enjoyed by citizens in adjoining authorities, while other local authorities were enjoying the benefits of public goods provided by adjoining authorities to the cost of which they made no contribution. What was needed was an extension of the boundaries of the cities to embrace their hinterlands, thus internalising the public goods externalities of the existing system.

The Functional Criterion
The second condition for an effective local government system that it may be argued the old government system was unable to fulfil is the functional criterion, i.e. that it should be capable of providing the major services to currently accepted standards. But if the old local government system was deficient in this respect the evidence is less persuasive than that for the socio-geographic factor. One reason for this is that while the functional capacity criterion is undoubtedly a necessary condition of local government it is, none the less, extremely difficult to demonstrate its fulfilment, except at the extremes. Thus we may say, for example, that an effective secondary education system can no longer be provided by a unit of government of the size of a village, and we may go on to say that it is unnecessary to have units of government for secondary schools as big as half a million population, but it is much more difficult to demonstrate what the *optimum* secondary education authority ought to be. Such difficulties, however, did not deter critics of the old system who were convinced that there were too many local authorities that were too small in population terms to provide the major services. Essentially, these critics rested their case on the application of economies of scale theories derived from theories of the firm. That is to say, they argued that the range of services that local government was required to provide involved inescapable fixed costs which if the units of local government were larger could be spread over a larger output. Whether or not this theory had any substance remained to be proven, but there seemed to be a fairly plausible version of it that does warrant our attention.

This argued that there has been a secular trend within the educational, social, health and welfare services in the direction of providing new services for increasingly more precisely defined client

groups. This process was a function of a growing recognition by the
State that all had to be given equal life chances and therefore tended
to involve the provision of more and more specialised services for
small and smaller proportions of the population. This process may be
traced, for example, in the field of education where originally public
education was seen simply as the provision by the State of certain
minimal standards of literacy and numeracy for the whole age
cohort except those in private education. In Britain when public
education was first established, this cohort ran from age 5 to 12. By
just after the turn of the century, State grammar schools with a
strong academic bias were felt to be necessary and they catered for
not 95 per cent of the age cohort but nearer 25 per cent. Later
there developed the need for post-school technical education which
catered for an even smaller proportion of the age cohort. At the
same time came special school provision for blind children, for the
handicapped and the mentally retarded and each was dealing with
tiny fractions of the total school age cohort. Now, depending on
the capital structure of the service, this steady reduction in the
proportion of the population to be catered for meant that the
administrative area for the service had to be made wider and wider
in order to provide enough clients to warrant in economic efficiency
terms the minimum provision of equipment and staff – the indivisible
element – necessary to making the service operative. Even for a
class of, say, twenty mentally handicapped children of school age,
the indivisibles would be, let us say, one specially trained teacher,
one classroom and one set of special equipment and materials. But
to get the optimal case load of twenty mentally handicapped children
it may be necessary to have a base population far larger than that
of the existing local authority.

At the other end of the scale in local education in Britain, the
Polytechnic level, where the indivisible commitment of capital and
staff is enormous, the base population necessary to provide the
students to make such a commitment economically viable broadens
into regional and perhaps national proportions. In short, an
important trend in the personal health, welfare and educational
services tends to require larger units of local government. Whereas
the fulfilment of criterion (2) demands larger units in spatial terms,
the fulfilment of the service desideratum (3) requires larger units of
output in population terms.

The Democratic Criterion
We must now turn to the most important criterion, namely, that
a local government system should be as democratic as possible. In
this respect the old system was seen to have fewest deficiencies, and
for that reason it has been left to the last for appraisal. This is not

to say that there have been no critics of what may be called the democratic quality of British local government, but that these alleged deficiencies involved fewer fundamental criticisms than did the alleged deficiencies cited under the other three criteria. The four most cited deficiencies were, first, that local government did not attract elected members of sufficient quality to carry out the tasks involved. The second criticism was the low proportion of the electorate voting at local elections. Thirdly, it was claimed that the complicated structure of local government made it difficult for ordinary electors to comprehend the system and thus to participate in it. Finally, it was said that in large urban areas there was a need for a more localised body at the neighbourhood level comparable to the parish council in rural areas.

Let us examine the first criticism on the quality of local elected members. Leaving aside the question as to whether the notion of quality can have any relevance in a democracy because the electorate's right to choose representatives must by definition be untrammelled, this issue appears to have been a peculiarly British problem and seems to be related to a form of cultural lag whereby the norms appropriate to a pre-democratic age when the social elite tended to be coterminous with political elite still persist in the democratic era. As an issue of official concern it first appeared in the late 1950s when it was an important subsidiary theme in the Herbert Report on London government.[36] It came to a head when the Maud Committee on Management, which was set up in the mid-1960s, was specifically charged with the task of recommending ways in which the quality of elected members could be maintained and improved. Its proposals were published in 1967,[37] but despite these terms of reference the major concern of the Committee's Report was the need radically to alter the internal power structure of local authorities. Now it could be argued that such proposals were somehow linked to questions of quality of councillors. Nevertheless, those of the Committee's proposals that were strictly relevant to the quality of elected members were a minor feature of the Committee's Report. These proposals included a compulsory age limit of 70 for election, the abolition of aldermen[38] and the payment of an attendance allowance for councillors. The last two proposals have been adopted and interest in the whole subject of quality of councillors seems to have waned.

The second alleged democratic defect of the British local government system is the low turnout at elections. Little more than 40 per cent of the electorate on average vote at local elections, whereas turnout at general elections averages about 75 per cent. Whether this is a defect that can be remedied by manipulating the structure of local government is open to doubt, however. Equally doubtful is the assumption that the level of turnout is a measure of democracy. Some have claimed that low turnout reflected public bewilderment at the complexity of local government, and this leads us conveniently to the third democratic defect of the system noted earlier. One of the recommendations common to all of the various public inquiries into the local government was the simplification of the structure. The case for simplification was at its strongest in relation to the old county system where a third, intermediate, level of administration between county and district had evolved. This was designed to allow the second-tier district authorities (themselves divided into three classes) to participate in some county services, notably planning, education and health, by means of so-called delegation schemes. This had the effect of creating a shadow tier of government which could have done little to enhance public understanding of the way the system worked and where power lay. To the extent that the new system reduced the number of local government units, simplified the second tier and abolished delegation it must be presumed that public comprehension has been enhanced.

The final democratic defect to be discussed was the absence of an urban grass-roots authority. This criticism seemed to be derived at least in part from a much wider change in public attitudes towards government, especially in relation to planning that we noted earlier. Briefly, the public was less quiescent than it had been and had become both more critical and more demanding of government. This change in attitudes often expressed itself on environmental issues in defence of neighbourhood interests in urban areas, and a directly elected neighbourhood council was seen as one way of articulating such conflicts on a permanent and formal basis.[39]

The Tax-Raising Criterion
The tax raising criterion is perhaps the most problematic of the four criteria for an effective local government system. But since the distinguishing characteristics of the British local financial system and the extent to which it meets the tax raising criterion is discussed elsewhere in this volume by G. W. Jones it will be considered very briefly. The claim that an effective local government system should have the power to raise taxes is derived from the assumption that the willingness of a local community to tax itself is a fundamental measure of its willingness to govern itself. Second, it may be argued that the tax-raising power strengthens the democratic link between the citizen and his local government by providing the elector with a measure of performance. Finally, it may be argued that an independent source of revenue is essential for the independence of local government. The Layfield Committee Report[40] certainly considered the financial independence and the local democracy

arguments to be crucial, and it makes a strong plea for changing the ambiguity of the present system in which no clear lines of accountability are apparent between the local tax payer and his local government precisely because such a high proportion of its income comes from the centre.

THE NEW LOCAL GOVERNMENT SYSTEM

Origins of New System
The first attempt at modernisation of local government after the Second World War began in 1945 and formed part of a much wider movement of structural change and policy innovation flowing from the ethos of social reconstruction generated by the war. It took the form of a Boundary Commission which, in the British tradition of public inquiries, consisted of a group of laymen and professionals appointed by the central government which meets on a part-time basis to examine the working of given government process, institution or policy by receiving memoranda of evidence from interested parties, both in writing and orally, and then formulating a series of policy recommendations in the form of a Report to the minister. The Boundary Commission soon found, however, that its terms of reference were too narrowly drawn for it to make an adequate assessment. This was because it was not allowed to consider functional redistribution but could only look at boundaries. Yet it was impossible to redraw the boundaries of local authorities without establishing first what services the authorities were to undertake. The Commission decided therefore to go beyond its remit and recommend functional redistribution (i.e. new *types* of local authorities) as well as boundary changes. In so doing it naturally created a great deal of resentment among existing local authorities who felt that their fate was being pronounced upon in contravention of the law, and in 1949 the Commission was wound up by the minister and none of its proposals was ever acted upon.

The issue of local government modernisation did not re-surface until 1958 when the Local Government Act of that year established a new Commission, or rather two Commissions, one for England and one for Wales. The Scottish system of local government has always been different from that of England and Wales and it is always considered separately. At the time the English and Welsh Commissions were set up no comparable inquiry was established for Scotland. The English Commission, it must be noted, was excluded from considering the area of Greater London,[41] but it was allowed to consider functional redistribution at least in the great urban concentrations around the cities of Birmingham, Liverpool, Manchester, Leeds and Newcastle – the so-called conurbations.[42]

Both the English and Welsh Commissions began their respective tasks in 1958 and the Welsh Commission completed its work in the early 1960s and its Report formed the basis for the new system that was established in 1974. Because the area it covered was much larger, the English Commission divided up the country into regions and considered each in turn *seriatim*. This meant that it was still in the process of considering change in one part of England when its earlier recommendations were being implemented by the central government for other parts of the country. It also meant that because its own ideas and the general climate of public opinion about local government reorganisation changed over time, it was suggesting different and more drastic solutions by the mid-1960s than it had been just after it was first established in 1958.

For this reason and because of the somewhat cumbersome procedures devised for translating its recommendations into law, the Commission came into disfavour, and in 1966 the minister responsible at the time wound it up. Another motive for ending the Commission's life before it had completed its task was also that of party advantages. Because under the British electoral system for electing the House of Commons emphasis is given to representing communities as well as achieving numerical equality of electors, parliamentary electoral boundaries are, wherever possible, tied to local government boundaries in the sense that a parliamentary constituency seldom overlaps a local government boundary. Since one of the characteristics of the changes the commission was recommending was the extension of urban authority boundaries to embrace peripheral settlements that were mainly of a middle-class character, this meant that, in general, the effect of the Commission's activities was to put a number of parliamentary seats variously estimated at between eight and twenty then held by the Labour party (then in power nationally) at risk. This became particularly evident following the Commission's draft recommendations for the conurbations. The winding up of the Commission was one way of delaying any change in local government boundaries, and thus protecting the Labour Party's majority in the Commons until at least after the following general election.[13]

Party advantage was clearly not the only motive for winding up the Local Government Commissions, however, since the government at the same time that it wound up the Commission also created a third, Royal, Commission on local government reorganisation that is known as the Redcliffe-Maud Commission after its Chairman, Lord Redcliffe-Maud. Moreover, this Commission was given an even wider remit than its predecessor and could consider boundaries and functions in their entirety over the whole of England. A separate Commission with the same remit was set up simultaneously for

Scotland. This was the Wheatley Commission which reported in 1970 and whose proposals are discussed later. The Redcliffe-Maud Commission sat for three years and reported in 1969.[44] Unlike its two predecessors its proposals were endorsed by the government with only minor amendments in a White Paper published in February 1970.[45]

The 1972 Act

The White Paper was not, however, supported by the Conservative Opposition and when the Labour government was defeated in June 1970 their proposals based on the Redcliffe-Maud Report died with them. The new Conservative government set about devising its own scheme which appeared in the early part of 1971 and eventually became law in September 1972. The ostensible reason for the incoming Conservative government's rejection of the Redcliffe-Maud Report was that they disliked the central feature of its proposals which was the unitary authority. This was a new concept that involved creating a single-tier system throughout the country of very large authorities with a population range from 250,000 to 1,000,000 and each centred on a major city with its boundaries embracing the surrounding hinterland of the city. Instead, the Conservatives favoured a two-tier system which they felt was a more democratic system, since it would make it possible to have smaller and more localised authorities for minor services. However strong this motive was, it is clear that the Conservatives also sought to devise a new system that favoured their party locally. In England outside the conurbations they achieved this by abolishing the system of separate city authorities where the Labour Party was strong (formerly called county boroughs) and extending the two-tier system to cover the whole country in the form of county councils and district councils, incorporating the county boroughs (which became district councils) into the adjacent county where in all but a few cases the Conservatives, or the Independents, were usually in a majority. In the conurbation areas the Labour Party interest was less affected and existing county boroughs were in effect strengthened in terms of population and area, becoming metropolitan districts within the metropolitan counties created for each conurbation.

Two years were allowed for winding up the old system and laying down the foundations of the new including the holding of elections for the new authorities in 1973. In April 1974 the new system came into being.

The new system comprises two levels, or tiers, of local authorities; the top tier are the counties and below these are the districts. In the six great urban conurbations around Birmingham, Liverpool, Manchester, Leeds, Sheffield and Newcastle a special type of county has been created called a metropolitan county, and corresponding metropolitan districts below them. Metropolitan counties and metropolitan districts both tend to have larger populations than normal counties and districts. The distribution of functions is also different in that the metropolitan counties have fewer functions than normal counties and the metropolitan districts have correspondingly more functions.

In rural areas there is a third tier, the parish, which embraces a village and its surrounding farmland. Parishes have a very narrow range of very local amenity responsibilities. There are in England and Wales 47 counties and 333 districts, 6 metropolitan counties and 36 metropolitan districts. The distribution of the main functions between these different types is as follows:

County ($N=47$)
- Education
- Health, welfare and child care
- Main roads
- Traffic management
- Public transport
- Structure planning
- Police
- Libraries

Metropolitan county ($N=6$)
- Structure planning
- Main roads
- Traffic
- Public transport
- Police

District ($N=333$)
- Housing
- Local planning and control
- Street cleansing and refuse collection
- Local roads
- Sport and recreation

Metropolitan district ($N=36$)
- Education
- Health, welfare and child care
- Housing
- Traffic
- Local roads
- Local planning and control
- Street cleansing and refuse collection
- Sports and recreation

Parish (rural areas only)
- Village hall
- Footpaths
- Recreation etc.

This system which in total comprises 422 new authorities (excluding parishes) was a drastic change by any standard, replacing as it did a much more complex combined two-tier and single-tier system consisting of 83 county boroughs (single tier covering most of the cities) and 58 counties. The latter were the top tier of a two-tier system, the lower tier of which consisted of 1,252 districts divided into three categories: municipal boroughs, urban districts and rural districts. Below the latter were the parishes which have been retained unchanged in the new system. Excluding the parishes, the 1,400 or so authorities of the old system have been reduced by a factor of 3·3.

Scotland

At the same time as the Redcliffe-Maud Commission was set up in 1966 a parallel Royal Commission was established to examine local government in Scotland under the chairmanship of Lord Wheatley. The Wheatley Commission Report[46] was published in 1970 and much the same arguments are deployed in favour of the radical restructuring of local government that were discussed in the second section of this paper. The socio-geographic criterion was, if anything, even more dominant in the case made out for the new Scottish structure than it was in relation to the English. This seems to have had the result that in relation to Scotland as a whole the new primary local authorities, called significantly regions and not counties, are very much larger than the English counties. Unlike the proposals of its sister Commission, the Wheatley proposals were, with one or two exceptions, usually in the direction of moderating the extent of change, largely accepted by the government and translated into law which came into force in May 1975. The new system seems to have been accepted with somewhat less misgivings and recriminations than was apparent, certainly in the parliamentary debates, in relation to the new system in England and Wales.[47] This is no doubt attributable to the fact that the new Scottish system bore a much closer relationship to the recommendations of an impartial Commission and was, therefore, absolved of the accusation of party bias or just plain wrongheadedness that was levelled against the new system in England.

Like the new English system the new Scottish structure comprises two levels, but in many other respects the systems are different. Even in this respect there is the difference that not all of Scotland will have two levels, for the three island groups to the west and north of the Scottish mainland will have single-tier government and one of them, Shetland, has subsequently won for itself by means of a private Act further powers, particularly in relation to its own economic development which make it largely independent of the Scottish Office in relation to the exploitation of the massive oil reserves within its territorial waters. There are nine regions which, as we have noted, are in proportion to the total population of Scotland much larger than English counties. The largest region – Strathclyde – which covers Glasgow and its hinterland embraces a population of 2·6 million which is over half of the total Scottish population. Below the nine regions are fifty-three district councils and at the very local level there is the possibility of elected community councils. These bodies will have no statutory functions but they are intended to express local views and act on behalf of the local community. The distribution of functions in the new structure

– which is broadly similar to that between county and district in England and Wales – is as follows:

Island
authorities
(*N* = 3)

Regional
council
(*N* = 9)

- Education
- Health, welfare and children
- Main roads
- Traffic movement
- Public transport
- Strategic planning
- Police

District
councils
(*N* = 53)

- Housing
- Local planning
- Street cleansing and refuse collection
- Minor roads
- Sport and recreation
- Local libraries

Community
councils

No statutory functions

This system, which comprises (excluding community councils which have yet to be established) 64 authorities in all, replaces a much more variegated pattern of 430 authorities. This represents a reduction in numbers by a factor of almost 7, which is about twice as big a reduction as for England and Wales. If the English and Welsh reform was drastic, the Scottish reform can only be described as revolutionary.

The electoral system follows broadly the British pattern and also as in the rest of the country important changes have taken place in the internal decision-making system. These are aimed at creating more coherent and co-ordinated policy making and breaking down departmental boundaries.

The new Scottish system is even younger than the new local government system in the rest of the country so no adequate assessment can be made of its relative success. However, generally speaking, it was established on the same rationale as the new system in England and Wales and similar reservations apply both as to whether that rationale is justified and whether the new system will be able to fulfil the objectives which it was intended to achieve under the latter heading. For this reason there is no separate section assessing the new system in Scotland since there is no need to go over the same ground again. However, it should perhaps be emphasised that there is nothing comparable in the new Scottish system to the metropolitan counties which are perhaps the most problematic of the new bodies created in England.

The Internal Decision-making Process

Before going on to assess the operation of the new structure of local government since it was established, there remains one further aspect of the reorganisation process that merits our attention. This is the series of modifications that have been made to the internal decision-making processes of local authorities.

As at the central level, British local authorities adhere strictly to a tradition of a permanent, politically neutral, bureaucracy employed solely on merit. But unlike the central civil service where the non-specialist generalist manager dominates the higher posts, at the local government level it is the technical specialist who reigns supreme. This distinction between centre and locality reflects the two different and complementary roles that central and local government perform within the overall system of British government mentioned in the opening section of this paper. As befits the executant and operational arm of the central–local partnership, all the top levels of local government are manned by technical specialists (accountants, solicitors, engineers, surveyors etc.), and it is impossible to rise above the lowest rungs of the career ladder without the appropriate technical qualifications.

The structure of the local bureaucracy is thus strongly departmentalised with almost no movement of individuals between departments, and in the absence of any executive there is no hierarchy above the level of the departmental heads with the power to enforce co-ordination and direct departmental heads on pain of dismissal. This division is reinforced by the committee system. They direct the affairs of the departments and are manned by the councillors. It should be noted, however, that the annual budget-making process serves as an important co-ordinating instrument and in urban areas the leader and the officers of the major party and the leadership group in non-partisan rural authorities also constitute an informal executive and co-ordinating element. However, the absence of a·formal executive has been the cause of some considerable official concern over the last decade or so, since it has been claimed that such an absence makes adequate co-ordination and forward policy making difficult. The fragmented committee system, it is argued, also obscured the respective roles of councillor and bureaucrat. This concern has expressed itself in two official inquiries into local government management processes: these were the Maud Committee Report[48] (not to be confused with the Redcliffe-Maud Commission Report mentioned earlier), and the Bains Report,[49] and both are discussed within this volume by R. A. W. Rhodes.

AN ASSESSMENT OF THE NEW SYSTEM

How far has the new system of local government flowing from the 1972 Local Government Act (which came into operation in April 1974) corrected the alleged defects of the system as outlined earlier? We begin with the socio-geographic criterion which, it will be remembered, requires that the structure of local government reflects the population settlement pattern. There seem to be obvious reasons why the boundary of a local government system ought to reflect the living patterns of its citizens in the sense that it may be more equitable and be more rational for planning and transportation to 'internalise' the 'externalities' of the services provided by local government.[50] That is to say, to adjust the boundaries of adjacent authorities so as to ensure that both the benefits and the costs of such services which may overlap existing boundaries are shouldered by the same citizens. Examples of such externalities are the services provided by a city authority that are enjoyed by citizens living in surrounding areas, such as access roads to central shopping and services, public transport, car parks, specialised education, cultural and sports facilities.

It is also argued that such amalgamations reinforce subjective attitudes of community identity among the population as well. For instance, if a man works in one local government area and lives in another his sense of identity with local government may be weaker than if he lives and works in one authority. However, plausible as this theory may seem, there is some evidence to suggest that the extension of boundaries in order to internalise the former service externalities, far from generating new subjective loyalties to the new wider authority may weaken them, thus undermining rather than enhancing the social cohesion of the new local authorities.

The case for creating new units of local government that will be largely self-contained in planning and cognate service terms involves the integration of the urban centre with its service hinterland, or to put it in the simple terms of everyday political debate, joining up town with country. However, the undoubted integration of the environmental services that has been achieved in the new system by joining up towns with their contiguous penumbra – what may be called *horizontal* integration – has to be set against the vertical disintegration of the system that has also occurred because the districts have also been given powers in planning, highways and traffic. Under the old system these functions were centralised either on the county, in rural areas, or on the county borough in the larger towns. Now throughout the country they are divided between the two levels of local government. This division is perhaps at its most extreme in relation to planning where there is a fundamental split in the plan-making function; the formulation of local plans lying with the districts and the strategic plan-making function lying with the county. The bulk of day-to-day planning control is exercised by the district. In short, horizontal integration has been achieved at the cost of vertical *disintegration,* and in two senses the cost has been especially high in the urban areas. First, all the towns of any size were county boroughs under the old system, that is to say, they were single tier so that not only was planning integrated, but the related services of highways, traffic management and public transport were integrated too. In such urban areas centralisation might be thought to be essential, yet one of the effects of the new system is that for the first time there are now two planning, two highways and two traffic authorities in the very heart of all the urban centres.

The second sense in which the new system seems likely to be unable to fulfil its objectives concerns the metropolitan counties. This is because these counties, unlike the counties in the rest of the country, do not extend beyond the built-up area, so that they do not in practice integrate town with country. Given the fact that they will have more limited powers than ordinary counties and will have to operate in co-operation with substantially stronger districts, it is difficult to see how the metropolitan counties will be capable of functioning as the strategic planning and transportation authorities that were envisaged by the proponents of the new system.

To sum up, it seems doubtful whether the new structure can ever achieve the objective of providing a better integrated and co-ordinated system within self-contained socio-geographic areas. The question then arises as to whether the gains achieved by the new system in terms of reducing the externalities at the county level outweigh this deficiency. The enormous disruptive effects and the huge costs involved in the changeover has entailed widespread public disenchantment with the new system and must also be taken into account in such an assessment.

We now turn to assessing the new system against the second criterion of an effective local government system on modern democracy, namely, that relating to functional capacity. This requirement, it will be remembered, is in any case a vague one, involving assumptions about functional scale optima about which it is extremely difficult to obtain any convincing evidence one way or the other. Despite the many claims made in the debates about local government modernisation in Britain on behalf of larger units of government in terms of their greater efficiency and effectiveness, the fact remains that none of the studies that attempt by systematic analysis to relate scale (i.e. population) to service output shows scale as having much demonstrable impact on services.[51] Small authorities, in other words, as measured in conventional financial cost terms, do not appear to be any worse, or better, than large authorities. Moreover, even if it was possible to delineate such optima there would remain the need to reconcile those optima one with another since the new structure, like the old, has to be multi-functional. If, however, we accept the earlier (yet unproven) assumption that for the social welfare and educational services ever larger base populations are becoming necessary for efficiency, we may conclude that the new system is an improvement on the old. For, whereas the population of the smallest education and social welfare local authority under the old system was about 30,000, now it is about 150,000, and the average for such authorities is about 1,000,000.

There is little to say about the tax-raising criterion since the financial aspects of the new system are the same as the old, but, as was pointed out earlier, there is the Layfield Report that examined the whole question of local government finance, and it may be that changes will be made in the near future to combat the problems discussed elsewhere in this volume as a result of the Report's recommendations. However, as the Report makes clear, some of the alleged deficiencies of the financial system are perhaps not as critical as is often supposed. However, there is one aspect of the local financial system – the impact of central grants – that merits further discussion. The Layfield Committee places a strong emphasis on the link between local autonomy and the extent of central grants. Broadly speaking they argue the greater the extent of central funding the less the autonomy of local government. However, although there clearly must be some link between central grants and local autonomy, it is difficult to escape the conclusion that the Committee may have taken a too simplified view of the relationship.

In the first place, if we define autonomy as being able to do what you want, then it is equally plausible to assume that the reverse is true; that is to say, central grants make it possible for some local authorities – the relatively poor ones – to undertake projects and provide services that they would not otherwise be able to do. In other words, on one view of autonomy central funds can *enhance* local autonomy. Secondly, it is by no means clear that, in Britain at least, the proportion of the cost of local services carried by central government influences the degree of central government control. In planning, for example, which receives virtually no central funds, central government takes a very strong interest. Not only does it approve all the structure plans, but it also acts in a quasi-judicial capacity on planning approvals where there is a dispute. Similarly, central government makes precisely the same contribution to the cost of police as it does to the fire service, yet it has much more control over the former than the latter for obvious reasons. Beyond the undoubted necessity for central government to ensure that grants made to local authorities have been expended correctly, that is to say, the need to make sure that local authorities are properly accountable, there does not seem to be a necessary link between the extent of central financial aid and local freedom. Moreover, in Britain, as we noted earlier, the complementary nature of the roles of central and local government – especially the fact that executant expertise is locally employed – means that local government enjoys an irreducible degree of autonomy in any case – whatever the extent of financial aid from central government. Does this mean, then, that the right of local authorities to tax and raise some of their own revenue is of no importance? The answer must be 'no', for, as we saw earlier, willingness to tax itself is the primary test of the community's capacity for self-government. The power to tax also confers on local government a special status that is not enjoyed by any other government agency (in a unitary system at least) except central government itself. And this special status is cognisant with the fact that local government is the only other elective body in the State. Furthermore, it is also linked to local government's essential role as an efficient provider of services.

This role is derived from the fact that local government performs the task of common general superior at the local level. This is a primordial function of all local government systems and is derived from the fact that central government organises itself for the sake of efficiency into specialised departments administering cognate public services – roads, traffic and transportation, for example, or health, welfare and social services. However, the recipients of these services – the citizens – do not live in such ordered categories, but in mixtures of such categories: the old, the young, the unemployed, the mentally handicapped, the able-bodied and the chronically sick. In short, they live in communities, and each community varies in its composition, and this fact demands that another level of government be established nearer to the point of consumption of public services whose special task is to adjust the level of each public service coming down from the centre in accordance with the variation in need in each community and to co-ordinate public services one with the other. Not only must there be a common general superior to adjust the level of services to meet local variation and to co-ordinate, there is also the equally important function of setting priorities as between the competing demands of each service. All three functions involve decisions about values, and the link between them and the local tax is simply that in a democratic state such tasks not only imply some form of locally elected body but also the right to raise some revenue locally. This is especially so for the priority-setting function since it is the relative availability of resources that determines the need for priority setting in any case.

However, the functional case for local government just described does not exhaust the reasons for granting a local government system in the modern state the right to tax, since it is possible to define a range of services, albeit somewhat minor ones such as refuse collection, the maintenance of minor roads that are inherently local in character in the sense that they can be provided and are 'consumed' within each locality, there being no spill-over effects. These are public goods that have no externalities beyond the community boundary and as such are, therefore, of no concern to anyone but those who live in the community; they should, in logic, be financed solely by them as well.

There remains the democratic criterion, and here we may detect one or two changes introduced by the new system that demand appraisal. It will be remembered that there are four aspects of the democratic quality of local government that, it was claimed, were deficient in the old system. The first deficiency was the quality of elected members and it is much too early to make any assessment as to how far the new structure has affected this defect, for if the new system does affect the quality of councillors it will take some time for it to have an effect. But even if insufficient time has elapsed, there remains a serious problem of assessing the extent of change since, like functional capacity, quality in this context is an elusive characteristic to measure. Where the new system may have affected members' quality relates to the abolition of the aldermanic system (see note 38) for, in so far as this system tended to encourage elected members to remain on the council after their faculties began to decline, it could be said that the new system, by abolishing aldermen, has improved the quality of councillors. Similarly, it could be argued that the reduction in the total number of councillors (about a one-third reduction in numbers in aggregate) brought about by the new system has also raised their quality because party selection committees, faced with fewer places to fill, have been more discriminating in their choice of candidates. But this of necessity must remain even more of an inference than the assumption that the abolition of aldermen has led to an improvement in the quality of councillors.

On the question of low turnout, which was another alleged democratic defect of the old system, there does not appear to be any discernible change. Again, it is clearly too early to make any accurate assessment, but if the first elections to the new system are any guide, turnout has not been affected even though the structure has been simplified. Turnout is, of course, only one indication of public interest in local government and public comprehension of the new system, and if we want an accurate assessment of the effect of the new system on public participation some kind of national survey is required.

We now come to the last alleged democratic defect of the new system which was the absence of a localised representative body in urban areas at the neighbourhood level. No provision was made for such a body in the legislation that established the new system except in Wales and Scotland. However, the Labour government elected in 1974 has shown a strong interest in establishing some forms of very localised representative body in urban areas. These are called 'neighbourhood councils', and the government published a consultation paper setting out the case for such councils for England in July 1974 which was issued to interested bodies.[52]

To sum up, the changes under the democratic criterion have been relatively minor; the dominant changes in the system have been made in relation to the socio-geographic and functional criteria. These changes have been so far-reaching that Britain now has the largest local authorities in Western Europe and possibly the world. The district, for example, is now on average some 100 times larger in population terms than the average French commune! Whether such large units will ever command sufficient public support to give them some permanence remains doubtful and another round of reorganisation is possible in the near future.[53]

NOTES

1 A. F. Leemans, *Changing Patterns of Local Government* (The Hague: International Union of Local Authorities, 1970), Introduction.
2 E. Kalk (ed.), *Regional Planning and Regional Government in Europe* (The Hague: International Union of Local Authorities, 1971).
3 L. J. Sharpe, ' "Reforming" the grass roots: An alternative analysis', in D. E. Butler and A. H. Halsey (eds), *Policy and Politics* (London: Macmillan, 1978).
4 For example, P. G. Richards, *The Reformed Local Government System*, 2nd edn (London: Allen & Unwin, 1975); R. Buxton, *Local Government*, 2nd edn (Harmondsworth: Penguin, 1975); Lord Redcliffe-Maud and B. Wood, *English Local Government Reformed* (London: OUP, 1975); J. Brand, *Local Government Reform in England: 1888–1974* (London: Croom Helm, 1974); D. Hill, *Democratic Theory and Local Government* (London: Allen & Unwin, 1974); B. Wood, *The Process of Local Government Reform 1966–74* (London: Allen & Unwin, 1976).
5 For a discussion of the principal characteristics of the Anglo-Saxon functional tradition of central–local relations as compared with the prefectoral tradition see B. C. Smith, *Field Administration* (London: Routledge & Kegan Paul, 1967).
6 For a comprehensive account of central–local relations in Britain see J. A. G. Griffith, *Central Department and Local Authorities* (London: Allen & Unwin, 1967). Also see Lady Sharpe, *The Ministry of Housing and Local Government* (London: Allen & Unwin, 1969), and M. Kogan (ed.), *The Politics of Education* (Harmondsworth: Penguin, 1971).
7 For descriptions of the machinery of the nationalised sector see L. J. Tivey, *Nationalization in British Industry* (London: Cape, 1973), and R. Pryke, *Public Enterprise in Practice* (London: MacGibbon & Kee, 1974).

8   For an account of quasi-governmental and non-governmental bodies see
     D. C. Hague *et al.* (eds), *Public Policy and Private Interests: The Institu-
     tions of Compromise* (London: Macmillan, 1975).
9   M. Crozier, *The Bureaucratic Phenomenon* (London: Tavistock, 1964),
     and M. Crozier and J.-C. Thoenig, *The Regulation of Complex Organized
     Systems* (mimeo, 1975).
10   J. E. Milch, 'Influence as power: French local government reconsidered',
     British Journal of Political Science, vol. 4, no. 2 (1974).
11   V. Wright, 'Politics and administration under the French Fifth Republic',
     Political Studies, vol. XXII, no. 1 (1974), p. 65.
12   J.-C. Thoenig, *State Bureaucracies and Local Government in France*
     (Berkeley: University of California, Berkeley, Department of Political
     Science, 1975); Crozier, *The Bureaucratic Phenomenon,* pt 4; M. Kessel-
     man, *The Ambiguous Consensus* (New York: Knopf, 1967), Ch. 1.
13   J. E. S. Hayward, *The One and Indivisible French Republic* (London:
     Weidenfeld & Nicolson, 1973), ch. 2.
14   P. Gourevitch, 'Reforming the Napoleonic State', paper given to the
     IXth World Congress of the International Political Science Association,
     Montreal, 1973.
15   R. Gregory, *The Price of Amenity* (London: Macmillan, 1971), and R.
     Kimber and J. J. Richardson (eds), *Campaigning for the Environment*
     (London: Routledge & Kegan Paul, 1974).
16   P. Mawhood, 'Melting the iceberg: The struggle to reform communal
     government in France', *British Journal of Political Science*, vol. 2, no. 4
     (1972).
17   See the *Report of the Committee on Management in Local Government*
     (Maud) (London: HMSO, 1967), Vol. 4 for a discussion of the various
     forms of executive found in the local government systems of a selection
     of Western democracies.
18   Hayward, *The One and Indivisible French Republic*, ch. 2.
19   H. Machin, 'Local government change in France – The case of the 1964
     reforms', *Policy and Politics*, vol. 2, no. 3 (1974).
20   B. Donoughue and G. Jones, *Herbert Morrison: Portrait of a Politician*
     (London: Weidenfeld & Nicolson, 1973), p. 242.
21   Machin, 'Local government change in France', and J. E. S. Hayward,
     'Presidential suicide by plebiscite: De Gaulle's exit, April 1969', *Parlia-
     mentary Affairs*, 1969.
22   Mawhood, 'Melting the iceberg', p. 502 seems to have been the first to
     perceive the difference between the two countries' approach to local
     government modernisation. It is also noted by Hayward, *The One and
     Indivisible French Republic*, p. 36.
23   D. Ashford, 'The limits of consensus: The reorganization of British local
     government and the French contrast', *Western Societies Programme
     Occasional Paper No. 6* (Ithaca: Cornell University, 1976).
24   M. Kesselman, 'Over-institutionalization and political constraint: The case
     of France', *Comparative Politics.* vol. 3, no. 1 (1970); Milch, 'Influence as
     power'; Thoenig, *State Bureaucracies and Local Government in France*;
     and Wright, 'Politics and administration under the French Fifth Republic'.
25   H. Machin, *The Prefects in French Public Administration* (London:
     Croome, 1977).
26   Ashford, 'The limits of consensus', p. 62.
27   ibid, p. 27.
28   Thoenig, *State Bureaucracies and Local Government in France*, p. 67. See
     also Gourevitch, 'Reforming the Napoleonic State'.

29 Milch, 'Influence as power', *passim.*
30 D. Ashworth, 'Financial incentives for local reorganization in Britain and France', paper given at the Xth World Congress of the International Political Science Association, Edinburgh, 1976.
31 Crozier, *The Bureaucratic Phenomenon*, p. 225.
32 *Report of the Royal Commission on Local Government in England* (Redcliffe–Maud), Cmnd 4040, 3 Vols (London: HMSO, 1969).
33 *Report of the Royal Commission on Local Government in Scotland* (Wheatley), Cmnd 4150 (Edinburgh: HMSO, 1969).
34 *Report of the Local Government Commission for Wales* (London: HMSO, 1962).
35 *Reform of Local Government in England*, Cmnd 4276 (London: HMSO, 1970); *Local Government in England: Government Proposals for Reorganization*, Cmnd 4584 (London: HMSO, 1971).
36 *The Report of the Royal Commission on Local Government in Greater London* (Herbert), Cmnd 1164 (London: HMSO, 1960).
37 Volume 1, Report of the Committee on Management in Local Government.
38 An alderman was an indirectly elected member of local councils. They were elected by the ordinary councillors for a six-year term and numbered one-quarter of the council. The office was abolished by the 1972 Local Government Act.
39 For a discussion of the case for neighbourhood councils see J. Baker and M. Young, *The Hornsey Plan* (London: Association of Neighbourhood Councils, 1973).
40 *Report of the Committee on Local Government Finance* (Layfield), Cmnd 6453 (London: HMSO, 1976).
41 London local government was modernised in the mid-1960s under the London Government Act 1963. The new structure is broadly similar to that of the metropolitan counties. See G. Rhodes and S. K. Ruck, *The Government of Greater London* (London: Allen & Unwin, 1970).
42 For a detailed history and analysis of the work of the Local Government Commissions see J. Stanyer, 'The Local Government Commissions', in H. Victor Wiseman (ed.), *Local Government in England, 1958–1969* (London: Routledge & Kegan Paul, 1970).
43 R. Crossman, *The Diaries of a Cabinet Minister*, Vol. 1: *Minister of Housing 1964–66* (London: Hamilton & Cape, 1975), pp. 64, 91 and 380.
44 The Commission's recommendations are contained in Vol. 1: see note 32 for reference.
45 *Reform of Local Government in England*, Cmnd 4276, 1970.
46 See note 33.
47 For a description of the legislative passage of the 1972 English Local Government Reorganisation Act, see Wood, The *Process of Local Government Reform*, chs VI and VII.
48 See note 17.
49 *The New Local Authorities: Management and Structure* (Bains) (London: HMSO, 1971).
50 J. M. Buchanan and W. C. Stubblebine, 'Externality', *Economica*, vol. XXX (1963).
51 K. Newton, 'Community performance in Britain', *Current Sociology*, vol. XXII (1976), p. 54.
52 *Neighbourhood Councils in England*, Consultation Paper (London: Department of the Environment, 1974). Under the legislation establishing the new local government system in Wales and in Scotland provision

was made for comparable bodies to be called 'community councils'. For a discussion of the debate on neighbourhood councils and various attempts to set them up on a voluntary basis see S. Humble and J. Talbot, *Neighbourhood Councils in England: A Report to the Department of the Environment* (Birmingham University: Institute of Local Government Studies, 1977).

53 One substantial straw in the wind is the Labour Party's Consultative Document *Regional Authorities and Local Government Reform*, issued in July 1977.

Chapter V

LOCAL GOVERNMENT INSTITUTIONS
AND THE CONTEMPORARY EVOLUTION
OF FRENCH SOCIETY

From the end of the 1940s until the beginning of the 1970s, France experienced a period of profound and spectacular transformation. In little more than a generation lasting changes came about. At the outbreak of the Second World War French society remained, as evidenced by its local institutions, strongly marked by its rural past and was devoted to the administration of the heritage of the first industrial revolution accomplished in the nineteenth century. Today it stands in the forefront of the industrialised nations, having undergone a rapid phase of transformation and expansion. The most obvious characteristics are industrialisation and urbanisation. The French population has changed its professional composition, its domicile and its standard of living.

Table 5.1 *Evolution of Population According to Residence*

	Total population	*Urban population**	*Rural population*
1936	41·5 million (100%)	21·6 million (52%)	19·9 million (48%)
1954	42·8 million (100%)	23·9 million (56%)	18·9 million (44%)
1962	46·4 million (100%)	28·6 million (61·6%)	17·8 million (38·4%)
1968	49·8 million (100%)	34·8 million (70%)	15·0 million (30%)

Source: Commissariat général au Plan, *Les Villes: l'urbanisation* (Paris: Colin, 1970), p. 21.

*Population residing in towns of more than 50,000 inhabitants.

Table 5.2   *Evolution of the Working Population by Occupational Sector*

	1954 %	1962 %	1968 %
Agricultural production	26·8	19·9	15·0
Production industry: intermediary products	8·5	9·1	8·7
Production industry: *équipement*	12·5	15·8	17·5
Production industry: consumer goods	14·4	13·3	12·6
Transport, services industry, trade	24·4	26·6	29·6
Others (financial institutions, administration, local authorities, domestic)	13·5	15·2	16·6
TOTAL	100	100	100

This chapter will deal with the problem which the results of such a transformation pose for the territorial government of public affairs, more particularly that of the validity of the solutions and policies set in motion between the 1950s and the first half of the 1970s. Emphasis will be placed mainly on the institutional aspect.[1] One of the paradoxes of the French situation is that the theme of the crisis of local public institutions was seen, especially during the 1960s, as an important element in the analysis of the consequences of national socio-economic transformation, but no attempt at global institutional reform was ever really made or carried to a conclusion.

NEW DATA ON THE PROBLEMS OF LOCAL INSTITUTIONS

When the infrastructure of a society – notably the apparatus of economic production – has undergone profound changes, one might expect the new power relationships between social groups to modify the superstructure – in particular the political and administrative institutions. This is in fact what happened in France at the national level with the establishment in 1958 of the Fifth Republic. At the local level the territorial government of public affairs, a direct result of the Napoleonic Empire and the Third Republic, was also confronted from 1950 onwards by totally new factors. The rural exodus, the urban explosion, the internationalisation of the economy, the development of modern agriculture and full-scale industrialisation, exerted pressure for a substantial reform of both its institutions and its practices.

In this context the basic unit, the commune, is seen to be weak in spite of its deep historical roots. There are far too many communes, both in the urban agglomerations which are growing rapidly and in the country which is becoming depopulated. The boundaries of communal land now correspond even less than in the past to the actual population bloc and to the zones now subject to public works programmes. Communes are thus not only too weak but too small. They cannot afford officials of high calibre and are unable to confront the new problems of management and planning. Scattered and fragmented to a high degree – there are more than 36,000 of them – they are also divided and in competition with one another.[2] In such circumstances, mutual co-operation tends to be difficult and temporary.

Their budgetary resources are stagnant in relation to escalating costs of administration and the growth of a new variety of economic and social investment, notably in the field of public works programmes (road building programmes, sanitation, housing, schools etc.). Between 1945 and 1957 public expenditure in the communes and the *départements* rose from 500,000,000 francs to 12,000,000,000 francs. From 1953 to 1957 public works expenditure escalated from 1·34 thousand million francs to 2·58 thousand million francs.[3] In order to finance expenditure the communes were obliged to increase direct taxation at a rate of more than 14 per cent per annum between 1962 and 1966.[4] The ability of the communes to exercise the general powers accorded to them by law is limited by the size of their territory and the fact that they do not alone control the financial, administrative and technical resources necessary for carrying out their policies.

The same problems beset the intermediary unit of local government – the *département*. Whilst under the Third Republic this institution fulfilled its functions with vitality, it now finds difficulty in adapting itself to current changes. It does not have autonomous, technical and administrative means at its disposal. Its geographical boundaries no longer correspond to new economic developments. The impact of the urban agglomeration extends beyond the framework of the *département*. Their weakness and their lack of mutual co-operation make it impossible for the ninety *départements* to achieve integration between the economic and the spatial dimensions of public works problems.

The maladjustment of communal and departmental institutions is not only technical, financial, geographical and administrative, it is also, and above all, sociological and political. The composition of the municipal and departmental councils reflects less and less that of the population or at least of its elites. It has remained largely that of the society of the Third Republic.[5] Local tradesmen, solicitors, landowners and small industrialists predominate, whilst the new economic elites – top executives, modern farmers, trades unionists and managers – are conspicuous by their absence. But even more than composition it is the orientation of communal and departmental politics itself which seems to be a source of tension. The notables, accustomed to managing stable and, at times, stagnant communities, seem to have a certain difficulty in playing the expansion game, in administering urban growth and in planning economic growth.

Thus the political capacity of the commune and the *département* is seriously threatened. Local political power no longer represents relevant economic power. The local institutions have difficulty in getting the legitimacy of their decisions accepted and in deciding between particular interests. In many towns there is a political vacuum. Indeed, the new elites, a product of economic evolution, attempt to react at times, when necessary, through collective organisations on the fringe of the traditional institutions which they judge to be outmoded. Thus, in opposition to the traditional chambers of commerce and agriculture, generally the stamping-ground of conservative leadership, pressure groups like the *Jeunes Chambres Economiques* or the *Centres Départementaux des Jeunes Agriculteurs* are set up. These latter are controlled by groups who dream of modernising and reforming traditional institutions and, beyond this, the local political and departmental institutions. They give preference to planning at the regional level (that is, supra-departmental) and co-operation between the political decision makers and the socio-economic powers.

This unease does not spare the third partner in territorial government: the central State and its ministerial departments. The years 1950 to 1960 saw the development of a lack of confidence in the abilities of public administration, particularly amongst the top officials concerned with economic planning. There was talk of 'a crisis of bureaucracy'. A certain number of study groups concentrated on the political and technico-administrative aspect of State and administrative malaise, taking up and expanding upon the reformist perspective which had been expressed in particular by Mendès-France, president of the Council of Ministers in the Fourth Republic.[6] In fact, rapid urbanisation emphasised the extent to which the weakness of local institutions was accompanied by deficiencies in the State. The latter increased its power but the balance between its own responsibilities and those of the communes was confused and arbitrary. Increasing State power was enhanced by the communes' tendency to rely more and more upon State intervention to resolve their problems. But public central administration did not manage to deal with these in a satisfactory manner. The field services were well entrenched in the rural areas but had little influence in the urban zones. Trained in the subtleties required to deal with the traditional notables, they did not understand the new conditions obtaining in the urban network. Moreover, the clearcut division between ministerial departments prevented any global approach to the problem. There was an administration and a policy on housing, another on road building, another on school building, yet another on urbanisation etc., but there was no overall urban administration and policy. Control of the urban situation cannot easily be co-ordinated. High technical expertise cannot supplement the lack of political legitimacy. One of the consequences of these deficiencies is the reinforcement of the inequality of access to the public services guaranteed by the central State.

Everything seems to be inter-related. The problem of the commune is linked to that of the *département* and that of the central bureaucracy. The absence of an adequate local political organism prevents the satisfactory functioning of collective public works programmes. But this absence presupposes, at the same time, that between local requirements and national planning there exists an intermediary level capable of ensuring a minimum of coherence in the middle term. Malaise leads to the disintegration of a territorial apparatus which is both scattered and uniform. A clear differentiation has developed between communes and between *départements*.[7] It seems impossible to administer the whole country according to one single, repetitive model in which what is good for a village of 150 inhabitants in the south-west is also valid for an agglomeration of 500,000 inhabitants in the north. Centralisation, a particular relationship between the centre and the periphery, comes up against an increasingly complex social organisation. As Crozier remarks, centralisation is not the concentration of all activity in Paris but is rather a certain type of division and dissociation between two complementary functions: the conception of policies and their execution. The centre decides and the periphery executes.[8] The result is that each individual regards his function as a jealously guarded monopoly, information is hard to obtain and decisions are not explained.

Everything happens as though, from the 1950s onwards, the institutional fabric of the country had less and less in common with the social and economic fabric. Municipal powers, departmental powers and even State powers have lost their hold on economic and social phenomena. A process of disintegration has affected the local communities at the bases of society and has drained local institutions of much of their relevance.

THE POLICIES SET IN MOTION

The measures taken to counteract this situation between the years 1950 and 1975 were characterised by the essential role played by the governmental executive at national level. It was from Paris and by Paris that the solutions which attempted to cope with the problem were elaborated and decided upon. However, and of crucial importance, these measures did not conform to an overall plan aimed at restructuring public institutions from top to bottom. On the contrary, they were only a disparate catalogue of varied and limited acts of intervention with no particular coherence and which were grouped round three axes.

Functional regionalism[9]

In the past, in France, the creation of regions had often been considered as a political lever for the achievement of decentralisation and autonomy.[10] In 1900, Charles Brun created a regionalist movement inspired by federalist notions. The *département* was perceived as an instrument which had allowed the French Revolution to reduce France definitively to tatters. Philosophers of such diverse tendencies as Proudhon and Maurras supported the regionalist cause.[11] After the Second World War the notion of creating strong intermediary units re-emerged but with a different perspective. In 1947 Michel Debré, future Prime Minister under de Gaulle in 1959, proposed that the ninety *départements* should be reduced to forty-seven.[12] Gradually the political and decentralising concept gave way to a more technical and economic one. What was required essentially, it was felt, was to correct the inability of the territorial institutions to administer the new conditions of development. In the eyes of central government in particular it was increasingly necessary to set up a regional level capable of dealing in spatial terms with economic planning and the drawing up of public works programmes. The means and methods attempted are examined in the chapter devoted to regionalisation in France.

The functional concept of regionalism continued to gain ground and was well received by central government, particularly by the Planning Commission which sought local support to increase the effectiveness of public investment that planning had shown to be important but inefficient due to the phenomenon of incrementalism induced by the rural model of local government. The prefectoral corps also received it well as they were disturbed at the way in which the control of intersectoral co-ordination was escaping from their hands. Finally an institutional compromise was reached: the *département* would remain untouched but a new level of public planning would be interposed between Paris and the periphery. In each area of regional action (which corresponded to the regions of national planning), and under the aegis of the prefectoral administration, new administrative mechanisms were set up: the prefect of the most important *département* in the area was appointed co-ordinating prefect, interdepartmental conferences between high officials of the local State services were set up, a sub-prefect was appointed to assist the co-ordinating prefect in economic matters. At the same time and more informally this bureaucratic apparatus relied upon new local and regional forces, notably semi-private institutions of an economic nature: the economic expansion committees. These latter have a fairly long history. They bring together leading economic and social cadres who wish to accelerate the development of their regions and secure the leadership. They are rarely traditional notables, but rather the younger, more dynamic elites: the *forces vives,* as the innovators in agriculture, trades unions and the industrial sector were called at the time. In a certain number of areas a positive and effective co-operation developed between the active and economic sub-prefect and the innovative and well-entrenched expansion committee. Often their deliberations went beyond mere preparation of the economic plan and questions of public investment and touched upon perspectives for political reorganisation, particularly as the traditional deliberators seemed exhausted and banal in their ideas. Regional expansion became the main preoccupation of certain local elites and stimulated initiatives which, though private, had a collective and civic objective. Pressure groups exerting influence on the notables and the State field services joined with the *forces vives* encouraged by the economic sub-prefect. A new climate and a different style of action grew up at the periphery. Its political and intellectual dynamism was, however, to be 'recuperated', by the State, dammed up and broken by the reforms of March 1964 promulgated by central government.

On 14 March 1964, an important decree was published concerning the territorial administrative framework of the State. Its intention was two-fold: to reinforce the regional level and to modernise the departmental level. At the departmental level the prefect was given effective control of all the field services of the Parisian ministries and the co-ordination of the public works policies often set in motion in a discretionary and piecemeal fashion by the departmental directors. The decree went further at the regional level. The co-ordinating prefect, who had only been *primus inter pares* in relationship of his colleagues from the other *départements,* was officially designated 'regional prefect' whilst at the same time remaining at the head of the principal *département* in the region. From that moment on he enjoyed a certain hierarchical power over his colleagues through the regional administrative conference over which he presided. He had a certain power over the distribution of regional investment. The public works budget set up by the planners was regionalised. The region was given not only an economic sub-prefect but a general staff of high officials – the regional mission – and a council formed by political notables and socio-professional elites: 'the regional economic development commission' or CODER.[13] In more general terms, the decree of March 1964 was a major act. The region acquired an officially recognised geographical and administrative identity.

The region is now invested with a certain power over the *département* which, nevertheless, preserved its powers intact. It has become an effective framework for the budget and planning. Its pivot is the prefectoral institution. The local elites are associated with the administrative action but have no decision-making powers.

The regional reform of March 1964 seemed to force the *départements* to work together openly and to give up that competition which they had hitherto enjoyed. It also permitted a new group of elites and socio-economic leaders to become associated with the decisions of the central State. Indeed, in the beginning, the *forces vives* became involved in the new institutions. The president of the economic expansion committee, automatically a member of the local CODER, tended to play an important role in its functioning. Very soon, however, disillusionment set in, and a certain number of *forces vives* – trades unionists, convinced regionalists etc. – began to lose interest and a more traditional style of action and thought returned. The new apparatus rested too exclusively on the prefectoral corps, which was the only organ capable of mediating and arbitrating between competing local and sectarian interests (departmental councils, communes and ministries), and secondly on its alliance with the notables who assured it of a certain local legitimacy. The prefectoral corps appealed effectively to its proved local partners – the notables – and moderated the impulses of the *forces vives*. The establishment of the reform of 1964 succeeded in damming up the movement which had become fragmented over the preceding year. The economic expansion committees saw their influence diminished by the new-found strength of the CODER, under the aegis of the prefects and the old departmental notables; the innovating impulses of the economic sub-prefect suffocated in the new structure. The first reforming wave was overlapped by a larger yet more traditional one concerned with preserving, within the State system, local institutions and the practices of complicity between officials of the field services of the State and the locally elected representatives, even if this involved reducing the regional perspective to its most rudimentary form.

A new attempt at regional reform took place in 1969 after the trauma of May 1968. General de Gaulle, President of the Republic, commissioned one of his ministers, Jeanneney, to draw up a more ambitious project than that of the decree of 1964. The region was to become a political and territorial community in its own right. Its competence was to extend to public works programmes in which it was to replace the central State (sanitation, school building, road building, social services) except where the national interest was concerned. It was to have its own financial resources. It was to be governed by a regional prefect and by a regional council elected indirectly.[14] The project was formulated after preliminary consultation with thousands of formal and informal local institutions and was presented to the country in the form of a popular referendum, unlike the decree of March 1964 which had been elaborated within the secrecy of the Parisian ministerial *cabinet* and which had never been the subject of either parliamentary or electoral debate. It was rejected in April 1969 after a confused campaign. As a result of this failure, de Gaulle resigned as President of the Republic.

The preliminary consultations for the 1969 project indicated that the regional idea was gaining ground in local society and was an expression of the desire for general and radical transformation. Two-thirds of those consulted favoured direct election of local representatives to the regional assembly. (In fact the final text of the project did not institute an assembly with deliberative powers.) If it failed it was due to the clumsiness of the project itself which was submitted to popular referendum. The text was confused and difficult to understand and involved together with regional reform a reform of the Senate which was premature *vis-à-vis* public opinion and, furthermore, its corporatist nature created hostility to it. Its failure was basically due to a generally unfavourable political reaction to the policies of de Gaulle: instead of dealing with the problem in question the referendum was used to indicate a lack of confidence in the actions of the President. The opposition of the Left was joined almost unanimously by that of the traditional notables who feared that the modification of the role and composition of the Senate, coupled with the creation of a strong region, would weaken their importance as mediators between the centre and the periphery and diminish their political power. These latter were enough to tip the balance in the referendum in which 500,000 votes, or 2 per cent of the electoral body, determined the result.

The regional idea seemed to be doomed, particularly as, in the eyes of the new President of the Republic, Georges Pompidou, it symbolised the reason for his predecessor's political demise. Henceforth prudence was the order of the day. In a speech delivered at Lyons on 30 October 1970 Pompidou attempted to rally the traditional notables by declaring: '. . . the region should not be conceived as an administrative level superimposed on existing ones but above all as the union of *départements* which will permit the rational realisation and management of large public works programmes within the community'.

The law of 5 July 1972 confirmed this attitude and transformed the region from an administrative unit into a 'public territorial establishment'. Its powers and resources are greater than those intended in the decree of 1964 but are inferior to those proposed by Jeanneney in 1969. The law of 1972 did not signal a break with the orientation of that of 1964, but rather completed and reinforced it. The new region has an administrative and not a political vocation.[15] Its principal innovation is the regional council which is a sort of improved CODER in which Members of Parliament are a strong force: the pick of the notables can be found there.[16] It votes the regional budget and expresses views (*avis*) on regional planning and on works programmes of local interest. It is, indeed, less under the control of the prefect, but its powers remain limited. The prefect dominates the executive and the council has hardly any legitimacy, as its members are not directly elected. It in no way replaces the departmental councils or municipal councils.[17] It has, alongside it, a consultative assembly, the regional economic and social council, whose members are from the socio-professional classes. The region has its own financial resources obtained from driving licence tax, additional motor taxes and certain property taxes. This income must not represent more than 45 francs per capita. In short, the region is not a real public authority as are the *départements* and the communes and it has no political capacity: it is a functional institution, a public establishment, with the task of observing economic development. It must respect the prerogatives of the *départements* and the communes (and, it goes without saying, the State). Its power is consultative.

Intercommunal co-operation

A second axis of institutional reform concerns the basic unit, the commune. The struggle to combat the problems provoked by the existence of a mosaic of more than 36,000 communes is of long standing. The law of 1884 recognised the possibility of merger or at least of co-operation between communes and even municipal councils. However, the application of this law had always remained restrictive, as the process of merger was practically impossible under existing conditions. Even co-operation between the communes took the weak institutional form of a single-purpose syndicate of communes. This syndicate was a public establishment with the task of administering one single public service (for example, electricity supply, water supply or refuse collection): from the beginning of the 1950s it became evident that such a set-up was inadequate.

The statute of 5 January 1959 created the multi-purpose syndicate of communes, or SIVOM. The SIVOM is responsible for the administration of several public services at one and the same time.

Moreover, the rule which had hitherto required unanimity amongst the voting members of the constituent communes now requires only a simple majority.[18] A syndicate is created either by the votes of a certain number of municipal councils or on the initiative of the prefect who draws up a list of communes which should be involved in the syndicate, and obtains the consent of the departmental council and of two-thirds of the communes representing 50 per cent of the population (or 50 per cent of the involved communes representing two-thirds of the population). It is administered by a committee composed of two delegates per commune appointed by the municipal councils as well as an administrative board. It has the freedom to choose its powers on condition that these are concerned with questions of intercommunal interest. In the urban areas in which the absence of a single territorial authority complicated the decision-making process, the 1959 statute provided for the specific organisational set-up: the district. The district is an organism which is a little more than the limited instrument of intercommunal collaboration but a little less than a territorial authority lodged between the commune and the *département*. Its powers are either obligatory (housing, fire protection), or optional and decided upon by its members (refuse collection, water, sanitation, sports facilities etc.).[19]

As its legal basis is ill defined, the district can only exercise limited constraints on the communes. Its authority is weak in agglomerations of more than 50,000 inhabitants. From that point of view the law of 31 December 1966 represented a marked improvement, as it instituted the urban community. Four agglomerations were obligatorily formed into urban communities: Bordeaux, Lille, Lyons and Strasbourg. The urban community is a public administrative institution, not a territorial authority, endowed with a deliberative organism elected by universal suffrage. It has a constraining function: it is impossible for the communes involved to withdraw, its existence is not limited in time or by the accomplishment of its aims, its powers are considerable (urbanisation plans, establishment of property reserves, urban transport, the construction of secondary schools and colleges, public highways etc.).

These varied possibilities for intercommunal collaboration have produced results.[20] The idea of local solidarity gradually gained ground with the local leadership and the population concerned. However, they remain strictly functional – and non-political – and limited in time and space. The communes are grouped together in order to counteract the lack of resources but also in the hope that, via this functional grouping, more draconian measures of a political nature, such as the merger of the communes, might be avoided.[21] All the obstacles born of the partitioning and fragmentation of the communes are far from being surmounted by the above-mentioned procedures. The communes remained autonomous and the basic unit in the administrative and political system.

Whilst it encouraged intercommunal co-operation, the State also pursued a more draconian policy: a reduction in the number of communes. Nineteenth-century attempts at fusion had produced hardly any significant result. For this reason a law was promulgated on 16 July 1971, establishing a new method of regrouping by merger. This law was intended to be decentralising and democratic. This process of merger requires close co-operation between local leaders under the aegis of the prefect. At the outset a commission composed of departmental councillors and mayors and presided over by the chairman of the departmental council was set up in each *département* in order to study the situation in general and the characteristics of each commune in particular. It was aided by the technical expertise of the heads of the State's departmental services. It drew up proposals which it submitted to the prefect. In the light of these recommendations the prefect drew up a proposal for suitable mergers or for the creation of the requisite syndicates, districts and intercommunal authorities. Phase two involved the implementation of this proposal. If the municipal councils involved were in agreement then the prefect confirmed this agreement; if there was disagreement the departmental council had to consider the matter, and if it pronounced in favour then the prefect confirmed the merger. If the departmental council opposed the plan then it was population of the communes in question which decided in the last resort.

The results of the communal merger law of 1971 have been mediocre and the dynamism which it was supposed to engender did not manifest itself.[22] In May 1973 a survey showed that the prefects had proposed 3,482 mergers involving 9,761 communes but that only 581 mergers involving 1,465 communes had been carried out.[23] The mergers were primarily in rural areas and regrouped an average of two or three small communes. In communities of more than 5,000 inhabitants only 32 mergers involving 54 communes actually took place. As the law of 1971 fixed no time limit for the submission of proposals by the prefect and the locally elected representatives, delaying tactics were often employed. As a result of this general lack of enthusiasm the law has gradually been consigned to oblivion.

Administrative reform
The third axis of the reforms of the years 1960 to 1970 was concerned with correcting the deficiencies of the State bureaucracy.

The situation appeared most complex in Paris where, in 1961, General de Gaulle appointed a 'general delegate', Paul Delouvrier, for the Paris region. Delouvrier was a prefect, in the General's confidence, who set up a powerful instrument for urban study, the Institute for Urban Planning in the Paris Region. The decree of March 1964 confirmed the orientation and powers of this body. In 1963 the *Délégation à l'aménagement du territoire et à l'action régionale* (better known as the DATAR) was created. The DATAR is a regional and spatial planning agency set up to introduce a regional element into planning and work out the implications of the Plan for the regions. At its head was Olivier Guichard, a close collaborator of the General and an influential political strategist. Like the *Commissariat Général du Plan* the DATAR was intended to exemplify a new principle of political action: the administrative mission. Unlike management administration which is organised in a rigid and hierarchical fashion, the mission's staff is a flexible body concerned with reflection and intervention. The DATAR co-ordinates the actions of ministerial departments and orchestrates planning in urban terms. It formulates the strategy of 'balancing the urban centres', that is, the utilisation of the large provincial towns as poles of development around which the regions may be constructed and which can counterbalance the weight of Paris. Although it has no field services it intervenes directly in local politics, both by the funds which it distributes and by favouring the initiatives of the *forces vives*. Thus from 1965 onwards the DATAR encouraged the creation of important study groups, the regional study groups on planning in the metropolitan area (or OREAMs), in the large urban centres – Rouen, then Lille, Marseilles, Bordeaux, etc. Their function is to promote within the public service and at local level a global concept of the urban centre, linked to a national and even European perspective. At the operational level they formulate planning documents and structured public investment programmes for the metropolitan area.

The creation in 1966 of a Ministry of Infrastructure (*Equipement*) was an important political and administrative act. It emphasised the priority accorded by General de Gaulle to the problems of urbanisation, housing and urban transport. The ministry was formed by the fusion of the ministries and local field services of construction and *Ponts et Chaussées* and it reinforced the entrenchment of these in the urban area.[24] Edgard Pisani, the minister responsible, attempted to make it into the 'Ministry of the Towns'. Its policy was to be one of a global view of urban growth embracing questions of land and property, finance and economics. In this way the State would have at its disposal a unified and powerful administrative machine permitting the establishment, as a result of public investment programmes and contact with the locally elected representatives, of an urban framework compatible with the policy of industrialisation. This would have the effect of co-ordinating the activities and perspectives of a certain number of administrative sections of the State which are facing the same problems at the urban level. It was designed to strengthen State control country-wide. This action on the part of Paris was precipitated by the threat of seeing certain large towns, in particular Lyons, taking the initiative at the instigation of their mayor and creating their own urban planning organs.

The State resolutely took control of the situation. The reorganisation of local authorities became subordinate and complementary to administrative reform. Thus it is possible to talk of a depoliticisation of the problem of local government. The main aim was not to respond to aspirations towards local autonomy or to develop a new type of urban politics but rather to improve the techniques necessary for the activity of central government and its bureaucracy to be carried out 'rationally'. Between 1954 and 1968 the State attempted to bring administrative decision making closer to the population concerned exclusively through the concept of planning: regional plans, transference of decisions concerning public works programmes from Paris to the prefect, the regionalisation of public works programmes in the Fifth Plan.

At the end of 1969 the Chaban-Delmas government embarked on a programme of reform with the aim of 'unblocking' the administrative structure through a sustained deconcentration of public administration. In December 1970 an attempt was made to modify the relationship between the State and the local authorities by means of planning contracts (*contrats de plan*) between the State and the urban communities.[25] Henceforth the relationship between the administration and the local authorities was to be negotiated by a contract which would commit each partner to the financing and realisation of a series of projects, instead of being regulated, as previously, by a series of separate arrangements which were negotiated with difficulty and openly committed neither of the parties concerned. In fact this contractual notion merely standard-ised the practice which already existed and in no way substantially modified the power relationship between the two parties.[26]

Another attempt at administrative deconcentration was made between 1969 and 1973. It was becoming indispensable to alleviate the increasing mass of decisions concerning local affairs which had to be made at national level. Paris was submerged by matters of secondary importance and had to contend with details without really grasping the actual context in which the decisions had to be made. The weight of administrative centralisation was too great. It was not a question of decentralising by transferring central State authority to the powerful local political authorities but rather of devolving the tasks attributed mainly to Paris on to the local echelons of the State bureaucracy (regional and departmental echelons) and on to local institutions (departmental and municipal councils) without at the same time giving these latter any real decision-making power independent of the State's representatives (prefects etc.). Thus, in 1969, control over local finances was conferred on the paymaster-general of the *département* instead of being exercised by the Ministry of Finance of Paris. In 1969, more than a hundred types of State decision were devolved on to the regional and departmental services. A large deconcentration programme was put into operation, but this had very little advantage for the local authorities, as the trumps remained in the hands of State officials and informal channels remained more important than the official ones.[27] Deconcentration did not change much, it merely permitted the improvement of certain inadequacies in the State method of choosing community public works programmes.

In 1973, President Pompidou launched the notion of devolving on to the *département*. He appointed Peyrefitte as Minister of Administrative Reform. This attempt, which was interrupted by the death of Pompidou in spring 1974, was extremely ambiguous. The *département* furnishes both the possibility of delegating central power to the field services of the State and even to the departmental council and also permits the ridiculing of the regionalist demon which continues to haunt the reformers.

Marginal adjustments

The policy followed until 1975 can be characterised as one which maintained the essential features of the institutional system corrected by significant and yet marginal adjustments. Everything was geared towards adapting procedures and institutions in order to administer urban and industrial development more efficiently. Emphasis was laid on local administration rather than local democracy. Not one institutional or legal principle was modified and the local public authorities remained unchanged. The State remained both strong – it decided the rules of the game and there was no autonomous local power – and, at the same time, weak – it could not function without the notables and was incapable of instituting new rules concerning local government. At best, it improved technical procedures and middle-term co-ordination and perspectives and had its legitimacy to act confirmed.

If one looks beyond the constitutional trimmings it is clear that this policy of adjustment rather than change was also applied to the practices and powers of the public leaders.[28] Although they may be a little more complex than they were fifteen or twenty years ago, procedures and regulations remain basically the same: this is, for example, true of the relationship between the prefect and the chairman of the departmental council, the keystone of departmental government.[29] The State bureaucracy has become marginally more hierarchical at the top. The deconcentrated field services of the State intervene more intensively in communal matters and with the exception of a few large regional agglomerations they have reduced communal competence to a residual and specialised role. The prefect and the paymaster-general at departmental and regional level now guarantee better financial and economic co-ordination. The possibilities for locally elected representatives to apply pressure on the central State appear to be somewhat reduced. Reforms carried out under the Fifth Republic have been neither innovative nor disruptive and they certainly have not penetrated local institutions and practices, either because from the outset they were intended to preserve the essential structure and only introduce technical modifications or because in practice decisions taken in Paris have not produced the hoped-for result.

Transformations which have taken place in the economic and spatial infrastructure do not appear to have been complemented by significant transformations in the institutional superstructure. There is a yawning gap between the sociological upheaval which took place, for example, at national level with the creation of the Fifth Republic (the emergence of a strong presidential power, growing influence of the technocrats in top administration, eclipse of parliamentary power, transformation of the party system etc.), and the modifications to the public institutions which may be observed at local level. The State has retained its control over local government, and whilst, in practice, certain local notables may dictate to the State and the large towns impose their will, in the final analysis, ultimate choice remains the prerogative of the State.

LOCAL GOVERNMENT AS A FACTOR IN THE POLITICAL DEBATE

Is local government a prime and specific motivating factor for society and the political forces in contemporary France?

This question must be asked for, as we have just seen, it is not geographical or administrative factors which, as such, furnish the irresistible need for change. In local government, as in other areas, institutional or legal change can only be achieved if the problem is raised to the level of political debate by a coalition of interests sufficiently powerful and convinced of its importance. In this context developments over the last twenty years are quite significant. Certain phenomena, at least, need to be emphasised in an attempt to throw light upon the way in which the problem of local government has been formulated and treated at the level of political debate: the strategy for change adopted by central government, the political policy pursued by the government, and the decline of the problem of local government as a political factor.

Central government has kept a tight rein on local government reforms. More precisely, initiatives have been controlled and, with one or two exceptions, confined to the executive, the President of the Republic, his ministers and their top officials. In general terms the strategy adopted has been one of depoliticisation – decisions are not taken by Parliament, and the measures decided upon do not form the subject of broad national political debate involving public opinion and the political parties. On the contrary, everything is controlled by the ministerial *cabinet,* and the measures undertaken are presented as a response by means of decentralisation to the demands of technical and administrative rationalisation. Paris does not adopt a global and authoritarian approach but rather attempts to involve local interests as closely as possible to the extent that, in some cases, it is they who decide upon the measures to be taken. This strategy was adopted in the decree of March 1964 which created the regions, and in the Communal Merger Act promulgated in 1971.

Even if the numerous measures taken since the 1950s were not aimed at totally disrupting the mode of local government, certain of them had enough potential to provoke a dynamic change. The decree of March 1964 which created the regions (and to a lesser degree the 1971 law merging the communes) is an example of this.[30] A climate favourable to reform which was in vogue in an influential sector of the public service – in the planning commission and in certain sections of the prefectoral corps – allied with the local pressure of the *forces vives* permitted the unleashing of an irreversible regional awareness and a dynamism which far exceeded the prudent objectives outlined by Paris. When the decree was put into practice its results were more restricted than had been expected, for the reform reinforced the role of the notables and the traditionally influential bodies. Thus, the move for change made at the top became inhibited and distorted in practice. There was resistance to change, even dysfunction. The system of depoliticisation adopted by Paris did not give rise to a dynamic change at the local level.[31]

Those who should have advocated greater autonomy at the local level, the notables, in fact desired at all costs to maintain the *status quo.* For them the solution to the problem of local administration was not the creation of a new entity, the region, but the reinforcement of traditional structures, in particular the combination of prefect–departmental council, and thus the retention of the direct and attentive presence of the State in local affairs.

The problem in this context resides in the existence of a local political and administrative system which is relatively specific in the sense that it imposes a logic of action and a particular code of rules upon its members. It is a complex and stable system which varies little from one region and *département* to another and forms the backbone of local government. Its characteristics will be described in the following paragraphs.[32]

At each geographical level from the commune to the region and even at the centre, two threads which are institutionally independent of one another become closely interwoven: the administrative and public services of the State and the local political and socio-economic leadership. The system is structured around the principle of cross-functioning controls. No local leader, no head of a local State agency may react really autonomously. Neither the hierarchical authority of the bureaucracy nor a vote in the local legislative assembly is sufficient to ensure choice and co-ordination. There may be interdependence, co-ordination and influence, but they are only achieved by the direct intervention of a third party. Thus the local State officials – sub-prefect, tax-collector, sub-divisional engineer for the Ministry of Infrastructure – each exercise direct influence on the choices and initiatives of the mayors and municipal councils in their area to a far greater extent than the law itself intended. But in their turn they are subject to the direct influence of the departmental councillor in their canton. This cross-functioning control is continued at a higher level. The departmental councillors in their capacity as members of a legislative organism have many of their decisions either inspired, formulated or imposed by the prefect. He, in his turn, like the other heads of departmental services, takes account of the desires and initiatives of the most powerful politicians, notably the Deputies and Senators.

This structure, like a beehive, interlinks autonomous institutions from the local base through to central government in Paris. Each participant both regulates and is regulated. The control is external, cross-functional and informal, instead of being dictated from within, either horizontally by the peer group as is the case in political assemblies, or vertically through the bureaucratic hierarchy. At one and the same time State technocrats intervene in local political life and local politicians intervene in the administrative management of the State. There are, however, certain exceptions to this rule which, though minor, are of considerable importance: local representatives who hold several offices concurrently. They play an entirely different role. The mayor who is also a Deputy and chairman of the departmental council has direct personal access to various levels of the administration which tend not to communicate with one another. He thus becomes for the other local representatives a mediator, a means of bypassing the beehive and dealing directly with the summit, and in turn he may trade favours and obtain important privileges.[33]

Such a system fulfils two essential functions: it is through this network that leadership, influence and co-ordination are guaranteed in local government, and it is through these cross-relationships between the two institutional threads that the periphery is guaranteed access to the centre and vice versa. Unlike countries such as Belgium where the relationship between the centre and the periphery is conducted mainly through the political parties according to party affiliation, in France this relationship is conducted above all through the politico-administrative system.

The very characteristics of the system largely explain why it has not been rejected *en bloc* either by its members or by those it was created to serve: the population. Of course, decisions are taken in secret by a handful of initiates, far from the prying eyes of public opinion. There is mistrust of universal suffrage and public debate. Access to decision making and to the centre is the monopoly of a few notables who acquire personal advantage from it: prestige, security, income.[34] The system is so constructed that no one person epitomises its failings and, therefore, the fault can be attributed to no one in particular. The system is not totally hermetic and does incorporate a real ability to assimilate new generations of slightly more open and dynamic notables and bureaucrats. Even centralisation is not as strong as people have claimed. To a large extent centralisation does not work only from the centre to the periphery as a means of retaining power, but is in fact maintained and reinforced by the periphery itself which uses it to promote its particular interests and to put pressure on the centre in the most direct way possible at the highest possible level. The system survives by the competition thus engendered and by granting enough people the possibility, however slight, of putting pressure on the centre through the intermediary notables. If it exists, local democracy, far from being a deliberative democracy, is in fact a democracy of access. There is hardly any desire to do the administering oneself – that would be far too risky. It is preferable for problems to be solved at a higher level without there being any need to negotiate with others in the same situation or at the same level. The system makes prisoners of those whom it administers and serves, for it offers a solution to problems which it has itself helped to create or maintain. Each case is treated as a special case. All are in competition to obtain the favours of the notables. The notables block direct access to decision making, but they function as effective intermediaries and spokesmen dedicated to the interests they represent. If the notables are at times completely overburdened by the weight of demands made upon them this is the price they must pay for their continued acceptance of support by the population.

The French local politico-administrative system is homeostatic and conservative. The notables and bureaucrats who control it do not wish it to evolve and even if they did they would not manage to find the resources necessary to carry this out. Politically active citizens horrify them; the political parties have other interests; the most underprivileged of the administered are also those who have the least possibility for collective action.

In short, if reforms like those of 1964 and 1971 have failed, it is because the type of strategy employed by central government – depoliticisation, decentralisation and progressive diffusion – entrusted the implementation of those reforms to the system itself. This strategy was doomed to failure because none of the members of the system had the slightest personal interest in changing or modifying it. So, the reform was smothered by the paradoxical alliance of reforming technocrats from Paris and local notables.

At the beginning of the 1960s the French political situation was characterised by the growth at the national level of Gaullism, a political movement which had no solid base at local level. The municipal and departmental councils remained firmly in the hands of the moderate and Right-wing parties, the Radicals and the Socialists, which had their roots in the Third and Fourth Republics. The main and essential objective of Gaullism was to create a solid local base and to dislodge the opposition from its traditional strongholds. Various tactics were employed to this end. The most brutal of these was electoral confrontation. Another was to rally the moderate notables to the cause and thus to create a clientele.[35] For this purpose State subsidies were distributed in such a way as to make a certain number of local representatives dependent on central government. Thus the rapid completion of public works programmes was not merely a response to industrialisation but also a symbolic political act. The State encouraged the local authorities to complete public works programmes even if they did not have the requisite financial resources. As a result the community got into debt and had to rely on government subsidies and, therefore, became dependent on government favour. The Left-wing opposition mayor learned to curb his anti-government feelings, and the moderate departmental councillor not to shun co-operation with the prefect or the Gaullist Deputy. Thus the 'depoliticisation' of local administration was a means by which central power might become accepted and entrenched at the base. Conversely the mayor, or departmental councillor, used the improvement in public works programmes as a sign to the electorate of his efficiency. What could be more spectacular than a new swimming pool or sports stadium, especially when the mayor was the first to construct one in his area? That neither of them was used by the population seemed irrelevant. The prefect or the minister in Paris apportioned public funds astutely whilst local public demands for new community projects was stimulated artifically by the mass media and the State technocrats. The local community functioned as a producer of goods and the citizen's role was reduced uniquely to that of consumer.

The creation of the DATAR in 1963 was a decisive act. Its General Delegate had direct access to the Prime Minister, and it was associated with those central government decisions which had a bearing on local or regional matters. However, land use planning was a highly political act (and not merely an economic or technical gesture). Guichard, the General Delegate, an expert in electoral techniques, did no doubt wish to redress the regional balance between east and west and to create regional centres with some political muscle, but the distribution of subsidies, the construction of factories and the formulation of urbanisation projects were not without political significance of a discreet and subtle nature. Even if the DATAR spoke of national development programmes and long-term plans, it acted, in fact, in a piecemeal fashion if it felt a situation to be opportune, and through personal contact with the local leadership concerned.

The creation in 1964 of the CODER, a regional, consultative organ composed of elected leaders and socio-professionals, was a way for central government to kill two birds with one stone; it might win over the *forces vives* to Gaullism without alienating the traditional notables. De Gaulle was not fond of the notables in whom he saw the personification both of the 'party system' and the 'politicians' policies' which he had many a time castigated. But at the same time he did not wish to provoke their animosity. Thus the decree of March 1964 was ambiguous. It was regionalist but not threatening, since the prefect remained dominant. Can one, therefore, speak of the 'failure' of a regional reform? The results are more ambivalent than that. Certainly the *forces vives* were brought under control. A number of young farmers and trades unionists, once tempted by the overtures made to them by central government, were to become disillusioned and sink into political apathy. But other new economic leaders were gradually incorporated into the system, became young traditional notables and even joined the ruling political coalition. For some time to come, in fact until 1969, the government continued to play an ambiguous game. It presented itself both as reformist and conservative on the question of territorial government, it manifested stray impulses towards regionalism and leaned heavily on the disciplined ranks of the prefectoral corps and the notables. It was not until the rebellion of the 1969 referendum and the call made to the notables in Pompidou's Lyons speech that government policy became unequivocal. From then on Pompidou took a conservative line. This attitude was embodied in the regional law of 1972. The presidential majority by then controlled a majority of regional councils and local entrenchment was guaranteed.[36]

Viewed from this perspective it is easier to interpret the failure of the 1971 law merging the communes. The Minister of the Interior at the time, Marcellin, did not wish for sweeping changes. The solution adopted consisted in appearing to be extremely daring from a legal standpoint, but actually limiting the effects of the legislation through a broad decentralisation of procedure. The law of 1971 was, in fact, a typically symbolic innovation: the local politico-administrative system, comprising those local interests which had shown themselves to be the most conservative and which would be most threatened by the consequences, was entrusted with the task of deciding upon and applying the changes. In other European countries where substantial remodelling at local level has taken place (as in Great Britain, Belgium and Sweden), this has been done with authority and by means of a global strategy formulated by Parliament. But the law of 1971, in the guise of a modernist and democratic document, avoided any upheaval at the base and proved that the country, at local level, did not desire substantial reform.

Thus the 'failure' of local reform in France takes on a different complexion. It is as though the Fifth Republic, and in particular President Pompidou, had reached agreement with the local notables on the following terms: 'I will leave your local power intact but give me a free hand to industrialise the country.' There is no need to change territorial government whilst Paris has the means to administer the spatial results of economic development and whilst the local notables, and through them the local institutions, present no obstacle to the strategies and demands of what the Marxists call 'State Monopoly Capitalism'. Why risk the dangers of regionalisation when industrialisation programmes might, at a pinch, be adequate? This was the lesson which Pompidou felt he had learned from the regional referendum of 1969. In his opinion, de Gaulle had made the mistake of wishing to change political institutions at a time when France's economic infrastructure was changing. Pompidou was convinced that in a period of economic change it would be quite wrong to change the political institutions. For this reason he chose the *département* as the instrument of deconcentration.

There is a feeling in certain circles in Paris that the present system of local government is no longer viable, since the local authorities are too weak and State intervention too strong, notably at the technical level. But these same circles are wary of stripping the State bureaucracy of its technical functions and bestowing them upon the

local authorities, for it is through technology that the State intervenes at the local level. There is, of course, the possibility of side-
stepping the bureaucratic apparatus and re-establishing a client relationship with certain local authorities. A method like 'area contracts'
(*contrats de pays*) is used as a means to bypass the weightiness and
incrementalism created by the bureaucracy and to favour a certain
number of rural and semi-urban communes which are regrouped
within 'communities'. This regrouping reduces the number of intermediaries, and at the same time is thought to pay dividends in those
areas whose electoral support is desired.

The attitude of the Left opposition to the local issue has appeared,
in the mid-1970s, to be scarcely more dynamic than that of the
governmental coalition. In an almost ritual fashion they extol the
strengthening of the financial position of the local institutions.
Everything they advocate is tinged with references to local democracy and citizen participation in public affairs.[37] The Socialist Party
promotes self-management and the Communist Party speaks of
communal liberties. But no real overall and in-depth debate has
taken place on this subject, as the parliamentary Left finds the
theme embarrassing. As for the trades unions their attitude is
similar, for they are aware of the power which they wield in the
centralised nationalised, public sector.

The political elite and the parties are in agreement not to place
the question of the reform of local institutions on the government
agenda. Their reasons are tactical but also deep seated. They cannot
risk offending the national associations of locally elected representatives by adopting measures which would threaten their privileges,
not to mention their very existence, especially as this might lead to
electoral defeat. On the other hand, the Right is not prepared either
to give up a strong State apparatus which would enable it to exercise
strong control over society when it achieved power.

Whilst certain minority, but active, elements supported the regional
idea at the beginning of the 1960s – from the New Left to the more
dynamic elements of the employers' associations – the issue subsequently lost a lot of its impetus. It is no longer one of the prime
issues in public opinion.[38] Not one coalition of interests of sufficient
political and social standing has taken up this cause, for all are too
preoccupied with the problem of power at the national level – some
of them wishing to preserve it and others to conquer it. For a long
time local government in France has only been of relevance in
relationship to the general problem of power relationships within
society as a whole.

The weakened substance of the territorial framework
Is the reform of territorial institutions in post-industrial society of

any real significance or is it merely a rearguard action? The commune and the *département* have, in real terms, even less control now than in the past over economic and social power.[39] The Italian experience of the 1960s seems to indicate the following. The region was perceived there as a spatial political framework within which, through the concept of planning, decisions by the large multinationals and public powers concerning investment might be better controlled. In fact, though stronger than the local framework, the regional framework was inadequate. In the course of the last twenty years, post-industrial societies have experienced an increasing divorce between public and economic power and a growing difficulty in setting up frameworks within which these two powers can be coordinated and brought together. Even at the national level, control over decisions eludes government as a result of the development of an international economic dimension.

The local institutions' loss of power has been accelerated not only by the irruption of new decision-making dimensions – international economy, urbanisation – but also by the immobility of the politico-administrative system itself. The departmental councils of the late 1950s and 1960s provide us with an example of this. They preferred to ignore the problems of urban growth in their respective *départements* rather than to have to modify their practices and characteristics. Thus a parallel local government in the urban areas grew up outside the traditional system, with its own subsidiaries, its own bureaucratic and political institutions, both at the urban level and at the level of central government. It was the preserve of the State public administration. The large towns, politically powerful (through their mayors and their role of structuring the urban agglomeration) and strong administrative machines (through the sheer quantity of their officials), stood outside any intermediary local set-up between Paris and themselves. They negotiated directly with the centres and were able, to a large extent, to dictate policy to the authorities which were nominally entrusted with their supervision. In fact, working outside the normal channels is not necessarily a handicap, it may even prove a trump card for the bodies concerned, as they do not have to pass via the notables for the solution of their problems, and may organise themselves in an autonomous fashion in order to exercise direct pressure on the centre. The farmers furnish us with an exceptional example of this. Farming policy is not in the control of the notables and prefects. Representation of farming interests is guaranteed by professional organisations which have direct access to Paris and negotiate without intermediaries. The powerful *Fédération Nationale des Syndicats d'Exploitants Agricoles* (FNSEA) represents a large proportion of all farmers, is extremely active politically (in contrast to organisations in other economic sectors), and guarantees a minimum of arbitration and integration between the particular interests of its members. The Ministry of Agriculture is its privileged partner. They overlap to such an extent that it appears at times as if the Federation is the representative of the government confronting the farmers and the ministry the farmers' representative. Furthermore, the farmers exert considerable pressure on the notables who are obliged to humour them, given their electoral strength under the French electoral system. There are, also, many other interest groups which attempt to escape the system, set up their own representative organs and their own means of access to Paris. The same is also true of the large towns which have succeeded, far more than the *départements*, the small towns or villages, in setting up their own channel of access for negotiation with Paris. This has a two-fold result. The channels which run parallel with the formal local political institutions tend to multiply on a sectarian and often corporative basis. At the same time there is a certain flexibility offered for the solution of public problems. In contrast to the rigidity and impotence of the traditional local channels, the parallel channel permits a certain measure of subtlety and innovation. Mediation and the representation of interests escapes the control of the intermediary bodies which are organised according to the dual principle of local suffrage and universal competence. This serves only to accelerate the disintegration of the local community.

The State bureaucracy, for its part, also multiplies the sectoral and specialised organs which are grafted onto local problems in a concealed way and are not subject to political control. The alienation of local society, far from being checked, is in fact reinforced as a result.

Local solidarity based on the commune or the *département* is destroyed and replaced by a solidarity based on a bargaining relationship. The individual is no longer the citizen of an integrated political community but scarcely more than a consumer torn between an infinity of services and public networks which each have their own particular territory and no common frontiers.[40]

Is this local government structure an unbearable and serious handicap for France? Given the tendency over the last twenty years to subordinate the problems of local administration to the primary objective of economic and industrial development, the results do not appear to be too bad, in spite of bureaucratic slothfulness, obvious wastage and regional disparities. After an initial delay the urbanisation programme was administered in an adequate fashion without inhibiting the move towards a new type of economy. In comparison with other countries like Great Britain, the effectiveness of the French system of allocating public resources appears proven: the relationship between the centre and the periphery seems to allow a more rapid rhythm of progress and a more genuine global co-ordination.[41] Dangerous errors and threatening excesses have been avoided. The same is true for urban policy which underwent a change of direction in the 1960s. For administrative reasons – collective costs linked to the excessive size of urban areas – and for electoral ones – the loss of control by the presidential coalition in the large towns and their suburbs – the formation of large agglomerations was abandoned in favour of the development of medium or small towns, units which are more easily governed by the prefect–notable combination. The question still remains whether the present mode of local government is capable of dealing effectively with other present or future problems such as the reduction of regional differences and the social inequalities caused or accentuated by industrial or urban development. The potentially explosive element in the sphere of regionalism is not so much ethnic differences or cultural minorities, but rather the aggravation of inequalities between developed and underdeveloped regions, town and country, and rich and poor agricultural areas.

A possible reopening of the debate
One might have imagined that the accession of Giscard d'Estaing to the Presidency in June 1974 would have modified the conservative orientation of territorial government policy. From the outset he entrusted the Ministry of Administrative Reform to Servan-Schreiber, a dedicated supporter of regional power. But Servan-Schreiber was dismissed after a week.

In a speech at Dijon in November 1975 the President pronounced himself in favour of decentralisation but explicitly condemned the region, advocating the development of the commune and the *département* as did his predecessor. In December 1975 he announced that local reform would soon be given priority. He set up a 'Commission for the development of local responsibility' based on the British model of the Royal Commission. Its task was to offer suggestions, and it was presided over by Guichard. The Commission took its work seriously, and in October 1976 it presented a voluminous Report. This Report was a significant document in so far as it was the first official pronouncement for decades which dealt with problems of local administration in global terms and not according to specific aspects.[42] The so-called Guichard Report was anti-regional in content, giving priority to reform at communal and departmental level and to State action. It was also conservative, in the sense that it did not regard the disappearance of the communes in their present form as a necessary precondition for reform. The principal concrete measures which it proposed were:

- that the 36,000 communes should form themselves into strong, multi-purpose and permanent federations (ordinary communities where there are less than 30,000 inhabitants; freedom of choice between the two proposals for communes with a total of between 30,000 and 200,000 inhabitants);
- that these federations would be directed by a council presided over by a committee appointed for six years and composed of members elected, not by universal suffrage but by the municipal councils;
- the creation of a national conference of local institutions to ensure close co-operation between the State and the local authorities;
- a clearer redistribution of a certain number of responsibilities between the communes, the *départements* and the State, notably in the case of community works projects;
- the allocation *in toto* of the four current local taxes to the communes and communities, and in addition they may also benefit from a transfer of funds from the Public Exchequer.

But more important than these concrete proposals is the fact that this Report has created the opportunity to reopen public debate on the whole subject of local government. It criticises the *status quo* and stresses the urgent need for global action. And above all it proposes that a clear and legal differentiation be made between the responsibilities of the State and local institutions. Hand in hand with this must go a realisation of the fiscal and administrative changes which must accompany this differentiation in order for it to be effective. The role of local institutions cannot be discussed without discussing that of the State. The cards must be redealt. The local boundaries must also be redrawn according to correct principles, and the complex and manifold communities of interest must be grouped around political poles. Although the debate has been reopened, it remains to be seen whether this problem will in fact ever become a political priority.

One thing is certain: even if spectacular reforms have not been achieved in the last two decades, an important transformation has gradually taken place in the sense that the ideology of the nation-state has lost its impact. From now on local government is no longer an addendum to the controversy between the Jacobins and the Girondins: it is a specific social problem and its possible solutions are far from being clear or definable in advance.

NOTES

1 Other chapters in the book will deal with financial and economic problems and more specific aspects such as regionalisation.
2 P. Germain, 'Grandeur, décadence et possibilités de renaissance de

l'institution communale française', *Administration*, no. 59 (1971); P. Bernard, *Le Grand Tournant des communes de France* (Paris: Colin, 1969).

3 *Statistiques et études financières, octobre 1958: la situation financière des collectivités locales en 1955 et 1956.*

4 P. Lalumière, 'L'Aide financière aux collectivités locales', *Revue de science financière*, vol. 54, 1962.

5 M. Marchand, *Les Conseillers généraux depuis 1945* (Paris: Colin, 1970).

6 One of the groups which was particularly active during the 1960s was the Club Jean Moulin (named after one of the organisers of the French Resistance during the Nazi occupation); it produced a document on political reform which was to have a considerable influence, *L'Etat et le citoyen* (Paris: Le Seuil, 1963). M. Crozier's work, *La Société bloquée* (Paris: Le Seuil, 1969) resembles the analysis which the reformers of the Club Jean Moulin give of the problems of French society and their possible solution.

7 *Division of communes according to the size of population*

Number of inhabitants	Number of communes			Proportion of the national population		
	1851	*1968*	*1975*	*1851* %	*1968* %	*1975* %
Less than 100	433	3,877	4,012 ⎫			
100–500	15,251	20,130	18,719 ⎭	13·52	10·65	9·33
500–5,000	20,734	12,380	12,168	67·03	30·47	29·50
5,000–30,000	384	1,124	1,266 ⎫			
30,000–100,000	28	160	190 ⎬	19·45	58·88	61·17
100,000 and over	5	37	39 ⎭			
TOTAL	36,835	37,708	36,394	100 (35,787,170 inhabitants)	100 (50,840,577 inhabitants)	100 (53,696,777 inhabitants)

One notes an increase, up to 1968, in the number of small communes and an increase in the size of large communes.

8 M. Crozier, *Le Phénomène bureaucratique* (Paris: Le Seuil, 1964).

9 J. L. Quermonne, 'Vers un régionalisme fonctionnel', *Revue française de science politique*, vol. XIII, no. 4 (December 1963), p. 350.

10 Th. Flory, *Le Mouvement régionaliste français* (Paris: PUF, 1966).

11 Ch. Maurras, *L'Idée de decentralisation* (Paris, 1898); Proudhon, *Du Principe fédératif* (Paris: Rivière, 1959); Ch. Brun, *Le Régionalisme* (Paris, 1911).

12 M. Debré, *La Mort de l'Etat républicain* (Paris: Gallimard, 1947).

13 This commission was composed of twenty to fifty members appointed for a period of five years. Half its members were appointed by departmental consular institutions (chambers of commerce, industry, agriculture, trade associations) and by employer and salaried staff organisations; a quarter at least were mayors appointed by the departmental council and the rest individuals appointed by the Prime Minister. The CODER expressed opinions on matters arising out of economic and social questions and town and country planning and was consulted on the regional functioning of the national economic plan. In fact, the CODER was entirely controlled by the prefect who set up its agenda, fixed the dates for its sittings, was responsible for its secretariat and nominated its members or had them nominated by the traditional notables.

14 '... the regional council is composed:
of – National Assembly Deputies elected in the region

of – territorial regional councillors elected by the departmental councils and the municipal councils or their delegates

of – socio-professional regional councillors appointed by representative organ'.

This is Article 12 of the reform submitted to referendum on 27 April 1969.

15 These powers comprise: studies concerning regional development, the implementation of community public works programmes of regional interest, voluntary participation in the financing of public works programmes carried out by other institutions (the State, *département* and commune), proposals about public investment policy in the region.

16 The regional council is composed of: (1) Deputies and Senators elected in the region (2) The representatives of the local authorities elected by the departmental councils . . . (3) The representatives of agglomerations appointed from within the municipal councils . . .

A number of seats equal to that of the Members of Parliament (1) is attributed to the representatives from the departmental and municipal councils. These seats are distributed in proportion to the population of each *département*.

17 H. Detton, *L'Administration régionale et locale de la France* (Paris: PUF, 1975).

18 R. Maurice, *Les Syndicats de commune* (Paris: Massou, 1976); M. Bourjol, *La Réforme municipale* (Paris: Berger-Levrault, 1975).

19 M. Bourjol, *Les Districts urbains* (Paris: Berger-Levrault, 1963).

20   *Grouped communes (on 1 January 1975)*

	Number of groupings	Number of communes	Regrouped population
Single-purpose syndicates	10,210	—	—
Multiple-purpose syndicates	1,738	16,940	19,381,397
Districts	148	1,269	4,564,713
Urban communities	9*	251	4,142,526

Source: Commission de Développement des Responsabilités Locales, *Vivre ensemble* (Paris: La Documentation Française, 1976).

* Apart from the four agglomerations mentioned above, the following were also involved: Dunkirk, Cherbourg, Le Mans, Brest, Le Creusot-Montceau-les-Mines.

21 The Ministry of the Interior was of the opinion that out of the 1,738 SIVOM existing on 1 January 1975, 10·7% fulfilled no function at all, 11·33% had been created too recently to be analysed and 26% fulfilled only one function and were thus unauthentic SIVOM. Cf. Commission de Développement des Responsabilités Locales, op. cit.

22   *Communes merged by 1 May 1970*

Number of mergers	350
Number of communes regrouped	746
Regrouped population	3,700,000
Regrouped population as percentage of total French population	7·4%

Source: J. de Savigny, *L'Etat contre les communes?* (Paris: Le Seuil, 1971), p. 198.

23 *Le Monde*, 7 June 1973.

24 J.-C. Thoenig, *L'Ere des technocrates* (Paris: Les Editions d'Organisation, 1973).

25 Decree of 23 November 1970.

26 Subsequently 'area contracts' (*contrats de pays*), modelled on the 'planning contracts', were instituted between the State and the communes, grouped together for this purpose into a community which confronted the State in the negotiations concerning middle-term public works programmes.

27 Decree of 10 March 1972 on the reform of subsidies: creation of a global subsidy for public works programmes at local level (never brought into effect); decree of 13 November 1970 giving the prefect real power in matters concerning the State and the local authority '(globalisation of credit, extension of the list of devolved public works projects).

28 A. Peyrefitte *et al.*, *Décentraliser les responsabilités, Pourquoi? Comment?* (Paris: La Documentation Française, 1975).

29 The results of the study carried out between 1961 and 1962 in the *département* of Oise by Worms can be broadly applied to the present situation: J. P. Worms, 'Le prefet et ses notables', *Sociologie du Travail*, vol. III (1966).

30 For the reform of 1964, P. Grémion, *Le Pouvoir périphérique* (Paris: Le Seuil, 1976).

31 Thus, the reformers underestimated the level of resistance to change, all the more so as, before they formulated a definitive reform for the whole country, they did not experiment sufficiently in one or two regions and as they applied a strategy of change by means of structures which were both abstract and foreign to local experience.

32 J.-C. Thoenig, 'La relation entre le centre et la périphérie en France', *Bulletin de l'Institut International d'Administration Publique*, no. 36 (December 1975).

33 The accumulation of offices is not a disease within the system but an essential mechanism for its functioning. The representative who holds a number of offices offers the possibility of a more direct communication and a greater suppleness, particularly for those authorities which are too small and would otherwise be obliged to pass through a long and complex labyrinth and cross-functioning control. Accumulation of offices is a common practice legitimised by universal suffrage.

Accumulation of offices by Members of Parliament (1975)

	Deputies	Senators
Are also: Mayors	84	46
Departmental councillors	61	39
Mayors and departmental councillors	167	122
Total accumulated offices	312	207

Source: Commission de Développement des Responsabilités Locales, op. cit.

Accumulation of offices by chairmen of the departmental councils (April 1970)

Ministers	8 ⎫	out of a total of 94 presidents
Former ministers	20 ⎭	
Senators or Deputies	51 ⎫	out of a total of 94 presidents
Former Senators or Deputies	16 ⎬	
Without parliamentary office	27 ⎭	

Source: Le Monde, 15 March 1970.

34 Of the forty mayors of medium-sized communes in the *département* of the Pas-de-Calais, six are enjoying their fifth term of office and the average term of office as mayor is thirteen years. Every second mayor is the son of a locally elected representative. Cf. J. Becquart, *Paradoxes du pouvoir local* (Paris: Fondation Nationale des Sciences Politiques, 1976).

In the *département* of the Ardennes, between 1945 and 1973 only one departmental councillor was not re-elected at the end of his first term of office. Six councillors out of thirty-one have sat on the departmental council without interruption since 1945. Cf. J. C. Fortier, 'Les Ardennes' (unpublished thesis, University of Lille, 1973).

There is evidence of a surprising stability of elected officials in the large towns in which political life is however more 'politicised' than in many villages. E. Herriot, for example, was mayor of Lyons for almost forty-five years.

35　The government in Paris sent top officials or ministers into the provinces to conquer for the Gaullist party *départements* held by the opposition. This practice is called *parachutage*. The candidate presents himself with a pocket full of subsidies promised by Paris which the *département* will have if it votes for him. A well-known example of this is the case of J. Chirac, protégé of Pompidou and Prime Minister, who conquered Corrèze, a former bastion of radicalism, in this way. On the tactics of the government in 1965 and 1971, see J. Hayward and V. Wright, 'The 37,708 microcosms of an indivisible Republic', *Parliamentary Affairs*, Autumn 1971.

36　In 1974, eleven presidencies of the regional councils were in the hands of the parties of the presidential coalition and eight in the hands of the opposition.

37　Parti Socialiste, *Citoyen dans sa commune* (Paris: Flammarion, 1977).

38　A national opinion poll carried out by IFOP at the beginning of 1976 indicates that among the principal issues with which the French are discontented, communal taxes are classed as sixth (53% of people interviewed mentioned them); the living situation in the towns as twelfth (39%) and communal administration as twenty-fourth (26%).

39　S. Biarez *et al.*, *Institution communale et pouvoir politique: le cas de Roanne* (Paris: Mouton, 1972).

40　In the case of public services like water, gas, urbanisation, roads, electricity, telecommunications and employment there are separate agencies whose areas of activity do not correspond to political constituencies.

41　D. Ashford, 'French pragmatism and British idealism: financial aspects of local reorganisation', paper delivered at Edinburgh IPSA Congress, 16–21 August 1976.

42　Commission de Développement des Responsabilités Locales, *Vivre ensemble* (Paris: La Documentation Française, 1976).

—————◆—————

Chapter VI

THE LOCAL POLITICAL ELITE
IN ENGLAND AND WALES

Out of a total electorate of about 36 million people, only 24,000 serve as elected members on the local councils of England and Wales. In other words, only a tiny proportion of adult citizens are elected to local political office. Moreover, councillors are not drawn from a broad cross-section of society, but are generally recruited from a rather restricted range of social and economic groups in the population as a whole. The purpose of this essay is to describe, in general terms, the social and economic characteristics of elected representatives in the local government system of England and Wales, and to explain why this particular group is recruited. The essay then goes on to describe the process which involves people in local government work, the nature of the work itself, and the different types of councils and councillors. The essay concentrates on district and county councillors because they are the most important of the elected representatives in the system.

RULES FOR CANDIDACY AND ELECTIONS

Few people are legally disqualified from holding public office in local government. Lunatics, bankrupts, and those sentenced to more than three months' imprisonment within five years of the election are not allowed to stand, nor are those who have been convicted of illegal election practices. No one can serve on the council which employs them, but local government employees are free to sit on the councils of other areas. In addition, candidates must either be on the electoral register of the local authority they wish to serve, or they must live in it, or own land in it, or have some other special connection with it. Other than the relatively small number of people who are disqualified by these rules, anyone who is a British citizen and an adult may stand for election. Unlike in national elections, local candidates do not pay a deposit, although they must have a proposer, and seconder, and eight other signatures on their nomination papers.

In the more rural areas, where the party system is less well developed, many candidates stand as independents, with no party connection at all, or as the representatives of small, local groups. In the towns and cities, most candidates represent one of the main national parties (Labour, Conservative, Liberal), or for one of the smaller or newer parties (Scottish Nationalist, Welsh Nationalist, Communist). While this pattern still generally holds, it has started to change in the past few years because increasing numbers of independent and minor party candidates are fighting elections in the urban areas, while rural elections are becoming more partisan.

The development of competitive party politics in urban authorities means that most of their elections are contested by at least two candidates from the major parties, but it is not at all uncommon for candidates to be returned unopposed in rural areas. Indeed, it has been suggested that some people in the rural areas are happy to serve on their councils provided they do not have to fight an election campaign, and that they withdraw from local politics when their seat is contested. Election is by secret ballot, each elector having one vote for each vacancy in the area. Towns and cities are almost always divided into wards, with three councillors representing each ward. Strict rules govern the conduct of election campaigns, including the amount of money which may be spent on them.

THE SOCIAL AND ECONOMIC COMPOSITION OF COUNCILS

The political elites of most countries in the West tend to be dominated, numerically at any rate, by middle-class, middle-aged, males. So it is with British local government. Council members have a markedly higher social status, income and education than the average elector, and they are much more likely to own the house they live in than to rent it. Women are under-represented quite considerably, for although they make up over half the adult population they take only 17 per cent of council seats. Councillors are also much older than the adult population, having an average age of over 55. The broad outlines of the socio-economic composition of council members are presented in Table 6.1.

Closer inspection shows that council members are drawn from an even narrower range of social groups than Table 6.1 suggests. At the turn of the century big landowners and businessmen tended to dominate local politics, but they have largely withdrawn from public life in the last fifty years, leaving local councils dominated numerically by small businessmen and farmers. The largest single occupational group now comprises employers and managers of small businesses, while farmers and farm managers are also heavily over-represented in rural authorities. Taken together, small businessmen, managers, farmers and farm managers make up about a third of all councillors, although they form less than 10 per cent of the population as a whole. Among the businessmen, the self-employed figure rather largely, and among them there are fairly large numbers of

Table 6.1 *The Social Composition of Councils in England and Wales compared with the Adult Population, 1976*

		Councillors %	Adult population %
Age	21–34	9	27
	35–54	41	33
	55 and over	50	41
Sex	Male	83	48
	Female	17	52
Education			
	Higher education	50	8
	Other qualifications	13	25
	No qualifications	37	67
Social class			
	Professional and technical	27	10
	Administrative and managerial	14	6
	Sales and services	17	15
	Clerical	6	7
	Manual	33	60
	Others	2	2

Source: Report of the Committee of Inquiry into the System of Remuneration of Members of Local Authorities, Vol. II, The Surveys of Councillors and Local Authorities. (London: HMSO, 1977), pp. 8–13.

shopkeepers, estate agents, property developers, builders, hoteliers, publicans and merchants. People with a business interest in land and property form quite a large group, one study showing that their numbers have increased steadily over the years as local government has broadened its concern with land, housing and planning.

On the other hand, manual workers, and particularly unskilled workers and farm labourers, are considerably under-represented. Manual workers form almost two-thirds of the total adult male population, but they fill only a third of council seats. And while slightly more than a third of the adult male population is made up of skilled manual workers, only an eighth of councillors fall into this category. This, however, represents a marked change from the earlier part of the century when manual workers were even less well represented. By and large, the more urban the area, and the more active the political parties in recruiting candidates for local elections, the more socially representative the council. This seems to be due mainly to the efforts of the three main political parties to recruit a wider range of people to public office, and particularly to the rise of the Labour Party which has done a good deal to broaden the social composition of councils.

Meanwhile some of the counties retain their old middle- and

upper-class composition, and even their old aristocratic flavour. Non-metropolitan county councils have a higher average income, a higher average age, and a higher social and economic status than most other councils, and the contrast with the larger urban authorities is most marked. However, the 1972 Reform Act had the effect of introducing more party politics into county government, and it is to be expected that this will result in county councils becoming more representative of the general population.

Although the political elites of most Western societies are not generally socially representative of the population, two points about the British local elite should be made. First, although only a third of council members have working-class occupations, even this figure is higher than some other Western societies, and this is due mainly to the competitive party system which exists at the local level. Parties are important because they often make it a point of honour to contest seats, and because they provide ordinary people with the organisational and financial resources necessary to fight effective election campaigns.

Second, while the social composition of councils is determined primarily by wider social and economic forces, there are some local factors which effect the pattern. One of the main features of British politics is 'the cult of the amateur' which places a great emphasis on unpaid public service. Since many council meetings are held during normal working hours, and since the hours involved are often long and arduous, council membership is easier for retired people, and for those who, like the self-employed, can adjust their working hours around council business. The principle of unpaid public service may also increase the number of middle- and upper-class members, for they can better afford the loss of earnings which often goes with council work. Since 1974 a maximum attendance allowance of £11 per day has been paid, and it is possible that this will broaden the social composition of councils, although the evidence is not clear as yet.

In recent years some critical comments about local councillors have been made on the grounds that they are of rather low and declining quality. It is, of course, difficult to know how to interpret political quality, since this is entirely a matter of personal opinion, but it is worth pointing out that in so far as councillors have higher educational qualifications than the population as a whole, have more responsible jobs, and can bring a wide range of occupational, professional and administrative expertise to bear upon council work, claims about low quality are somewhat dubious.

THE RECRUITMENT OF COUNCILLORS

Most people seem to be drawn into council work as a result of a long-standing connection with the community, its people and its voluntary organisations. In 1964, over a third of councillors had been born in their local authority, and almost two-thirds had lived in it for more than twenty-five years. Moreover, they generally had an extensive range of contacts with local voluntary organisations, belonging to an average of almost seven organisations each, while a significant minority belonged to many more. By comparison, the average elector is a member of only one voluntary organisation. One study of council members in Barking (a borough of the old London County Council) found that they held an average of twenty-six official positions in voluntary organisations. While some of these positions were themselves tied to council membership, this very high figure does indicate the level of group activity among local representatives.

Having associations with a large number of organisations not only gives the council member deep roots in the community, but these organisations seem to be important recruiting agents for new members. Almost half of a national sample of council members said they were brought into touch with council work through these organisations, and the largest number said they were first invited to stand for election by one of them. Other evidence suggests that trade unions, the Co-operative movement and the Labour Party are instrumental in the recruitment of Labour councillors, while a broader range of sports, charity, business and religious organisations, and the Conservative Party, play the same function for Conservative members.

If it is clear that close contact with the community over many years draws local citizens into council work, it is also clear that many are not exactly eager to take up public work. Most council members, it seems, do not actively seek office; on the contrary, it appears that they have to be pushed, cajoled and persuaded – only one in five state that it was their own idea to stand for election. Whatever the motives which push councillors into public service, a desire for power seems to be relatively unimportant. In contrast to their French counterparts, British councillors generally stay in local politics, and rarely use their community position as a launching pad for a national political career. And unlike France, the few who do move from the local to the national political arena retain their local positions.

THE WORK OF THE COUNCILLOR

Council work is an arduous business. Although two-thirds of all council members have a full-time job, their public duties take up an average of almost twenty hours a week. Members with special responsibilities, such as the chairmen of council committees or the leading members of the party groups, will spend many more hours than this on their public duties, while a large minority, especially in the big cities, will devote a full working week, or more, to the job. The time spent on different activities will depend partly on the nature of the local authority – county councillors spend more time on travelling – and partly on the seniority of the councillor. Overall, however, members spend most of their time at council and committee meetings, at meetings of their party groups, with electors and their problems, and with a variety of voluntary and public bodies. Most of these meetings involve a good deal of paper work and preparation.

The average councillor sits on about four council committees, and each committee produces quantities of documents which have to be read and assimilated. As they gain experience of the work, which involves a wide variety of different public services, members tend to specialise in one or two committees. This is inevitable as the work of running large local authorities is enormous and since the technical and organisational complexities of the task are multiplying. Councillors also have to prepare for and attend meetings of the full council, as well as meetings of their party groups and their local party organisations.

Another important task involves dealing with the individual problems of electors at what are called 'advice bureaux' or 'surgeries', which give citizens a chance to discuss their problem with their elected representatives. Lastly, councillors are obliged to attend the meetings of a variety of public bodies and voluntary organisations. In some cases they represent the council on public or semi-public bodies, and in others they attend the meetings of organisations in their area in order to maintain contact with the community they represent.

The councillor's life is, therefore, an extremely busy one, and the long, hard hours of work involved seem to be a major cause of high turnover rates. About 6 per cent give up the work each year, and the figure is appreciably higher among those with relatively few years of council work behind them. About a third give up because of the hours involved, and a high proportion of them are younger people with professional and business careers which are, they feel, adversely affected by their public duties. Groups with a low turnover rate are workers in the nationalised industries (which have special arrangements for serving on public bodies), part-time workers, housewives, and those with low incomes. Most people, however, give up for personal reasons concerned with their family, their business or professional career, their health, or old age. In this respect it is interesting that the existence of political parties in local government, which is a common source of complaint among members of the general public, is not a factor which makes many councillors want to give up their council work.

On the whole most members seem to find deep satisfaction in their council work, especially their work in the fields of housing and old people's welfare. A large majority feel that public service has enabled them to develop and use a range of abilities denied to them in their other roles. Working-class councillors in particular are likely to say this. In fact, more than a third find their council work more satisfying than their jobs, and this proportion rises to almost two-thirds in the case of manual workers. This helps to explain the relatively low turnover rate among low income councillors. On the other hand, the job of the councillor also has its frustrations. Many feel that their council does not make full use of its powers, and they often feel that central government puts too many limitations and restrictions on its activities. In urban areas, in particular, there is a fairly strong feeling that councils should have greater freedom to make decisions about town planning, housing, traffic management and public utilities.

TYPES OF COUNCILS AND TYPES OF COUNCILLORS

It is clear from what has already been said that urban and rural councils differ quite considerably. The more urban the local authority, the more highly organised and competitive the local party system is likely to be, not only for the purpose of contesting elections but also for the purpose of conducting politics within the councils and its committees. Most city councillors are party representatives, and most (90 per cent) have to fight an election to get on to the council. In the counties about a third of the candidates are returned unopposed. The existence of a developed local party system affects the whole nature of local politics, not least in producing councils which are socially more representative of the general population than in the rural areas. By comparison with the counties, the cities have a high proportion of low income, low social status, female, and younger councillors. City councils and their committees are also organised along party lines in much the same way as the House of Commons, whereas the county councils, with their relatively high proportion of independents, are more likely to be composed of small groups and a more loosely organised set of individuals.

However, there are also considerable differences between members of the same council, whether urban or rural. These differences usually, but not always, coincide with the distinction between council leaders and ordinary members. The leaders include the present and past chairmen of council committees, and the leaders of the party groups. Ordinary members are those who have held less significant positions, or no official position within the council hierarchy at all. Council leaders are usually the older and longer-serving members, often with fifteen, twenty or even thirty or more years of experience behind them. They usually have a fairly high level of education, are often professionals or businessmen, most frequently male, and they spend anything between 80 and 120 hours a week on council business.

By and large council leaders know much more about local government in general, and about their own local authority in particular, than the ordinary members. Their grasp of complex policy issues is often impressive, and some of them have a formidable ability to analyse the subtleties of local issues and problems. They know a good deal about what is happening in other local authorities and about the activities of community organisations. They are involved primarily with making local policy and with running the local authority as a whole, rather than representing one small ward within it. They are also the most powerful and influential members of the local councils.

Ordinary members are rather different. They are younger, have less experience of council work, have a fairly high turnover rate, and spend fewer hours on council work. Most important, their view of their political role in the local system differs from that of the leaders quite considerably. The political world of the ordinary member consists primarily of his or her own ward, and of individual electors with problems. They see themselves not as policy makers so much as a special sort of unpaid social worker or ombudsman whose main job is to sort out the problems of their constituents, so far as these problems involve local public services. For these reasons, ordinary members are not highly partisan (although they may be highly ideological) and they are more likely than council leaders to oppose the existence of parties in local government. Their main concern is not public policy but individual problems, and they tend to take the view that if they look after the individuals, public policy will look after itself.

It is easy to draw too clear and rigid a distinction between council leaders and ordinary members. They are not completely distinct types, and they do fuse and merge into one another to some extent. The main merit of drawing a distinction between them, however, is to discourage easy generalisations about councillors. Some of the literature, including some of the academic literature which should know better, tends to dismiss local government councillors as rather ignorant, unintelligent, politically puny, and incapable of running modern, large-scale local government. While this picture may be accurate for some of the ordinary members, the council leaders are more usually of a much higher calibre, and, so far as elected members really make the decisions, it is the council leaders who have most influence in the local government systems.

FURTHER READING

Committee on the Management of Local Government, Vol. 2, *The Local Government Councillor* (London: HMSO, 1967).

Report of the Committee of Inquiry into the System of Remuneration of Members of Local Authorities, Vol. II, *The Surveys of Councillors and Local Authorities* (London: HMSO, 1977).

J. Dearlove, *The Politics of Policy in Local Government* (Cambridge: CUP, 1973).

W. Hampton, *Democracy and Community* (Oxford: OUP, 1970), especially ch. 8.

J. M. Lee, *Social Leaders and Public Persons* (London: OUP, 1963).

K. Newton, *Second City Politics* (Oxford: The Clarendon Press, 1976), especially ch. 6.

A. M. Rees and T. Smith, *Town Councillors* (London: The Acton Society Trust, 1964).

L. J. Sharpe, 'Elected representatives in local government', *British Journal of Sociology*, vol. 12 (1962).

Chapter VII

———◆———

OFFICE HOLDERS IN THE LOCAL POLITICS OF THE FRENCH FIFTH REPUBLIC

It is intended in this paper to give a systematic analysis of the political personnel in present-day France who are elected to local office at one level or another. Those notables, such as businessmen, who exercise considerable influence at the local level but whose legitimacy does not stem from the electoral process will, therefore, be excluded from consideration in this research.

In France elections take place at communal level to elect the municipal council which chooses the mayor from amongst its members, and at the level of the canton, with each canton electing a member to sit on the departmental council at the head of each *département,* which also elects a chairman from within its numbers; and, finally, since the regional reform of July 1972, regional councils have been created within the framework of each of the twenty-two regions. These councils are composed of Members of Parliament, delegates from the municipal councils and the departmental councils and representatives from the urban communities. These regional councils elect their chairman from within their number. This study will be limited to examples from these three categories of elected representatives and, due to the shortage of relevant data, will not be concerned with the members of the urban communities.

THE MAYORS

Each one of the 37,708 French communes has a deliberative organ, the municipal council, which is elected by direct universal suffrage every six years, the precise method of election varying according to the size of the commune in question. The mayor, elected in his turn by the municipal council, may either limit himself to executing the decisions of this council or he may, on the contrary, act on his own authority or he may even exercise his powers in his capacity as representative of the State, which retains the right to control the actions of the municipal council and the mayor. There are in France more than 500,000 mayors and municipal councillors of whom more than three-fifths represent communes of less than 500 inhabitants (that is to say, 6 million Frenchmen). By contrast, the 12 million Frenchmen who live in towns of more than 100,000 inhabitants

Table 7.1 Mayors According to Profession after the Local Elections of March 1971

	Farmers	Farm workers	Industrialists	Artisans	Tradesmen	Wholesalers	Doctors, surgeons ...	Secondary school teachers, intellectual professions	Engineers	Upper management (private sector)	Top civil servants	Elementary school teachers	Technicians, middle management	Office workers	Shop workers	Workers	Clergy, c. my	Retired	Landowners without profession	Others
1971 All Mayors Number	16,801	66	1,994	1,496	1,639	100	928	713	381	1,460	484	1,010	1,677	1,210	536	762	422	4,544	783	500
%	44·9	0·1	5·3	4·0	4·3	0·2	2·5	1·7	1·0	3·7	1·3	2·7	4·4	3·2	1·4	2·0	1·1	12·1	2·0	1·3
1971 Towns of more than 30,000 inhabitants Number	3	—	20	3	1	4	5	23	5	46	18	12	15	8	3	24	1	5	—	—
%	1·5	—	10·2	1·5	0·5	2·0	2·5	11·6	2·5	23·3	9·1	6·1	7·6	4·0	1·5	12·2	0·5	2·5	—	—

37,506 (All Mayors Number total); 196 (Towns Number total)

Source: Table constructed from information supplied by the Ministry of the Interior in: V. Aubert, Etude sur le personnel politique français, Maîtrise de Sociologie, Paris University.

(0·1 per cent of the communes) are only represented by about 1,500 councillors.

As it would be impossible to examine the municipal council in its entirety here, it seems indispensable to study the French mayor more particularly, as no exhaustive study has as yet been made of the subject: only works dealing with specific aspects of their functions have been published.[1] Table 7.1 gives a breakdown of the socio-professional origins of those mayors elected in March 1971 who were in office until March 1977. The table clearly indicates the pre-eminence of the agricultural sector which accounts for 44·9 per cent of the mayors elected. After these come the retired (12·1 per cent) and the tradesmen and artisans (8·3 per cent). On the other hand, the liberal professions are very poorly represented although since the Third Republic they have tended to furnish an essential element at the parliamentary level.

The poor participation of industrialists, higher executives and top civil servants in the management of local affairs should also be noted. The picture presented here is already in complete contrast to that offered by the political personnel at the national level, be they Deputies or ministers, for while the agricultural sector accounts for 44·9 per cent of all mayors it accounts for only 5·2 per cent of the Deputies elected in 1973 and a mere 1·6 per cent of the ministers appointed between 1969 and 1973, and this percentage has decreased further since 1974 due to the changes undergone by the political personnel under Giscard d'Estaing.[2] By the same token the retired are hardly better represented at parliamentary and ministerial level whilst they account for 12·1 per cent of all mayors. By contrast, the liberal professions which are very poorly represented at the mayoral level are the dominant element amongst Members of Parliament: doctors, for example, passing from 2·5 per cent of all mayors to 12 per cent of Deputies elected in 1973. The evolution in the representation of top civil servants should also be underlined: they constitute 1·3 per cent of all mayors, 11·4 per cent of Deputies elected in 1973 and 38·8 per cent of ministers appointed between 1969 and 1973.

Whatever the differences which separate parliamentary and ministerial personnel may be (the latter containing a smaller proportion of the liberal professions and a larger proportion of top civil servants and industrialists),[3] this personnel differs totally from mayoral personnel from the point of view of its socio-professional composition. This distortion reveals the great distance which separates the mayors from national affairs: they appear as people implanted locally by virtue of their profession as farmers or small traders; they are in no way in possession of an expertise identical to that of political personnel at the national level.

This helps to explain the profound 'localism' of the mayors and the paternalistic manner in which they manage their communes. The mayors 'share a common rhetoric which denies the existence of political divisions within the commune and which stresses the importance of communal harmony'.[4] As a group, the mayors, deeply integrated into their commune by virtue of their profession, appear as simple managers who claim to avoid any partisan commitment: in this connection it is important to note that about one-third of all mayors are elected from lists bearing no political label.

This conception which the mayor has of the neutrality of his own role is further reinforced by the fact that more than a half of the electorate (66 per cent in rural communes which, today, still represent the vast majority) consider that their mayor should have no political affiliation.[5] As it is managed by a personnel which differs radically from that of the national political class, the political life of the commune also evolves sheltered from attack by the political movements. Thus, the traditional political parties like the Socialist Party and the Radical Party easily manage to preserve their foothold, whilst the Communist Party and the UDR succeed only with difficulty in conquering the municipal councils.[6]

The quasi-exclusive domination of the farmers and small tradesmen also explains why the local political personnel is so deeply entrenched: a large proportion of French mayors are natives of their communes and have lived there almost permanently. They are very often the sons or grandsons of mayors of the same commune.[7] They tend to retain their seats from one election to the next over a long period of time.[8] One may also conclude that the absence of real expertise amongst mayors and the apparent 'depoliticisation' of political life in the majority of communes accounts for their lethargy: deprived of real power, the mayors are often reduced to seeking from departmental councillors or even Deputies on the one hand and from the administration on the other that impetus which alone can get things moving. Therefore, in the vast majority of cases, the mayors in France can no longer really be qualified as notables.

MAYORS IN TOWNS OF MORE THAN 30,000 INHABITANTS

An examination of a more limited sample of mayors – those elected in 1971 in towns of more than 30,000 inhabitants – indicates an entirely different socio-economic origin from the mayoral body in general. The agricultural sector is represented here by only 1·6 per cent as compared to 44·9 per cent of all mayors elected in 1971. By the same token, artisans and small traders account for only 2·0 per cent as compared to 8·3 per cent, and the retired 2·5 per cent as compared to 12·1 per cent. On the other hand, the number of industrialists is doubled (10·2 per cent as compared to 5·3 per cent) and, likewise, higher executives in the private sector represent 23·3 per cent as opposed to 3·7 per cent overall, whilst top civil servants pass from 1·3 to 9·1 per cent.

The mayors in large towns, then, form a very specific group which should be carefully distinguished from the group as a whole. These mayors in medium-sized towns or who hold office in the big provincial cities in fact do have an expertise which equates them more with the political personnel at national level. They are no longer characterised by mere 'localism' and a deep-rooted connection with their particular commune. They appear rather as true leaders with the competence necessary to manage their cities. They are also able to deal on a more egalitarian basis with the local field services and, by virtue of their professions, they have a network of contacts which enables them, in certain instances, to make themselves heard at national level. Thus they appear as real partners of the prefects with whom they are far more able than the mayors of small rural communes to co-operate in a way which reinforces their mutual power.[9] Unlike the mayors in small rural communes, or even those in small towns, the mayors in towns of more than 30,000 inhabitants, and especially those who govern the regional capitals like Lyons, Marseilles, Nice or Bordeaux, may be considered as notables whose power is even more secure than that of the notables who held power in traditional provincial France in the nineteenth century.

THE DEPARTMENTAL COUNCILLORS

The members of the departmental council, the elected organ at the head of the *département,* are elected by universal suffrage under a uninominal system and each represents a particular canton. The departmental council is the deliberative assembly of the *département* vested with a certain decentralising function. Thanks to the work of certain historians it is possible to attempt a few observations on the evolution of the recruitment of departmental councillors from the July Monarchy to the Fifth Republic. An examination of those departmental councillors elected through the system of 'scrutin censitaire' – a system of eligibility based on property qualification – in 1840 reveals a preponderance of property owners (28·0 per cent of the whole) and lawyers (19·2 per cent of the whole). The former were more often than not real estate owners, whilst the latter were sometimes recruited from among the less well-off sections of the population although they were, of course, also subject to the property qualification. One also finds in 1840 a group composed of bankers and industrialists which alone constituted 14·3 per cent of the departmental councillors.[10]

In 1870 real estate owners represented 29·7 per cent of the departmental councillors, the legal profession 21·4 per cent, industrialists and bankers 15·55 per cent and top civil servants 5 per cent.[11] There appears, therefore, to be considerable stability in the recruitment pattern between 1840 and 1870. However, it should be noted that the top civil servants managed to double their representation during this period, moving from 2·6 to 5·2 per cent. One can conclude from this that during the nineteenth century the departmental councillors were recruited from among the more affluent sections of the population and often played an important role at national level. They were notables in the true sense of the word who sometimes combined the possession of a private fortune with the exercise of a particular talent.

If we now look at those departmental councillors elected between 1945 and 1964, we will see that a certain change has taken place in the recruitment pattern. Whilst there is relative stability in agricultural representation (25·5 per cent of the whole), there is a decline in the representation of the legal profession but a considerable increase in the liberal professions into which the former has been integrated (29·9 per cent), and increasing influence from the industrial and commercial sectors which (and here we include the higher executives in the private sector) represent 25·5 per cent of all departmental councillors. Conversely, a considerable drop in the number of top civil servants is evident but is compensated for by an increase in the number of elementary school teachers elected.[12]

Whilst both mayors and departmental councillors are recruited to a large extent from the agricultural sector, the latter are nevertheless predominantly recruited from the liberal professions and from the world of industry and commerce. From this point of view, the departmental councillors have a stronger tendency to belong to the political personnel at national level: they share the socio-professional characteristics of the mayors of large towns and even of parliamentary personnel. At this point it is perhaps necessary to emphasise the two-way movement which is taking place simultaneously under the Fifth Republic and which is leading on the one hand to the 'nationalisation' of the departmental councillors and on the other to the 'localisation' of the parliamentary personnel, which is increasingly abandoning the management of national affairs to the executive. This growing 'localisation' of the parliamentary function which concentrates more and more on the transmission of local demands is marked by the strong increase in the number of Deputies who are also departmental councillors (28 per cent in 1946, 44 per cent in 1962).[13]

This is an indication of one of several profound transformations which the parliamentary personnel have undergone during the Fifth Republic. There seems to be an attempt to compensate for the loss of power at the national level by a greater entrenchment at the local level accompanied by an increased plurality of mandates. Correspondingly the increased proportion of local Deputies elected to Parliament has risen from 63 per cent in 1953 to 79·4 per cent in 1967, highlighting the growing local attachments of parliamentary personnel.[14] As a result, one can advance the hypothesis that the acquisition of the status of notable by Members of Parliament is even easier if they have first held elected office in local politics. Thus, that departmental councillors, like Deputies combining the function of departmental councillors, become notables 'results from the sanctioning of an intermediary position through the addition of the status of political elite',[15] and this definition could apparently not be applied to the mayors.

This 'nationalisation' of departmental councillors is finally evidenced by the most recent evolution in their socio-professional origin. The year 1974 witnessed, for example, a strong decline in the agricultural sector to a level of only 13·6 per cent whilst it still accounted for 45 per cent of all mayors. Conversely, the liberal professions and middle and upper management have either maintained or increased their level of representation. Therefore, the socio-professional origin of the departmental councillors can be increasingly identified with that of parliamentary personnel.

Table 7.2　*Departmental Councillors by Socio-professional Category, 1955–74*

	1955 %	1964 %	1974 %
Farmers	22·14	18·33	13·59
Employers, industrialists	22·33	20·05	15·30
Liberal professions and higher management	37·15	35·14	35·13
Middle management	5·70	7·01	17·42
Employees	1·75	3·24	3·53
Workers	0·93	1·32	1·72
Public service personnel	0·07	0·13	—
Other categories	1·88	4·17	0·01
Persons not in active employment	8·05	10·59	13·11

Source: Service d'information, Ministry of the Interior.

THE CHAIRMEN OF DEPARTMENTAL COUNCILS

One can measure the extent of the 'nationalisation' of certain local elective functions by examining the socio-professional origin of the chairmen of the departmental councils elected in 1976. It has been possible to assemble data on the socio-professional origins of 82 chairmen of departmental councils. Amongst these are to be found 10 farmers, 25 members of the liberal professions, 5 top civil servants (of whom 3 are members of the *grands corps*), 17 industrialists, 13 primary or secondary teachers, 8 middle-ranking civil servants, 2 workers and 2 artisans. In comparison with departmental councillors in general the agricultural sector falls back whilst the business world and high public office increase their representation. Therefore, one can say that the chairmen of the departmental councils are even closer to parliamentary personnel with regard to their socio-economic origins (see Table 7.3). Moreover, amongst these 82 men are to be found 32 Senators in office or who were elected to that function subsequently, 36 Deputies currently in office or who previously held such office and, finally, 20 ministers currently in office or who had resigned from office. One may, therefore, note the existence of a plurality of mandates, a sign of the progressive 'nationalisation' of local political life at a fairly high level.

THE REGIONAL CHAIRMEN

As already noted, the Law of 5 July 1972 confirmed the creation of twenty-two regions which grouped together varying numbers of *départements*. They were intended to aid economic development and regional planning by strengthening decentralisation of the decision-making process. Apart from the regional prefect who represents the central administration at this level, the regions are headed by a regional council composed of Members of Parliament, departmental councillors and municipal councillors to whom are added the representatives of the urban communities every four years. These councils elect from among their members a chairman who wields considerable power.

An analysis of the socio-economic origins of the chairmen of the regional councils elected in 1976 yields the following results: 5 top civil servants (4 of whom are members of the *grands corps*), 4 industrialists, 1 teacher in higher education, 3 lawyers, 3 doctors, 3 professional politicians, 1 journalist, 1 librarian and 1 auctioneer. It can be seen that the socio-professional distribution here differs considerably from that of either mayors or departmental councillors.

Here, for the first time at local level, one can observe the presence of a high proportion of top civil servants and industrialists, categories

Table 7.3 Political Functions and Initial Professions of Political Personnel in the Fifth Republic

	% Workers	% Employees	% Civil servants	% Farmers	% Elementary teachers	% Secondary school teachers	% Journalists	% Doctors	% Lawyers	% Upper management liberal professions	% Top civil servants	% Engineers, architects	% Middle management technicians	% Tradesmen	% Industrialists	% Clergy	% Others	% Retired	% Total
All mayors (elections 1971)	2·1	4·6	—	44·9	2·7	1·7	—	2·5	—	3·7	1·3	1·0	4·4	8·5	5·3	1·1	3·3	12·1	100
Senators (elections 1971)	1·8	2·2	3·3	22·1	2·7	7·0	3·3	7·7	11·7	1·8	6·2	1·4	3·3	5·5	11·7	—	7·3	—	100
Mayors in towns of more than 30,000 inhabitants (1971)	12·2	5·5	—	1·5	6·1	11·6	—	2·5	—	23·3	9·1	2·5	7·6	4·0	10·2	0·5	2·5	—	100
Candidates in legislative elections (1973)	6·5	8·3	7·1	3·6	4·9	13·4	3·6	7·6	5·5	1·3	3·0	2·8	12·6	3·6	7·3	0·5	7·3	—	100
Deputies (1973 elections)	4·8	3·3	2·9	5·2	3·5	10·1	2·9	12·0	8·0	7·6	11·4	3·5	5·0	2·8	11·4	0·2	4·4	—	100
Ministers (1969–73)	—	—	—	1·6	—	8·9	1·6	5·9	8·9	13·4	38·8	2·9	—	2·9	13·4	—	1·6	—	100
Active population (1971)	37·4	15·7		11·4						5·9		11·9		10·0					

Note: The categories 'middle-ranking civil servants' and 'elementary school teachers' are included in the category 'middle management technicians'.

Source: Aubert, *Etude sur le personnel politique français,* p. 51.

which, under the Fifth Republic, are more characteristic of the ministerial than the parliamentary stratum. One the other hand, the farmers disappear and the liberal professions are marginally less well represented. Even more significant, all the chairmen of the regional councils are, or have been, either Deputies or Senators (20 being currently in office), most of them are or have been departmental councillors (18 out of 22; 17 still holding office), many of them are or have been mayors (13 of them still are) and 7 chairmen are, or have been, chairmen of CODER (7 having also been chairmen of a departmental council). But, most important of all, 12 of them have, in fact, been ministers and one of them is still holding ministerial office.

The progressive 'nationalisation' of local political personnel attains its highest expression here. Already apparent in the large towns whose mayors are, more often than not, Members of Parliament, it is equally evident amongst the chairmen of the departmental councils who are themselves almost always former Members of Parliament, but reaches its peak with the chairmen of regional councils who are not all Deputies or Senators, but of whom more than half are former ministers,[16] and therefore share the socio-professional characteristics of ministers of the Republic.[17]

It only remains to emphasise the accumulation of offices (*cumul des mandats*) which increases in proportion to the position held by the local political personnel in the hierarchy: from the mayoral body in general to mayors of large cities, from departmental councillors to the chairmen of these councils, right up to those who are to be found at the head of the regional councils. As these people are extremely influential they may make the, often complementary, relations between the prefects and certain locally elected personnel more unstable. In particular, the mayors of large cities who are often chairmen of departmental or regional councils and who often belong over and above to parliamentary or ministerial circles can, without difficulty, exercise influence on central government.[18] The progressive 'nationalisation' of the most important elements in the local political personnel goes hand in hand with an increasing entrenchment which reinforces both their prestige and their power.

Table 7.4   *Offices Held by Chairmen of Regional Councils Elected in 1976*

Region	Mayor	Departmental councillor	Chairman of departmental council	Chairman of CODER	Deputy or Senator	Minister or staff of minister
Alsace	F	O			O	F
Aquitaine	O			F	O	F
Auvergne	F	O			O	
Bourgogne		O	F		O	F
Bretagne		O	F	F	F	F
Centre	O				O	F
Champagne-Ardennes		O			O	
Corse	O	O	O	F	O	F
Franche-Comté	O	O		F	O	F
Languedoc-Roussillon	F	O			O	
Limousin	O	O	O		O	
Lorraine		O			O	F
Midi-Pyrénées		F			O	F
Nord-Pas-de-Calais	O	O	F		O	
Basse-Normandie	O			F	O	
Haute-Normandie	O	O		F	O	F
Pays de la Loire	O	O			F	O
Picardie	O				O	
Poitou-Charentes	O	O	F	F	O	
Provence-Côte de d'Azur	O	O			O	F
Région-Parisienne		O			O	
Rhône-Alpes	O	O	F		O	F

Key: O = in office
F = formerly in office

NOTES

1 See J. Verdès-Leroux, 'Caractéristiques des maires des communes de plus de 2000 habitants', *Revue française de science politique*, October 1970, p. 986. See also J. Becquart-Leclerq, *Paradoxes du pouvoir local* (Paris: Presses de la Fondation nationale des sciences politiques, 1976), p. 37.

2 See P. Birnbaum, *La Nouvelle Classe politique* (Paris: Le Seuil, 1976), ch. 6.

3 ibid., ch. 4.

4 M. Kesselman, *Le Consensus ambigu* (Paris: Cujas, 1972), p. 17.

5 SOFRES opinion poll, January 1971. See also P. Weil, 'Quelques brèves remarques sur les différences de comportement observées aux élections locales et nationales à Marseille', *Les Facteurs locaux de la vie politique nationale* (Paris: Pédone, 1972), p. 275. Also J. P. Gilli, 'Le maire dans le département des Alpes-Maritimes', *Revue française de science politique*, June 1968.

6 J. Hayward and V. Wright, 'The 37,708 microcosms of an indivisible Republic', *Parliamentary Affairs*, Autumn 1971.

7 J. Becquart-Leclercq, *Paradoxes du pouvoir local* (Paris: FNSP, 1976).

8 See M. Kesselman, 'French local politics: a statistical examination of grassroots consensus', *American Political Science Review*, December 1966, pp. 970–2. See also M.-F. Souchon, *Le Maire, élu local dans une société en changement* (Paris: Cujas, 1968), pp. 71–3.

9 See J.-P. Worms, 'Le préfet et ses notables', *Sociologie du travail*, July–September 1966. For a critique of too functional approaches to these relationships which neglect the socio-professional origins of the personnel holding such offices see P. Birnbaum, 'Le pouvoir local: de la décision au système, *Revue française de sociologie*, July–September 1973, pp. 349–50.

10 A.-J. Tudesq, *Les Conseillers généraux en France au temps de Guizot* (Paris: Colin, 1967), Vol. 2, ch. 1.

11 L. Girard, A. Prost and R. Gossez, *Les Conseillers généraux en 1870* (Paris: PUF, 1967), pp. 47–8.

12 M. H. Marchand, *Les Conseillers généraux en France depuis 1945* (Paris: Colin, 1970), p. 59.

13 ibid., p. 161.

14 See J. F. Médard, 'La recherche du cumul des mandats par les candidats aux élections législatives sous la 5ème République', *Les Facteurs locaux de la vie politique nationale* (Paris: Pédone, 1972), p. 143. For a study of this problem under the Third and Fourth Republics see M. Dogan, 'Les filières de la carrière politique', *Revue française de sociologie*, October–December 1967, pp. 480–1.

15 M. Longepierre, *Les Conseillers généraux dans le système administratif français* (Paris: Cujas, 1971), p. 114.

16 Jacques Chaban-Delmas is a good example of the political personnel which combines both national and local functions, from the post of elected mayor to the position of minister, passing via the election to Deputy, the chairmanships of the urban community and the regional council and the CODER. See J. Lagroye, *Chaban-Delmas à Bordeaux* (Paris: Pédone, 1973).

17 See P. Birnbaum, *La Nouvelle Classe politique*, ch. 4; M. Dogan, 'Comment on devient ministre en France, 1870–1976', *paper to the Internation Political Science Association*, Edinburgh, 1976; P. Antoni and J. D. Antoni, *Les Ministres de la 5ème République* (Paris: PUF, 1976). These

authors note that only 12·66 per cent of the ministers of the Fifth Republic began their careers with election at local level. One should thus lay stress on the great importance which ministers attach, today, to the holding of seats as chairmen of the regional council, thanks to which they can strengthen their entrenchment at the local level whilst they, more often than not, began their career by attaining high public office straight away.

18 P. Grémion, *Le Pouvoir périphérique* (Paris: Le Seuil, 1976), pp. 429–34.

Chapter VIII

ORDERING URBAN CHANGE: CORPORATE PLANNING IN THE GOVERNMENT OF ENGLISH CITIES*

INTRODUCTION

English cities, like cities the world over, have been plagued by a wide range of ever-intensifying problems. At times it seems that all we understand is that the problems are complex – so complex that they defy effective solutions. Poverty had become the forgotten Englishman. It was 'rediscovered' in the 1960s and despite various, if somewhat desultory, government initiatives it has remained an ever-present feature of the cities. The brand new housing estates did not, as some anticipated, eradicate the old social problems. Good houses did not make good people. Equality of opportunity in education came to have the ring of hollow slogan. The limited educational facilities and resources made available to the inner city schools illustrated that some were very much more equal than others – a fact mirrored in the results, or lack of such, produced by this part of the educational system. And then there was the motor car with its incessant demands upon scarce land and its side effects of pollution and social dislocation. Allied to growing financial problems, this picture of urban areas is scarcely unique. City government has almost become a synonym for the above problems irrespective of the country under discussion.

No one essay could possibly describe and evaluate all the changes in the government of cities which attempted to deal with their problems. However, the attempts to improve the management of local government represent one strand which has run throughout much of the advice and many of the reforms. In considering government problems and policies, the study of management can take second place. It is dismissed as limited to means, whereas the ends, the policies of government, are seen as the most important, and certainly the more glamorous, objects of study. But managers and management in government can be of decisive importance.

The term management is an elusive one and no one definition

*I should like to thank John Stewart for his comments on this paper and Douglas Ashford for helpful discussions on the comparison of local government in England and France.

commands agreement. Commonly it is defined in terms of planning, organising and co-ordinating the activities of an organisation. For the purposes of this essay the various nuances of meaning associated with the term are less important than the recognition that the paid official in local government has the important role of planning, organising and co-ordinating the activities of the local authority. In this role, he can exercise substantial influence on the substance of policy. He does not just implement the policies of his political masters. Moreover, through his involvement in decision making, he injects his own values and preferences into the decision-making process. Technical considerations arising out of his professional training, and bureaucratic considerations arising out of the historically defined organisational routines of his department, are part of the 'advice' offered to his political masters. As a result, management must be seen as an integral aspect of any attempt to order urban change.

The focus on management in this essay is not wholly idiosyncratic. Recognition of the prominence of the paid official in decision making prompted the Committee on the Civil Service (Fulton) to express their concern with the quality of the advice proffered to the politician (*Report,* Cmnd 3638, London: HMSO, 1968). In addition, concern has been expressed about the extent to which problems have been defined in technical and organisational terms rather than political ones (e.g. Dennis, 1972). Thus, the problems of cities can be defined in terms of 'managing a complex system' rather than in terms of (to select only one alternative definition) affecting a redistribution of wealth and power. If, the argument goes, problems were recognised in all their complexity; if departments no longer dealt only with their part of the problem; if local government dealt with problems as a whole; then government would be more effective. This essay describes the changing conceptions of management in local government between 1967 and 1974. It argues that these changes represent not a minor isolated aspect of attempts to deal with the problems of cities but a major attempt to impose order on rapid urban change.

In view of the scope for misunderstanding, one point should be emphasised. I am *not* arguing that the managerial response has been the only response to urban problems. This essay simply seeks to establish that there has been a significant managerial component in the attempt to order urban change. It attempts to do so because, as already noted, this aspect of policy making is often disregarded especially by political scientists; and because by focusing on management, it will be possible to identify some distinctive features of the government of English cities. The exclusiveness of my focus should not be mistaken for the boundaries of the subject.

FROM MAUD TO BAINS

The changes which have taken place in the management of local government are not simply improvements in methods and techniques. They are, if not exclusively, then to a substantial extent, a manifestation of changing conceptions of the role of local government. There has been a shift from a *traditional* conception wherein local government services were provided in isolation from each other to a *federal* conception wherein departments were merged, the committee structure simplified and co-ordination improved. Finally, there has been a shift to a *governmental* conception which emphasised the need to reform the process of management rather than the formal internal structure. Such reforms would include the review of activities in relation to the needs and problems in the environment, the setting of objectives and, above all, the need for management in local government to be directed at supporting the development of corporate policy rather than the limited goals of co-ordination and efficiency (Greenwood and Stewart (eds), 1974, pp. 1–2).

These changes in the definition of the scope of management can be plotted through a series of official, government reports beginning with the *Report of the Committee on the Management of Local Government* (London: HMSO, 1967) – hereafter referred to as the Maud Report after its Chairman Sir John Maud; the *Report of The Royal Commission on Local Government in England* (Cmnd 4040, London: HMSO, 1969) – hereafter referred to as the Redcliffe-Maud Report; and the Report entitled *The New Local Authorities: Management and Structure* (London: HMSO for the Department of the Environment, 1972) – hereafter referred to as the Bains Report. The differences between the Maud and the Bains Reports reflect the shift from the traditional to the governmental conception of local authority management.[1]

The Maud Report represents a major critique of the traditional conception of management. This conception involves 'the management of separate services directed at separate problems. It is specialist management. The role of general management – the management of the affairs of the authority as a whole – is barely recognised' (Stewart, 1971, p. 1). The local authority is 'a collection of essentially separate services brought together more by historical accident or for administrative convenience than for anything they have in common' (Stewart, 1971, p. 2). This separation was enshrined in the internal structure of the authority. Each service constituted a department headed by a professional officer. The clerk of the authority was not in charge of the professional officers, he was *primus inter pares*. For each department there was a corresponding committee of elected members. This form of organisation led to a profusion of departments and committees. For example, the all-purpose authorities found predominantly in urban areas – known as county boroughs – could have up to thirty committees. Although some authorities were experimenting already with new forms of internal organisation, these changes were given added impetus by the Maud Report which criticised the committee system and the absence of unity of direction in the management of authorities. It is argued that the committee system wasted time, proliferated paper, involved elected members in the minutiae of administration and, ultimately, discouraged people of talent from serving on councils. Furthermore, the proliferation of committees and departments was said to give excessive departmentalism or fragmentation with corresponding difficulties in obtaining co-ordination.

In order to cure these ills, the Committee proposed a series of changes in the internal structure of local government. Its major recommendations were:

(1) the creation of a management board to formulate the principal objectives of the authority, to review progress and assess results and to co-ordinate the authority (para. 162);
(2) 'Committees should not be directing or controlling bodies nor should they be concerned with routine administration' (para. 165);
(3) a drastic reduction in the number of committees (para. 169);
(4) 'that the Clerk be recognised as head of the authority's paid service, and have authority over the other principal officers . . .' (para. 179);
(5) principal officers should 'work as members of a team of managers and specialist advisers . . .' (para. 182);
(6) 'that local authorities examine their departmental structure with a view to a drastic reduction in the number of separate departments' (para. 227).

Although most commentators on the Report have emphasised the proposed structural changes, in fact the Report did make some important recommendations about the process of management. It attempted to make a distinction between strategic decisions and their implementation, arguing that the management board should set objectives (para. 162) and that elected members should delegate far more to officers and not become involved in administrative detail. The local authority, it was argued, 'must necessarily study the present physical and social environment of the area and assess its future needs and developments' (para. 144). In order to do this, a systematic approach was essential.

'Systematic management is a cyclical process requiring a time-table which does not leave direction and control to chance. The time-table should provide for periodic review by the management board and by committees of the long term objectives of the authority, and for decisions to be taken by the management board and where appropriate by the council. It should also provide for review by the committees and the management board of the short term objectives such as the budget and the annual programmes of the various services. The time-table should also provide fixed times for the review by the committees and the management board of the performance by the various services, and of the progress on various schemes so that results may be assessed. These reviews in themselves may lead to modification of the long and short-term objectives.' (para. 183).

This description of the process of management may be vague but in it lies the beginning of the governmental conception of local authority management. At the time of the Report's publication, however, the whole emphasis fell on the proposed structural changes. With its emphasis on unity of direction, there is undoubtedly a classical management, or principles of management, feel to the whole Report. This orientation led to some scathing criticisms both on academic grounds (Stanyer, 1967) and on practical grounds (Chester, 1968). In particular, the twin proposals of a Management Board and non-executive committees were rejected because, it was argued, they were totally at variance with the political and human realities of local government. But the Report, almost independently of its intrinsic merits or demerits, fed the groundswell of local authority opinion. The time was ripe for change and change there was, although virtually no authorities adopted the Maud proposals in their entirety.

None the less, throughout the country there was a reduction of the number of committees and departments. The position of the Clerk was strengthened and some form of central, co-ordinating or policy committee was created. A survey carried out by the Institute of Local Government Studies found that in 34 county boroughs which had made changes, the average number of committees had fallen from 24 to 12·5 (Stewart, 1971, p. 164). Thus, although many authorities rejected the Maud Report's specific recommendations, they recognised the validity of the diagnosis and prescribed their own brand of more compatible medicine. In other words, the traditional conception of management was modified to admit of the need for improved co-ordination. The federal conception of management became the new orthodoxy. The seeds of a more all-embracing conception of management had been sown, however, in the Maud

Report. They now began to germinate in the form of 'local authority policy planning', or, as it subsequently became known, 'corporate planning'.

Perhaps the most influential apologists for corporate planning resided at the University of Birmingham's Institute of Local Government Studies (Inlogov). It is through the work emanating from Inlogov from 1967 onwards that the next steps in the development of management in local government can be traced. Unfortunately, it is difficult to describe corporate planning in a concise way. In many respects it is best described as a managerial ideology or philosophy rather than a management technique and, as is so often the case with philosophies, there are many nuances of meaning and emphasis. It will be useful, therefore, to distinguish between the general characteristics of corporate planning and the structures and processes of management associated with it.

The characteristics can best be summarised using the following four dichotomies:

Structure	–	Process
Efficiency	–	Effectiveness
Administration	–	Planning
Departmentalism	–	Corporatism

The basic arguments underlying these dichotomies are, first, that in the concern to introduce new management structures, little or no consideration had been given to the process which the structures were designed to support, thereby condemning the changes to impotence. Second, that the process of management should not be directed solely to the attainment of efficiency. There was no point in efficiently failing to achieve objectives. Rather, attention had to be directed towards the results of action. Were the needs of the community being met? Were policies giving the anticipated results? Third, local authorities should not be concerned solely to act as the mere agents of central government. Rather they should plan to meet the ever-growing, ever-changing needs and problems of their community. Their policies should be explicit and continuously reviewed in the light of such changing needs and problems. Finally, and consistent with the stress on effectiveness and planning, is the need to look at the activities and policies of the authority as a whole – i.e. corporately – rather than on a separate departmental basis. Problems do not respect departmental boundaries. Policies must be designed to meet problems in all their complexity rather than to respect the artificial pigeon-holes of local authority departments.

In sum, this general philosophy of management

'rests on the view that the local authority is the "primary" organ of government within the area for which it is responsible. Within the area it administers, individuals, families and organisations have developed a pattern of life. This pattern has been deeply influenced by the environment – both the natural, physical environment and the social, economic, political and technical environment, and has itself moulded that environment. In a very real sense, the general management of a local authority is the management of that environment, for the individuals, groups and organisations that live within that environment.' (Stewart, 1971, p. 17).

Turning from the philosophy of corporate management to the processes of management associated with corporate planning, the general prescription can be translated into a more specific form. The process of management, it is argued, should be as follows:

(a) 'The organisation identifies certain needs, present and foreseen, in its environment.
(b) It sets objectives in relation to those needs, i.e. the extent to which it will plan to meet those needs.
(c) It considers alternative ways of achieving those objectives.
(d) It evaluates those alternatives in terms of their use of resources and of their effects.
(e) Decisions are made in the light of that evaluation.
(f) Those decisions are translated into managerial action.
(g) The results of the action taken is monitored and fed back to modify the continuing process; by altering the perception of needs, the objectives set, the alternatives considered, the evaluation, the decision made or the action taken' (Stewart, 1971, p. 30).

At this time, it was thought that the corporate planning process could be implemented by the introduction of a Planning Programming Budgeting System (PPBS). PPBS was developed in America and its main constituents are:

(a) the programme structure;
    The activities of the authority are classified under the objectives they serve.
(b) programme analysis;
    Current and proposed alternatives (or policies) are systematically analysed in the light of the objectives they are serving;

(c) programme review;
      Current policies are reviewed and modified in the light of
      the analysis carried out (e.g. Schultze, 1969).

Given that the above process of management is introduced, the
following structural changes are commonly suggested:

  (i)   the Clerk should become the Chief Executive with authority
        over other paid officials;
  (ii) a chief officers group should be established, under the leader-
        ship of the Chief Executive, as the corporate decision-making
        body paralleling;
  (iii) a policy committee of elected members responsible for the
        development and review of local authority policies;
  (iv) the process of policy making should be supported by a
        corporate planning unit attached to the Chief Executive; and
  (v)   department structures must be seen as flexible structures
        capable of being adjusted to changing needs and problems
        (Stewart, 1971, pp. 168–78).

In the discussion of structural change, however, the emphasis falls
on the need for structures to support new processes of management.
Structural change for its own sake is seen as a fruitless exercise.

It might appear that this view of how local authorities ought to
manage themselves is a typical, rational piece of academic theorising.
This may well be true, but unlike much theorising it was not thereby
rendered of no practical significance. These views can be found in
the Report of the Redcliffe-Maud Commission. It argued that
'Arrangements to ensure a corporate, as opposed to a departmental
view, must be an integral part of an authority's organisation' (para.
480). It spoke of the need to set objectives, and to appoint a central
committee, a chief executive and a chief officers group. And more
significantly it opined that 'Local Government has moved a long way
from the days when its task was to provide a number of isolated
services. Authorities are now responsible for a great deal of the
context in which the lives of citizens are lived. Control of the
physical environment, economic development, collaboration with
other agencies of all kinds, public and private, as well as the
provision of local services, are now their business. *They have a duty
positively to promote the welfare of the community*' (para. 486, my
emphasis). Nor should this grand conception be dismissed as a side
issue in a Report devoted to other more important matters. An
important reason for its recommendation in favour of the large,
new all-purpose authority was that it can relate its programmes 'for
all services to coherent objectives for the future progress of its area

considered as a whole' (para. 253). Not only were the managerial activities of local government given a broad interpretation, but this interpretation was also an important reason underlying the Redcliffe-Maud Commission's proposals to reform local government.

Although the Royal Commission's proposals were rejected by the Conservative government and a very different reorganisation was carried into law (for details see Richards, 1973), it should not be thought that the concern with management was similarly consigned to oblivion. To the contrary, the then Secretary of State for the Environment established the Bains Committee 'to set out the considerations which . . . should be borne in mind by local authorities in determining their structures of management at elected members and officer levels . . .' (para. 1.1). In a Foreword to the final Report he commented: 'I look upon this report as being one of the most important and vital aspects of local government reform. Local Government tends to be only reformed once a century and we therefore have a unique opportunity to study carefully the best management practices within local government and to see that these practices are in future carried out by all' (p. vii). The concern with management was very much alive and the Bains Report exercised enormous influence on the new authorities. The governmental conception of management became the new orthodoxy. At the risk of repetition, the Report's central axiom is worth noting: 'Local Government is not, in our view, limited to the narrow provision of a series of services to the local community . . . It has within its purview the overall economic, cultural and physical well being of that community . . .' (para. 2.10). The remainder of the Report covers ground that should by now be very familiar to the reader. The elected members' role in deciding the policies of the authority is emphasised with the usual call for improved delegation to officers. In this case, however, far more attention is paid to the sheer variety of roles the elected member can play in addition to that of policy maker, e.g. constituency representative. The appointment of a Policy and Resources Committee, a Chief Executive and Chief Officers Group is recommended. The process of management is seen to involve the identification of need, the setting of objectives, establishing priorities and monitoring and reviewing performance. To this latter end, the Report recommends the appointment of a Performance Review Sub-Committee. Finally, the Report recommends a number of internal structures that could be adopted by the new authorities.

The most significant aspect of the Report, however, concerns the broadening of the scope of corporate planning. The reorganisation of local government has removed some of its functions and vested their control in *ad hoc* nominated bodies. Services such as water, sewerage and the personal health services were seen as integral to many other functions of the local authority – you can't build a housing estate without piped water and sewerage disposal facilities. In recognition of this new situation, the horizons of local authority management broadened. If the community as a whole is to be served, 'We believe that this concept of "community" interest must involve not only the new local authorities, but also other voluntary and public agencies . . .' (para. 8.4). Corporate planning has to become concerned, therefore, 'with planning to meet the problems and needs of the community within a specified area, irrespective of the particular organisation that might be involved – or even whether any organisation would be involved' (Stewart, 1974, p. 68). Here is the governmental conception of local authority management at its widest.

FROM THEORY TO PRACTICE

To this point, it has simply been established that there has been a concern with, and redefinition of, management in local government. It is perfectly possible that, in spite of the exhortations, little has changed. As far as the internal structure of local authorities is concerned, however, there has been a massive change. Almost without exception, Chief Executives, Chief Officers Groups and Policy and Resources Committees have been appointed by the new authorities (Greenwood *et al.*, 1975; Richards, 1975). There have been variations from the recommendations of the Bains Report on departmental and committee structures but even here there has been a substantial change usually involving a reduction in the number of departments and committees.

As far as changes in the process of management are concerned the situation is less clear. A survey of 615 local authorities carried out before the Bains Report found that 215 were engaged in, or seriously examining, all or part of PPBS (Butt, 1970, pp. 43–9). Since 1970 there has been a growing awareness of the limitation of PPBS and, as a result of these dissatisfactions, there has been considerable variation in the processes adopted to change methods of decision making. In an article written very shortly after the publication of the Bains Report, Stewart commented that 'Probably less than twenty out of the existing county boroughs, county councils and London Boroughs, have taken serious steps towards the development of corporate planning' (Stewart, 1974, p. 45). These numbers have undoubtedly expanded since the implementation of Bains's recommendations on reorganisation (e.g. Earwicker, 1975, pp. 1–10). From the, albeit limited, research available, it would appear that changes in the process of management have not been as extensive as those in management structures. More recently the comprehensive PPBS approach has given way to a more selective one: dogmatism has taken second place to flexible experimentation. In particular, since the Bains Report, three areas of experimentation seem to have become prominent. First, there has been the development of new systems of resource forecasting. Second, new systems for describing and reviewing the existing policies of local authorities have been introduced. These are commonly termed position statements. Finally, there has been an increase in the efforts to identify and analyse specific problems, both within departments and within newly established corporate planning or research and intelligence units (for examples see Greenwood *et al.*, 1976).[2]

The important point for the theme of this essay, however, is not that all should have undergone large-scale changes, or even that these changes should have successfully modified traditional patterns of decision making, but that time, money and effort have been expended on translating management ideas into practice at the levels of either structure or process or both. It is sufficient to establish that there has been a concern to improve local authority management, that this concern has been widespread and that attempts have been made to translate the ideas into practice. The next step is to determine in what ways this concern with management is relevant to the problems of urban change.

CORPORATE PLANNING AND URBAN CHANGE

One of the major reasons for the introduction of corporate planning, it has been argued, has been the concern over the fragmentation of the traditional management process. This was not the only or even the major reason. Three others can be identified:

(1) the inadequacy of traditional methods of resource allocation and planning in a situation of financial scarcity;
(2) dissatisfaction with architectural determinism (or the belief that changing the physical environment changes behaviour) coupled with reservations about the limited subject-matter of physical planning; and
(3) the failure to recognise the complexity of urban problems (cf. Stewart, 1974, pp. 29–36).

In other words, the corporate planning movement has its origins in the problems of urban change. It arose in response to the ever-changing over-intensifying problems with which local authorities, particularly the urban authorities, had to deal. It is an attempt to order that change.

The financial pressures on local government have been intensifying over the past decade. The Redcliffe-Maud Commission noted 'that the forces which have been pushing expenditure up are likely to persist and that local expenditure will continue to expand both absolutely and as a percentage of GNP' (para. 509). But the problems of the British economy did not admit of an unrestrained growth in public expenditure. The pressure to restrain growth meant that critical choices had to be made. But on what basis should these choices be made? Should each department make its bid for resources? If so, there would be 'a night of the long knives' in which these bids would be cut back, to a more realistic level. And in this process the well-planned and necessary programme suffered along with the less essential. Alternatively, there would be a target rate of growth and all departments would have to remain within this. But this did not permit decisions on priorities between departments. Baths had the same increase as education. Parks had the same increase as social services. Neither of these procedures was satisfactory. As a result, local authorities began to experiment with, *inter alia,* cost benefit analysis and output budgeting. And, of course, the financial pressures have intensified since 1974.

The dissatisfaction with land use planning has become part of the conventional wisdom about the problems of local government. The Redcliffe-Maud Commission included the inadequacies of planning as one of the major defects of the old local government system (paras 47–61). More specifically critics have argued that planning jurisdictions were fragmented; that the planning procedures were slow, detailed and cumbersome, that plans ignored the financial implications of their proposals, and, most importantly, that planning was divorced from social and economic considerations. Creating the city beautiful in spatial and architectural terms did not solve existing social problems and, if anything, it simply intensified them. Efforts were made to broaden the horizons of planning (for details see Sharpe, 1975), but the need to plan for the social and economic problems of the local authority's area remained unsatisfied. Physical planning, in spite of increasing sensitivity to its social and economic implication, remained too narrow to meet this need. A broader conception was required which encompassed all facets of the environment and local government's impact on that environment. Corporate planning provided that broader conception.

Of all the factors giving rise to corporate planning – departmentalism, inadequate resource allocation procedures and the inadequacies of physical planning – none is more important than the growing realisation of the complexity of urban problems. In all probability, it is this single fact which underpins all the other factors discussed. Policies in education, social services, planning, housing, highways, affect each other in different ways to differing degrees. Numerous official reports have made this very point. Thus the Plowden Report, *Children and their Primary Schools* (London: HMSO, 1967) argued that 'educational policy should explicitly recognise the power of the environment upon the school and of the school on the environment' (para. 80), and they noted the effect of children's homes and changes in the wider society on educational attainment. The *Report of the Committee on Local Authority and Allied Personal Services* (Cmnd 3703, London: HMSO, 1968) pointed to the crucial inter-relationship between health, housing, education and special services. The Buchanan Report, *Traffic in Towns* (London: HMSO, 1963) argued that traffic flows are only one aspect of the problem and pointed to safety and pollution as equally important facets. The list of examples could be extended. There would be little point. The import of the above examples is clear. Management as the separate provision of separate services failed to meet the problems existing in the environment. The reconstruction of town centres, urban renewal, the impact of the motor car and the massive development of individual services all forced home the realisation that physical solutions were inadequate and that problems could not be treated in isolation from one another. Unless the management of a local authority recognised the full complexity of its environment it was doomed to impotence.

Corporate planning offers a solution to these problems. By focusing on needs and problems in the environment it directs attention away from the parochial, historically defined concerns of a particular department, and develops an awareness that the service exists for those who need it, not those who provide it. The obvious department-based solutions did not work. As quotation after quotation from official reports has illustrated (often at the risk of repetition), local authorities were being urged to direct their attention to the needs and problems of the community and the importance of planning the activities of the authority as a whole. The response to this message was corporate planning – indeed it could almost not exist without the notions that problems are complex and will not fit meekly into those pigeon-holes we call departments. In brief, corporate planning is a major attempt to bring order to the baffling complexity of urban change.

THE LIMITS TO CORPORATE PLANNING

To this point I have argued that corporate planning represents a major attempt to order urban change. It is an attempt which has many problems associated with it; problems which are particularly acute in the context of urban problems, politics and policies. At the risk of some oversimplification, it can be suggested that there are four major problem areas. These are the operational or implementation problems; the organisational or human problems; the political problems; and the problems associated with inter-governmental or inter-authority relations.

The operational problems of corporate planning will be well known to any reader conversant with the problems of making government decision making more rational. At the practical level, analysis is costly; analysts are a rare commodity; information is scarce and, when available, often of either poor quality or limited relevance. One of the major tools of analysis, cost-benefit analysis, is plagued with problems – e.g. putting monetary values to aesthetic or qualitative aspects of the environment.

At a more fundamental level there are the problems of defining need and planning under conditions of uncertainty. Need is an elusive concept. For example, in meeting the needs of the community, does the local authority respond to those needs expressed as demands by groups/individuals or to the needs perceived by councillors and officers? Expressed need may not encompass the most deprived who are often politically apathetic, but can/should councillors/officers define other people's needs for them? The problems surrounding planning are no less intractable. However defined, planning involves the notion of predicting a future state of affairs, and yet predicting the future physical, let alone social, environment is notoriously difficult. Yesterday's experience can be a poor guide to tomorrow's problems. Moreover, the greater the degree of uncertainty surrounding any issue or problem, the greater the problems faced by a local authority in controlling its environment. Adaptive planning (or planning as a learning process) is an attempt, at the conceptual level, to overcome this problem. Plans should no longer specify fixed targets. Rather they should be based on a process of the regular review of objectives in the light of changing circumstances. But this still leaves the problems of identifying when circumstances have changed and why, in sufficient time for the authority to respond.

Even assuming that need can be defined and realistic plans devised, the evaluation of alternative courses of action is problematic. The more an alternative is similar to current practice, the easier it is to evaluate but the less applicable it will be as circumstances change. On the other hand, an original alternative is more difficult to evaluate. It is easy to call for more planning and better analysis. The problem is how to do it.

The organisational problems are equally intransigent. Departments evolve their own procedures and criteria for making decisions. Individuals are socialised or trained in using these procedures. They are resistant to change. Moreover, the paid official is often a skilled organisational politician. He will support analysis when it increases the resources available to his department. But when it means cutting his programme or deferring a beloved project . . . ! Moreover, even when analysis is available, there is the difficulty of ensuring that it permeates the organisational routines of an authority and informs the implementation of a policy. The transition from analysis to action can be fraught with problems.

The political problems of corporate planning have been widely discussed (Wildavsky, 1966 and 1969), and for convenience this debate can be summarised under three headings – the incrementalist critique, the centralisation critique and the structuralist critique.

The incrementalist critique argues that the politician's criterion of choice is not derived from rational analysis – it is not a ratio of costs to benefits. Rather, it is what he can get in a bargaining, negotiating situation with other politicians, pressure groups and officials. For selecting any one course of action, 'agreement' is the major criterion. As a result, the politician is reluctant to state his objectives precisely because it will provoke controversy. He avoids major changes in policy because they are unlikely to be easy to agree upon. Moreover, the analysis generated by corporate planning is of limited use in his attempts to negotiate agreements (Lindblom, 1959).

The centralisation critique forms part of the case against corporate planning put forward by the incrementalists but it is not always necessarily linked to the other aspects of their argument. In the context of English local government, it is argued that the creation of the Policy and Resources Committee and of the Chief Officers Group has centralised decision making in chief officers and leading politicians. Not only is this centralisation supported by the recent structural reforms, it is supported also by the new information system of corporate planning. Information is geared to the needs of policy makers and disregards the different information needs of the backbench councillor and the general public. The analysis is of such a technical nature that it is at best indigestible, and at worst incomprehensible, to all but the *cognoscente* of chief officials and leading politicians. Finally, the technical superstructure of the analysis obscures important value judgements, thereby accentuating the difficulties of the politician in exercising choice. The results of these problems, it is argued, are the increasing separation of the political leaders from their backbench supporters and a decrease in the responsiveness of local authorities to community demands. And this latter point leads us neatly into a consideration of the structuralist critique.

In recent years, central government has both encouraged and

mandated local government to improve its links with the local community and with community groups. One such experiment was the creation of the Community Development Projects (CDPs) which were designed to introduce new methods of tackling poverty on a small area basis. This involved CDPs in building up links with community groups in these areas. The experiment led to some important criticisms of corporate planning. It was argued that the local authority was unresponsive to the demands of community groups. Moreover, the more such demands were politically contentious and involved the redistribution of local resources between social groups, the more likely it was that the demands would not even be listened to. This led to the conclusion that corporate planning simply served to reinforce the existing distribution of wealth and power at the local level – a distribution which was itself a product of the national political and economic structure. (A useful selection of relevant articles can be found in Jones and Mayo (eds), 1974.)

Although many of these criticisms of the political aspects of corporate planning have indirect empirical support in the experience of the American government with PPBS (e.g. Schick, 1973) there has been no direct research into the political implications of the introduction of corporate planning into English local government. However, even convinced advocates of corporate planning concede that in practice it has produced objectives which are of little use for action and inhibit controversy; that the production of documents such as the programme structure have taken precedence over the policy analysis which would aid the politician in making policy explicit; that the flow of information is not geared to the politician's needs; and that politicians receive very little support from the authority in carrying out their various tasks. Concern has been expressed also about the possibilities of there being a centralisation of power in the hands of a few leading politicians and chief officers, with the attendant problems of unresponsiveness to both backbench councillors and community groups (Stewart, 1974, pp. 58, 59, 118, 140, 141, 142 and 156).

The final problem area – inter-governmental and inter-authority relations – points to the fact that the authority to take decisions does not lie, in many circumstances, with local government or even with government at all (irrespective of the quality of its corporate or community planning). For example, local government is dependent on central government's annual decisions on the level of grant – a decision taken independently of any local resource planning. Of equal importance are the decisions taken in isolation from each other by central departments which require the expansion or contraction of particular services. Thus, in a year when the Treasury attempts to limit local expenditure, the Department of the Environment can require local authorities to increase expenditure in order to implement a new Act. In these circumstances, the local authority has difficulty in rationally establishing its priorities. (For supporting evidence see: Committee of Inquiry into Local Government Finance (Layfield), *Report,* Cmnd 6453, London: HMSO, 1976).

Quite clearly many criticisms can be made of the ability of corporate planning to order urban change, and in particular the alleged disregard of the political context of management would appear to be a severe limitation. Urban problems invariably raise such crucial political issues as the distribution of wealth and power. To disregard them is to ignore possibly *the* major problem. But is the case against corporate planning so clear-cut? Do the above problems invalidate and render futile the experiments of the last decade? Certainly, a number of caveats to the foregoing criticisms should be noted. It cannot be assumed that the political problems associated with corporate planning were caused by it. Some local authorities were already centralised and unresponsive. Corporate planning has supported centralisation in those local authorities where it existed already, and it has attempted to create some degree of central co-ordination in those authorities fragmented on a departmental basis. And this simple fact reveals a stark contrast with French local authorities. In English local government there is not always a strong political executive. In those local authorities with party systems, the leader of the majority party and his senior colleagues may constitute the executive but this is not invariably the case. There is no direct equivalent to the French mayor. Accordingly, where a political executive exists, the criticism of excessive centralism may be valid. On the other hand, where local authorities have no such leadership, it can be suggested that corporate planning is an attempt to *create a political executive.* In these circumstances, it can be argued that the weakness of corporate planning is that it has not led to a sufficient degree of centralisation.[3]

Corporate planning does not necessarily create or reinforce centralisation in local government. Similarly, it does not necessarily weaken the role of the politician. John Stewart's work has always stressed that corporate planning can help the politician make explicit choices and that the emphasis should fall on the co-ordination and coherence of policy rather than detailed procedural and structural change. His later work shows an increasing concern with the political aspects of corporate planning and a desire to avoid apolitical local policy making (Stewart, 1974). More specifically, he has argued that such explicit choices ought to be about the redistribution of wealth and power (Stewart, 1975) and he has proposed a number of mechanisms for making local authorities more responsive to community needs.

The political case against corporate planning is not, therefore, inviolate. It can be argued that, in some circumstances, centralisation is desirable and that corporate planning can aid the politician to make explicit choices. Above all, Stewart has emphasised that the implementation of corporate planning is a learning process. Even if, in the early days, corporate planning had many of the weaknesses attributed to it, local authorities have learned from their mistakes and adapted accordingly.[4]

The problem in evaluating this line of defence lies in separating the arguments of the more sophisticated proponents from those in official reports; in separating the prescription and the reality. The awareness of the analytical, organisational, political and intergovernmental problems shown in official reports is limited. These weaknesses may not be *inherent* in corporate planning but they are present in the 'official' version. For example, the Bains Report contains no specific recommendations for supporting the backbench councillor, only a general recognition that he plays an important role (pp. 11–12). Similarly, the description of the corporate planning process contains no guide on how to analyse issues. The corporate approach is argued for at a very general level (e.g. pp. xv, 5–7). As Stewart (1974) has pointed out: 'The new authorities that seek to develop corporate planning will find too little guidance in the report . . .' (p. 59).

But have local authorities found guidance elsewhere? Have they learned to do corporate planning as they tried to implement the Bains recommendations? This survey covers the period 1967–74. In this period, PPBS and the Bains Report were, in many respects, synonymous with corporate planning. As noted earlier, it is only in more recent years that there has been a more flexible, a more experimental approach to corporate planning. In other words, in so far as local authorities introduced corporate planning in the period under review, their ideas and approaches bear a marked similarity to the procedures and structures of PPBS and the Bains Report. The uniformity of the internal management structures of the new local authorities is clear evidence of this. I do not wish to deny that local authorities have continued to experiment or to assert that the weaknesses of corporate planning are both inherent and invalidate it. I do want to suggest, however, that for the period 1967–74, the view of corporate planning contained in official reports and, in many respects, adopted by local authorities had many weaknesses – weaknesses which prompt the conclusion that this particular reform, although it aimed to combat complex urban problems, was managerial in its orientation because it devalued the political aspects of urban problems and emphasised the virtues of co-ordination and planning.[5]

THE PARADOX OF CORPORATE PLANNING

Corporate planning, irrespective of one's views on its intrinsic merits, constitutes a major expenditure of time, effort and money directed at devising better policies for the government of cities. And yet many of the problems associated with such rational, managerial systems were well known before they were implemented in British cities. The experience of the American government with PPBS attested to the difficulties and that experiment was terminated in 1971. Academics had found the rational model of decision making wanting many years earlier. (For a summary discussion see Dror, 1968, ch. 12.) Hence the following paradox: 'Why has there been such an emphasis on the contribution of corporate planning to the solution of the problems of English cities given the demonstrated lack of success of such systems in other countries?' There are a number of possible answers to this question.

In part, it reflects a national concern with more rational decision making. It appealed to the Conservative Party because of their ideological belief that government needed an injection of business efficiency, and to the Labour Party because it offered the prospect of more services for the same expenditure. At the local level, it could be argued that it reflects the power of the paid official in local decision making. With his distrust of politics and his preference for 'technical solutions' to problems, corporate planning had a very direct appeal to him. Alternatively, it could be argued that it was a solution to urban problems which offered the politician the possibility of reform without disturbing the *status quo*. It would solve problems because resources could be used more efficiently and effectively. The local authority would appear to be doing something without opening up the politically contentious issue of the redistribution of resources. Yet another reason arises from the distinctive features of centre–local relations in England, and because it will suggest some interesting contrasts between English and French local government, this facet will be explored in a little more detail.

One point links together the federal and the governmental conceptions of local management – the need for co-ordination. Almost *ad nauseam,* the management exhorts local government to look at its activities *as a whole.* Why is co-ordination seen as such a problem? A major part of this question can be found in the nature of centre-local relations in England. In comparison to French local government, local politics in England is insulated from national politics. It is only rarely that a local political issue is transferred to the national political arena. National politicians rarely retain a base in local government politics and such a base is not a key prerequisite of a rise to national prominence. There is probably no finer tribute to local government's lack of political influence than the weakness of the national associations of local authorities. The contrast with French local government's links with national politics is very marked. Allied to this feature of English centre–local relations is the functional nature of the links between the two levels of government. The expansion in the functions of central government is scarcely unique but the absence of any integrative institutional device is noteworthy. There is no machinery performing the integrative role of the French prefect. Instead there is a patchwork quilt of bodies, with each central department having its own institutional arrangements and areas of administration. An explanation of the origins of these two features would require a lengthy historical essay. Suffice it to note, therefore, the absence of integrating mechanisms of either a political or an administrative nature. The major consequence for local government of these features is the problem of co-ordinated planning. The recent *Report of the Committee of Inquiry into Local Government Finance* (London: HMSO, 1976) laid considerable emphasis on the problem, and through its proposal for a consultative forum it attempts to create a link between national and local elites. In addition, it endorsed the need for corporate planning in both central and local government. Thus the emphasis on corporate planning reflects not simply the need to cope with the problems of urban areas but the distinctive nature of centre–local relations in England. It arises from the need to co-ordinate the separate function-specific links between central and local government in the absence of mechanisms of political co-ordination. The contrast with the complex of linking and linked organisational structures of French government and administration is very marked. (On France see: Crozier and Thoenig, 1976; Kesselman, 1967; Thoenig 1975; Wright, 1974.) The concern, even obsession, with corporate planning in local government is very much a product of the national system of government and administration. Obviously, other systems of government have introduced their own variants of corporate planning. Equally obviously, the function-specific nature of centre–local links in England are not a necessary condition of corporate planning. But, in the English context, the nature of centre–local relations was an added imperative to the need for some such co-ordinating mechanism.

CONCLUDING SUMMARY

English cities, like their counterparts throughout Western Europe, have been the loci of ever-changing, ever-intensifying problems. There has been a variety of responses to these problems and one of the most prominent has been the redefinitions of the concept and the scope of management. This has involved a shift from a traditional, through a federal, to a governmental conception. These changes have been expressed in a series of official reports over the past decade, and the adoption of a governmental conception (of corporate planning) has resulted in a comprehensive reorganisation of the internal structure of local authorities and (to a lesser extent) reforms in the process of management. The reforms are a direct contribution to the solution of urban problems because of their emphasis on planning for the needs and problems of the community as a whole. Moreover, the origins of corporate planning lie in the growing realisation of the complexity of urban problems (amongst other factors).

Although corporate planning has become the new orthodoxy, it is not without its problems. These include operational, human and political problems as well as the problems stemming from the pattern of inter-governmental and inter-authority relations. In particular, the political problems raise serious doubts about the ability of corporate planning to cope with urban problems. Thus corporate planning was widely adopted in spite of the fact that its weaknesses were well known, especially following the demise of PPBS in America. The explanation of this paradox lies in a number of factors including the pattern of centre–local relations in England. In direct contrast to French government administration, English local political elites have failed to penetrate the national political arena and there is no institutional mechanism to co-ordinate the function-specific links between centre and locality.

Corporate planning's popularity stems in part from the need to compensate for the absence of integrating mechanisms in the pattern of centre–local relations. It is not wholly a product of local needs and problems. It is also a product of the national political-administrative system.

NOTES

1 The changing conception of management can be seen also in the follow-ing Reports: Committee on the Staffing of Local Government (Mallaby) *Report* (London: HMSO, 1967); Working Party on the Staffing of Local Government in Scotland (Hughes) *Report* (Edinburgh: HMSO, 1968); Royal Commission on Local Government in Scotland 1966–1969 (Wheatley) *Report* (Cmnd 4150, London: HMSO, 1969); *The New Scottish Local Authorities: Organisation and Management Structures* (Paterson) (Edinburgh: HMSO, 1973). The Mallaby Report's recom-mendations complement those of the Maud Report and were published

at approximately the same time. They are not considered separately in the text. The remaining three Reports refer to Scotland. This essay concentrates on England and consequently these Reports are omitted. However, it is well worth noting that the same changes in the conception of management can be plotted through the three Scottish Reports.

2 This essay concentrates on the period 1967–74 – hence the prominence of PPBS in the discussion. However, it is worth emphasising that local authorities continue to experiment with ways of introducing corporate planning (see Greenwood *et al.*, 1975 and 1976).

3 Like so many words in the vocabulary of politics, centralisation has many meanings and it is often used as an epithet. But centralisation is neither good nor bad. It is a question of the degree of centralisation in various circumstances. This point is clearly illustrated by the foregoing discussion of corporate planning. In some circumstances it has led to excessive centralisation, whilst in others it has not been able to overcome either political or departmental fragmentation.

4 A similar line of defence can be adopted towards the operational, organisational and inter-governmental relations problems. For example, it is argued that many of the analytical problems will be overcome in the future with the improvement in information systems and analytical techniques. For some, the behavioural sciences, in the form of organisational development, will help to overcome the resistance to change of bureaucrats. Finally, for inter-governmental relations, the Layfield Committee recommended a central Forum to co-ordinate centre–local relations. All of these proposals reflect the belief that corporate planning can gradually overcome its problems.

5 Support for this view can be adduced from the number of articles and letters in local government journals over the past two years (e.g. *Municipal Review* and *Local Government Chronicle*) which have discussed the political problems of corporate planning. Evidence on the fortunes of corporate planning for the period 1974–7 is limited – a major exception is Greenwood *et al.* (1976) – but it does suggest that many of the problems discussed above remain to plague local authorities.

REFERENCES

The references in the text and in this bibliography have been limited to the most relevant items. Full references to official reports can be found in the text.

Butt, R. (1970), 'PPBS in British local government', *Public Administration Bulletin*, no. 9 (November), pp. 43–9.

Chester, D. N. (1968), 'Local democracy and the internal organisation of local authorities', *Public Administration*, vol. 46. pp. 287–98.

Crozier, M. and Thoenig, J.-C. (1976), 'The regulation of complex organised systems', *Administrative Science Quarterly*, vol. 21, pp. 547–70.

Dennis, N. (1972), *Public Participation and Planner's Blight* (London: Faber).

Dror, Y. (1968), *Public Policymaking Re-examined* (Scranton, Penn.: Chandler Publishing Co.).

Earwicker, J. (1975), 'Position statements – the state of play, February 1975', *Corporate Planning*, vol. 2, no. 1 (February), pp. 1–10.

Greenwood, R., Hinings, C. R., Ranson, S. and Walsh, K. (1976), *In Pursuit of Corporate Rationality: organisational developments in the post-reorganisation period* (Birmingham: Institute of Local Government Studies).

Greenwood, R., Lomer, M. A., Hinings, C. R. and Ranson, S. (1975), *The Organisation of Local Authorities in England and Wales: 1967-75* (Birmingham: Institute of Local Government Studies, Discussion Paper Series L, no. 5).

Greenwood, R. and Stewart, J. D. (eds) (1974), *Corporate Planning in English Local Government* (London: Knight).

Jones, D. and Mayo, M. (eds) (1974), *Community Work – One* (London: Routledge & Kegan Paul).

Kesselman, M. (1967), *The Ambiguous Consensus* (New York: Knopf).

Lindblom, C. (1959), 'The science of muddling through', *Public Administration Review*, vol. 19, pp. 79–88.

Richards, P. G. (1973), *The Reformed Local Government System* (London: Allen & Unwin).

Richards, P. G. (1975), *The Local Government Act 1972: problems of implementation* (London: Allen & Unwin).

Schick, A. (1973), 'A death in the bureaucracy: the demise of Federal PPBS', *Public Administration Review*, vol. 33, pp. 146–56.

Schultze, C. (1969), *The Politics and Economics of Public Spending* (Washington, DC: The Brookings Institution).

Sharpe, L. J. (1975), 'Innovation and change in British land-use planning', in J. Hayward and M. Watson (eds), *Planning Politics and Public Policy: the British, French and Italian experience* (Cambridge: CUP), pp. 316–57.

Stanyer, J. (1967), 'The Maud Report: a critical review', *Social and Economic Administration*, vol. 1, no. 4, pp. 3–19.

Stewart, J. D. (1971), *Management in Local Government: a viewpoint* (London: Knight).

Stewart, J. D. (1974), *The Responsive Local Authority* (London: Knight).

Stewart, J. D. (1975), 'The government of cities and the politics of opportunity', *Local Government Studies* (new series), vol. 1, no. 1, pp. 3–20.

Thoenig, J.-C. (1975), *State Bureaucracies and Local Government in France* (Berkeley: University of California, Department of Political Science).

Wildavsky, A. (1966), 'The political economcy of efficiency', *Public Administration Review*, vol. 26, pp. 292–310.

Wildavsky, A. (1969), 'Rescuing policy analysis from PPBS', *Public Administration Review*, vol. 29, pp. 189–202.

Wright, V. (1974), 'Politics and administration under the Fifth French Republic', *Political Studies*, vol. 22, pp. 44–65.

Chapter IX

CONTROL OF URBAN DEVELOPMENT
IN FRANCE

It is a fact that the town has never been the result of totally spontaneous human activity. But it was not until after the Second World War that intervention by the public authorities in the structuring of urban areas became a primary necessity for regulating the contradictions in the social system as a whole. It should be noted that this public intervention was, in the first instance, a response to a combination of problems. This accounts, to a large extent, for the fact that the State, in the role of 'orchestrator' of economic growth, reacted for a time in a purely empirical fashion without having at hand the requisite conceptual instruments to explain its ultimate aims and objectives. As a result, under the heading of urban growth two separate phenomena have often been confused: the development of urbanisation and the transformation of the towns. Moreover, the connection between the redistribution of manpower and the rapid impoverishment of a certain number of French regions has been considered as part of the national Jacobin tradition and not as the logical outcome of industrial redeployment supported by the State apparatus.

Consequently, a moralistic reformism calling 'in the name of the general interest' for intervention by the political authorities in order to counteract the 'spontaneous' and 'unjust' tendencies of social change has become intermingled with a technocratic reformism aiming for the 'modernisation' of the productive apparatus and the 'nationalisation' of public investment in the name of economic expansion. The debate on the questions to be solved as a result of the 'anarchic' development of the towns (housing, community projects, urban animation etc.) is significant in this context in that it justifies voluntarist action in controlling the process of urban growth both through economic calculation (rationalising community projects) and through ecological considerations (planning and/or protecting the life of the town dweller).

The ideological laxity and obscurantism surrounding urban practices make an analysis of the policies relevant to the domain of urban planning difficult, even though it is true that the description of the organisms of land-use planning (*Aménagement du Territoire*) or the documents on urbanisation seem at first glance relatively easy to understand. But problems soon became evident: not only have the policies concerning land-use planning and urban planning changed with time and become more or less interlocking, as some concern for 'coherence' has motivated their evolution, but also the actions of officials responsible for planning, be they in the administration or the elected representatives of the local authorities, have tended to nullify any logic which existed in the legislation. What is even more serious is the contrast between the urban object dealt with by regulations and the actual urban area. Indeed, the text of the law conceals the fact that the town is a territorial projection of society and as such manifests the logical segregation which exists between the dominant and the dominated; it conceals, too, the class question arising out of the appropriation of urban space and the social struggles which take place within it.

The reformist, technical, voluntarist vision of urban planning can, in such a framework, use the term 'deficiencies' to account for the failures of the instruments for controlling urban development. The efficacious intervention of property developers, industrialists and supply companies etc. in the urbanisation process thus appears as 'abnormal', and as a feature of the derogatory practices, compared to the norm of the 'general interest'. This type of moralising also conflicts with social reality when it condemns a potential *affairisme*[1] on the part of locally elected representatives. Indeed, under the universal and abstract term 'local representatives' should be understood the institutionalised representation of the power relationships present in the area concerned and, in this respect, the defence of specific social interests which are organised therein. It follows, therefore, that to study tendencies in the practice of urban development implies that the existing instruments and institutions of planning should be perceived as indicative of the state of social relationships.

GLOBAL ACTION ON URBAN GROWTH

The development of urban politics in France is only comprehensible in terms of the politico-economic framework within which it is situated. In this respect it is closely dependent upon a political desire to exercise global action on the whole of social development which gradually became apparent among the national public authorities during the period of economic reconstruction (1945–50). The aim of giving the country a better geographical balance by attempting to 'redistribute the opportunities for expansion' was visible as early as 1955–6, even if it still appeared marked by notions of land-use planning and urban planning. In fact, two types of problems came into play in the orientation of national urban planning. On the one hand, as Jérôme Monod writes, urban planning should work towards 'correcting the regional deficiencies of industry and, as far as possible, direct the expanding industries towards determining the conditions of their growth'.[2] On the other hand, it will have come to terms with the acceleration of rural migration, particularly strong in France because of the lateness of urban growth. Whilst in Great Britain, the Netherlands or West Germany the urban population equalled and then overtook the rural population between the years 1870 and 1890, the same phenomenon only took place in France in 1928. It is, therefore, not surprising that there has been a high level of growth in the urban population since 1945: an average of 2·4 per cent between 1954 and 1962, and 2·9 per cent between 1962 and 1968. By this date seven out of ten Frenchmen lived in towns (see Table 9.1).

Table 9.1   *Evolution of the Rate of Urbanisation in France*

1851	1876	1911	1936	1954	1962	1968
26%	32%	44%	57%	60%	64%	70%

Source: INSEE population returns.

The whole programme for urban development laid emphasis on reinforcing the superior urban network chosen as a level suited to polarisation of economic growth, and at the same time able to counterbalance what was considered to be the excessively strong position of Paris.

The awareness of the importance and the complementary character of the towns for national economic development led to the formation of a plan of urban reinforcement which stressed the importance of the large regional capitals. As Professor Lajugie writes, such a plan should contribute 'to improving the coherence of decisions taken by persons in authority as regards urban development and the planning of public works programmes'. This plan was, as we shall see, to be extended by the *Schéma d'Aménagement des Aires Métropolitaines.*

The plan for urban reinforcement chosen in France led, in 1963, to the promotion of eight conglomerations to the level of *métropoles d'équilibre.* These poles of growth were destined at one and the same time to encourage the formation and implementation of strategies for regional development and to deal with the decline of certain regions due to changed economic circumstances. By favouring the economic development of metropolitan poles it was hoped to produce a similar effect throughout the whole zone of anchorage and thus to make optimal use of space.

This policy is closely associated with the activity of the *Délégation à l'Aménagement du Territoire et à l'Action Régionale* (the DATAR),[3] an organism (created by the decree of 15 February 1963) entrusted with preparing and co-ordinating the necessary elements in governmental decisions, using as a basis the general objectives as defined by the five-year Plan.

Considering that 'economic and social problems have a geographical dimension and that the policy of infrastructure should be adapted to the particular needs of each region', the DATAR became an active organ in the development of the regions, participating in the preparation of the reform of March 1964, organising the State's field services in the regions and setting up the Regional Development Commissions (the CODERs) – consultative assemblies, grouping together elected representatives, professional classes and the Regional Prefect assisted by the Regional Mission.[4] The coordination of industrial decentralisation based on the *métropoles d'équilibre* and the establishment of public works programmes linked to the regionalisation of the annual budget became the two principal axes of the DATAR's orientation.

The planning of urban public works programmes requires a more detailed examination, given its important influence on urban development. In the agglomerations of more than 50,000 inhabitants, the *Plan de Modernisation et d'Equipement* (PME) must plan ahead for public works programmes. Defined as a programme for providing for the 'spreading out and financing of public investment in the area of the principal urban agglomerations' by a circular of October 1961, the PME clearly revealed itself as an instrument which functioned with difficulty. Indeed, of the two stages comprising the PME, the first, that dealing with the long-term aspects, was carried out only by about fifteen agglomerations, and the second, that dealing with the middle-term aspects, was only carried out by two. A circular of 20 February 1969 took account of the difficulties encountered and opted for an attempt to institute a programme covering the five-year duration of the National Plan. But, there again, it is evident that the PME, far from becoming an organ for operational forecasting, very soon tended to deteriorate into a collection of promises and pious wishes. In elaborating it the local commission, created for this purpose, aimed first of all at provoking a greater financial commitment from the State. This is extremely important, for the PME should, theoretically, act in concordance with the *Plan Régional de Développement Economique* (PRDE), a projection, at regional level, of public investment objectives forecast by the National Plan, and the level at which funds are allocated.

The demand for a document dealing with land-use planning in the principal urban areas led to the establishment of the *Schéma d'Aménagement de l'Aire Métropolitaine* (SAAM). This plan dealt with long-term physical planning and should have been an instrument of cohesion and a framework of action facilitating the planning and carrying out of public works programmes. Before examining the terms under which the SAAM were implemented, it is necessary to establish their institutional origin. In 1966, the DATAR set up the *Organismes d'Etudes d'Aménagement des Aires Métropolitaines* (OREAM) which took charge of the forecasting of urban development in the large agglomerations within the regional perspective. The OREAMs were created, at first, in five urban complexes: Lyons-St-Etienne, Marseilles-Aix, Nantes-St Nazaire, Nancy-Metz, Lille-Roubaix, and later in Bordeaux, Toulouse and Strasbourg. The OREAMs were administrative bodies placed under the supervision of the DATAR for matters concerning general policy with regard to planning, and under the *Direction de l'Aménagement Foncier et de l'Urbanisme* (DAFU), a department of the Ministry of Infrastructure (*Equipement*) in matters concerning administration and the budget. The SAAM was the exclusive preserve of the OREAM even if consultation took place between the departmental council, the CODER and the urban community. Approved in the Council of Ministers, on the recommendation of the Interministerial Committee for land-use planning, the SAAM became a framework of reference for the administration, since it holds little interest for third parties.

Significantly, the locally elected representatives, only marginally associated with its implementation, tended to think that the plan did not commit them. The opinion of the Urban Community Council in Bordeaux was quite clear on this point: 'as it is important to control and direct urban growth for the next thirty years, it seems essential to take into account what has been planned for the future, that is, the options already decided on in the plan of PME and PRDE, but for the remainder those responsible for SDAU must be allowed their freedom of expression and conception'. This reference to SDAU, a document which, we shall see, belongs in the strict sense of the term to the instruments of urbanisation, clearly underlines the ambiguity of co-ordinating planning practices which are essentially heterogeneous and vary according to which authority has been called upon to intervene in the first instance. François d'Arcy notes: 'dilution in decision-making goes hand in hand with a certain haziness in the spread of responsibilities between the different public bodies, and the administration has created a theory round this phenomenon called harmonisation'.[5]

THE INSTRUMENTS OF URBAN DEVELOPMENT

In 1958 an important law was promulgated which dealt with the increasingly pressing need to create order in the development of towns. Thus the Urbanisation Plan (*Plan d'Urbanisme*) was created, and we will return to this later. It also established a certain number of operational instruments for co-ordinating the allocation of urban land. The process which had produced a disorganised growth at the periphery of the agglomeration could henceforth be dealt with by the public authorities by partially controlling the development of housing through the creation of *Priority Urbanisation Zones* (ZUP). The possibility given at the same time to the locally elected representatives to control the equipment of the Industrial Zones (ZI) and, therefore, to co-ordinate the creation of activities and housing, was supposed to permit the balancing of economic and spatial development. Policies – notably fiscal ones – favourable to industrialists were supposed to accompany this 'effort of rationalisation'. In fact, the legislation opened the gates for economic development to a crowd of locally responsible people by encouraging the hope of seeing business take root in their area in the multitude of ZI which were applied for and often granted. The competition between towns to attract industrialists likely to set up business in the area, called, evocatively, 'urban marketing' clearly indicates the awareness amongst some that if no new blood was injected the town would decline, since people would only go where they could sell their labour. The basic question here was not whether development took place in a coherent fashion, but whether it took place at all . . . The exceptional cases which demanded a deviation from the norm were, therefore, difficult to refuse. The impact of the rationalisation intended in the legislation of 1958 was directly affected by this. The aim of the originators of this legislation was, after all, ambitious: it presupposed that the scattered and disorganised practices of private actors could be replaced by a coherent voluntarist act of co-ordination. To this end, it was less a question of constraint than of exercising, by well-chosen measures (in particular the financing of infrastructures), a determining influence on the choice of those participating in urban development.

The ineffectiveness of the 1958 legislation gave rise not to a sweeping revision, but to a strengthening of the restrictive power of the instruments put at the disposal of the responsible authorities who were supposed to note the deficiencies of former legislation and to 'draw lessons from it'. This is especially true in the case of the *Plans d'Urbanisme* which were succeeded by *Schéma Directeur d'Aménagement et d'Urbanisme* (SDAU) and the *Plan d'Occupation des Sols* (POS).

The *Plan d'Urbanisme* was concerned with spatial planning. Consequently the *Plan d'Urbanisme Directeur* outlined the general framework of land-use planning and determined its essential elements: the *Plan d'Urbanisme de détail* dealt with certain sectors and districts and completed, as required, the *Plan d'Urbanisme Directeur*. In general terms, the *Plan d'Urbanisme* was made up of a plan and a set of rules. The Plan enumerated the projects envisaged and described the chosen area, the main highways and the position of the principal public services; the rules defined the conditions for using the land and for the construction of buildings.

As it had the legal character of an administrative statute the *Plan d'Urbanisme* could be contested by third parties (as could be the POS later). But the principal defect of the Plan was its static nature, attributable to the absence of a vision of the intermediary stages necessary to reach a long-term objective. This is one of the weaknesses of all fixed statutes dealing with spatial allocation; they describe a state without being able to control the process which, in reality, will determine the method of change. Of course, contrary to the *Plans d'Urbanisme,* the new legislation created the obligation, lacking until then, to have a coherent policy within the agglomerations covered by the Plans. However, the combination of temporal planning and physical planning can only partially overcome this 'deficiency'.

The framework law of December 1967 made the SDAU the document outlining the future development of towns and the POS the charter for land use. It is the SDAU which constitutes the main innovation: it represents an attempt to create coherent policy for both the years 1985 and 2000. 'The SDAU fix the basic orientation of land-use plannings notably with regard to urban expansion. The SDAU determine in particular the general use to be made of the land, the outlines of the large public works programmes, the general organisation of transport' (Article 22 of the *Code d'Urbanisme*). In its final version, the SDAU consists of two documents: a report describing the current situation, the perspectives for demographic and economic development, the justification for the type of development chosen; the second part consists of the blueprints. The objective of the SDAU is to break the evolution of urbanisation into separate units by defining the axes of development.

The principal weakness of the SDAU is not, in this case, the absence of elected representatives in the process of execution, but rather that it cannot be contested by third parties, since the POS which, in theory, should co-ordinate with the SDAU are often in practice worked out at the same time if not before the reference document.

It is here that the discrepancy between the extremely refined methods of formulating the schemes and their actual impact can be seen. The technical formulation of the SDAU is the responsibility of the *Commission Locale d'Aménagement et d'Urbanisme* (CLAU) which is supposed to monitor the work as it progresses and approve the final plans proposed by study groups which have sought the opinion of the State and the Departmental Council and have submitted the final report for the approval of the municipal councils. In this context the SDAU should in theory be, as Antoine Giraudon notes, 'a summary of the clearly expressed will to intervene in a given area'.

The POS which fixes the 'general rules and the constraints on land use' can be contested by third parties. It anticipates, within five- and ten-year periods, the development of the town by freeing the land upon which urban development is to take place, by reserving control of public works programmes for itself and by ordering the spatial distribution of men and activities. The final document is in five parts: an inquiry which reveals the general rules and the constraints on land usage, the actual plans for land use (outline of new highways, zoning, property set aside for public works programmes), the plan of the constraints, urbanisation regulations which fix the method of land use and, in particular, the coefficients for land use (COS) for each sector.

In practice, the move towards an urbanisation which may be qualified as operational and practical as opposed to the former urbanisation attempt which was liable to be institutional and static should not obscure the fact that it functions within a contradictory framework. Indeed, along with the implementation of these new regulations went another concept promoted by the government, a concept based on neo-liberal visions of the town which tended to subordinate production and organisation of urban land to the mechanics of the market. Thus, at the same time as awareness of the complexity of the urban unit was leading to a refinement of technical studies, the State authorities were modifying the orientation of their action by favouring concerted effort rather than constraint: concerted effort no longer merely on the part of those responsible in the administration and the locally elected representatives, but also on the part of the public authorities and private individuals concerned with urban development. The policy of the *Zones d'Aménagement Concerté* (ZAC) to which Chalandon, the minister, has attached his name, illustrates clearly the tendency towards public withdrawal and the institutionalisation of contractual procedures between public authorities and private developers, in order to define the principal characteristics and the mutual commitment of the parties involved in each property development project.

Once agreed by the authorities (the local prefect or Ministerial Council according to the size of the project in question), the contract removes, to the benefit of the property developer, the basic obstacle constituted by private ownership of the land. It must be understood, in fact, that the creation of the ZACs transfers public prerogatives such as public utility procedure or expropriation to private agents. Of course, in return the developer may be required to finance and execute certain collective public works projects (nurseries, schools etc.); but, in reality, these obligations do not counterbalance the profits which the large finance companies, benefiting from this legislation, make from the projects which they decide to undertake.

A top civil servant could thus write:

'Of course the POS can prevent development by defining zones as not for construction. In these non-construction zones urbanisation is merely deferred until the public works programme is carried out. However, it is enough for a firm to offer to undertake this public works programme for a construction permit to be granted. In the same way the creation of a ZAC makes the non-construction zone urbanisable. The law requires the compatibility of PAZ[6] with the SDAU but this relationship is difficult to verify. Finally, by defining construction rights in the urban areas the POS merely authorises. It is the market which decides on urbanisation, both whether it will take place and at what pace. In general terms, the POS are reduced to mere legal documents, a sort of ledger of the constraints which are applicable to construction permits. Urbanisation documents which propose a programme of action over five or ten years, supported by the elected representatives, are rare.' (*Source confidential*).

This policy orientation is, however, accompanied by a desire to transfer ever-increasing responsibility to the local authorities.

The Galley Law of 31 December 1975 which came into effect on 1 April 1976 reformed policy on land but aimed, at one and the same time, at 'strangling land speculation' and at favouring the communes in the allocation of new resources. This law is also somewhat ambiguous because, in the name of socially minded liberalism, it manages to limit the exercise of property rights in the centre of large towns and in Paris. The law institutes, in fact, a line of separation between the right to construct which the owner of a piece of land may use freely, and those portions of land above a certain size which he must 'repurchase' from the community. The communes are thus vested with authority in property transactions between private parties. At the same time, a new housing policy was prepared and approved on 22 July 1976. It aimed at giving easier and far wider access to housing property by a simplification of the system of financing.

The tendency towards State withdrawal, notable in the running down of the instruments of planning, is underlined by F. d'Arcy who writes:

'In connection with these private urbanisation agents: industrialists, large property developers and developers of large commercial areas, the public authorities have not the means of coercion which would permit them to outline in advance the spatial and temporal framework within which action should take place. It is capitalism which has become the planner, and whilst in previous plans the State, faced with a divided body of employers, has played a dominant role in the preparation of the Sixth Plan, the most dynamic section of the employers, reinforced today by a long policy of industrial concentration, plays the leading role.'[7]

This phenomenon is clearly visible in the housing domain. Whilst in the immediate post-war years the State intervened directly in the financing of the construction industry, there has been a gradual decrease in government support and a gradual increase in the capital invested by the banks (44 per cent in 1967, 65 per cent in 1972): on the one hand, a progressive substitution of the *Caisse des Dépôts et Consignations* (CDC) for the budget and, on the other, a decrease in the number of property investment companies. The CDC, a para-public organisation endowed with the task of centralising funds from a number of different sources, has developed its activity in the area of housing finance via the two central organisations which

Table 9.2   *Performance of Property Companies controlled by the Ten Largest French Finance Groups*

Companies	Date of formation	Actual starts	Dwellings sold up to 1970	Dwellings under construction in 1970	Groups
AGIM	1958	1958	4,083	306	Indochine
SERDI	1957	1963	3,655	598	BCP
GOGEDIM	1963	1963	1,897	1,750	Paribas
OCEFI	1961	1961	1,632	716	Paribas
UFIC	1956	1964	1,607	452	Snez
SGMI	1928	1961	1,522	2,003	Schneider
SOFAP	1964	1964	1,017	300	ICP
SIFRAM	1899	1961	654	367	Worms
SEPIMO	1963	1963	477	1,776	UFM

Source: D. Combes and E. Latapie, *L'Intervention des groupes financiers français dans l'immobilier* (Paris: Centre de Sociologie Urbaine, 1973), quoted in F. Ascher and J. Giard, *Demain la ville* (Paris: Editions Sociales, 1975), p. 158.

it set up (the *Société Centrale pour l'Equipement du Territoire* and the *Société Centrale Immobilière et de Construction*).

Banking capital and the large industrial groups also play an increasing role in the property and development sectors, especially since 1958. As J. P. Delilez writes, the withdrawal of the State should be perceived relatively; in fact, 'the State's role is to define and affirm selective bases for regulations which make the private banking system the privileged agent of the mobilisation of savings within the confines of State Monopoly Capitalism'.[8]

THE NATURE OF INTERVENTION IN URBAN PLANNING

To the questions 'what' and 'how' to control should be added 'who' should control and why, given that the former have been answered in terms of the ineffectiveness of urban policy without the criteria for making such a judgement being clearly stated. How often have the 'technicians' in the administration been heard to complain of their difficulties in overcoming 'private interests', of the lack of public support, of the electoralism of the politicians? In fact, by implicitly conveying the notion of the neutrality of the State apparatus, 'guarantor of the general interest', statements of this nature obscure the social issues contained within the production process, the appropriation process and the methods of allocating urban space, and conceal the role assumed by the State in the demand for expanded reproduction within the capitalist system. It is thus appropriate to examine the issue of urban planning at two levels: that of the specific nature of urban areas and that of the State's method of dealing with the urban question.

In an extremely enlightening article, Manuel Castells[9] distinguishes two main periods in the development of urban policy. In the first phase (1945–63) the State was in the forefront of the process of accumulation and assumed a central role in economic development. During this period urban policy is defined as 'social' because of the policy of promoting State-subsided housing schemes (HLM). In the subsequent period (1963–73) the State systematically aided the accumulation of monopoly capital. A transition has, therefore, taken place from 'an urban and regional State policy centred on the organisation of the means of production and the reproduction of the work force to a new policy which is entirely favourable to the accumulation of capital and which provoked such contradictions that in 1973–1974 an attempt was made to embark on an urban policy aimed primarily at reflecting social relationships'.

Such an analysis of the stages through which urban policy has passed enables us to arrive at a better understanding of certain practices in the planning field. It is clear, for example, that the increase in the number of private developers enjoying the support of the State is the most significant feature of the last decade. Charles Topalov notes that 'the help of the public authorities becomes indispensable in overcoming the resistance of the small urban property owners and in implementing large public works programmes . . . The intervention of the public authorities in the freeing of land is essential for the promotion of real estate development.'[10] This process has been accelerated since 1967 by the increasing intervention of the banks in this field. 'What has been done with regard to the consumer through advertising should also be done with regard to the State but through other means. A guaranteed turnover must be assured as must regular orders and a programme of associated public works programmes compatible with that of the constructor as well as, in many cases, the exclusive rights over a given area, not to mention a policy on land development.'[11]

The principal weakness of such an interpretation of the evolution of urban planning is that it tends to be over-mechanistic and over-systematic and thus presupposes a unity of practice throughout the State apparatus. An examination of the position of the local public works agents – *Directions Départmentales de l'Equipement* – is of considerable interest in this respect. J.-C. Thoenig and E. Friedberg have already described the diverging orientations of the town planners and the engineers with regard to urban policy.[12] It is also necessary to point out the increasingly inferior material position of the civil servants involved in public works programmes compared with private planners and developers and locally elected representatives. In the planning sector, the 'spearhead' of public works is the *Groupe d'Etude et de Programmation* (GEP), an organisation in charge of the programming of all operations and liaison between the different groups of the DDE and the outside world. Apart from various offices (statistics, programming, urbanisation, studies, land law) the GEP embraces two units of 'production': the *Groupe Infrastructure* (INFRA) which is concerned with management and works, and the *Groupe de l'Urbanisme Operationnel et de la Construction* (UOC) which deals essentially with land law. Due to lack of resources, officials of the Ministry of Infrastructure are often reduced to performing a mere administrative control function. The GEP, primarily concerned with the formulation of the POS, has difficulty in fulfilling its programming task; *Urbanisme Operationnel* is underequipped and almost non-existent. Consequently a contradictory practice develops: Infrastructure formulates POS and at the same time is reduced to the role of controlling operations already set in motion, for the most part by private initiative and especially by the *Sociétés d'Equipement*. These mixed economy companies hold great attraction for locally elected representatives, as they allow them to assert their authority as counsellors and planners and force the completion of a certain number of projects. As one locally elected member of the board of a *Société d'Equipement* notes: 'the pre-operational studies of this company and the ultimate realisation are far more effective than all the urbanisation studies carried out by the GEP'.

Is it, therefore, possible to detect a deep political hiatus between the voluntarist spirit of the law of 1967 and its actual practice? The Lyon OREAM writes:

'In matters of investment and management the CPURLY (Urban Community of Lyon) may appear to be a well adapted and effective instrument in matters of planning, but results do not bear this out. The communes' grievances still remain, and urbanisation is conceived of as a problem of the commune. Such a conception leads to a disorganised programming of public works programmes and urbanisation operations and, in general, to a non-optimal use both of local and State resources. The need for a global responsibility for the development of the towns is pressing.'

If one has to beware of oversimplification in perceiving 'the administration uniquely as the executive instrument of government policy with the task of assuring its implementation over the whole territory',[13] one must also, it seems, guard against a manichean view of the relationship between the State and local communities in order to comprehend the margin for manoeuvre and the local social logic existing at the various levels of municipal power. In this context, the conquest of the municipal institution is of real importance, as it permits participation in that decision-making process which is of direct interest to the social forces in competition for increased use of land (property owners, developers etc.). As H. Coing notes: 'In order to understand the nature of current urban planning it is necessary to know whence comes the intervention of the politician and when and why, from the point of view of the logic of the social system and its mode of production, a new form of control over the elements of the urban system is proved to be necessary. This analysis needs to be constantly amended.'[14]

Even if the global nature of State intervention in urban planning is only explicable in terms of the predominating mode of production and its consequences for the nation as a whole, it is also true that the practice of urbanisation is circumscribed by the framework set by the power relationships between the social groups which exist in the urban area in question. In contrast, what is common to all urban planning projects is the systematic absence of the population.

When provision for consultation with the population is made (for example, through a public inquiry, as provided for in the formulation of the POS, or when it is required by the municipal authorities) it generally fails, either as a result of the atomisation of urban existence or because organised local opposition groups are insufficiently strong. The insistence on the technical nature of decision making in urban policy only adds to the problem and reinforces the paradox: 'Resulting from class conflict, the urbanisation plans take on some of the characteristics of the general evolution of society: formalisation of democratic political structures, confiscation and personalisation of power. They rationalise urbanisation by neutralising it, planning it for capitalism and justifying social segregation.'[15]

NOTES

1   The intrusion of business into politics (Translator's note).
2   J. Monod, *Transformation d'un pays pour une géographie de la liberté* (Paris: Fayard, 1974).
3   DATAR was intended to introduce a regional element into planning and to work out the implications of planning for the regions (Translator's note). See pp. 86, 94.
4   See papers by Croisat and Souchon, and by Thoenig.
5   F. d'Arcy, 'Le contrôle de l'urbanisation échappe aux autorités publiques', *Projet*, April 1971.
6   PAZ = Plan d'Aménagement de Zone.
7   F. d'Arcy, op. cit.
8   CERM, *Urbanisme monopoliste, urbanisme démocratique* (Paris: CERM, 1974).
9   M. Castells, 'Crise de l'Etat, consommation collective et contradictions urbaines', in N. Poulantzas *et al.*, *La Crise de l'Etat* (Paris: PUF-Politiques, 1976), pp. 179–204.
10 Ch. Topalov, *Les Promoteurs immobiliers: Contribution à l'analyse de la production capitaliste du logement en France* (Paris: Mouton, 1974).
11 Y. Aubert, quoted in H. Coing, 'La planification urbaine existe-t-elle?', *Projet*, April 1971.
12 J.-C. Thoenig and E. Friedberg, *La Création des Directions Départementales de l'Equipement – Phénomènes de corps et réforme administrative* (Paris: CNRS, Groupe de Sociologie des Organisations, 1970).
13 F. d'Arcy, op. cit.
14 H. Coing, 'La planification urbaine existe-t-elle?', *Projet*, April 1971.
15 ibid.

BIBLIOGRAPHY

Bercoff-Ferry, R. and Coing, H., *La Planification urbaine à Dunkerque* (unpublished report, 1973).
Castells, M., *La Question urbaine* (Paris: Maspero, 1972).
Castells, M. and Godard, F., *Monopolville* (Paris: Mouton, 1974).

CNRS, *L'Analyse interdisciplinaire de la croissance urbaine* (Paris: Centre National de la Recherche Scientifique, 1972).

Lojkine, J., *La Politique urbaine dans la région parisienne, 1945-1971* (Paris: Mouton, 1972).

Lojkine, J., *La Politique urbaine dans la région lyonnaise, 1945-1972* (Paris: Mouton, 1973).

Monod, J., *Transformation d'un pays pour une géographie de la liberté* (Paris: Fayard, 1974).

Poulantzas, N. *et al.*, *La Crise de l'Etat* (Paris: PUF-Politiques, 1976).

Remy, J. and Voye, L., *La Ville phénomène économique* (Paris: Duculot, 1974).

Topalov, Ch., *Les Promoteurs immobiliers. Contribution à l'analyse de la production capitaliste du logement en France* (Paris: Mouton, 1974).

Chapter X

———————◆———————

LOCAL GOVERNMENT FINANCE
IN GREAT BRITAIN

This chapter has two parts. The first presents the salient features of
local government finance in Great Britain, and the second surveys
the main proposals of the Layfield Committee which in 1976 issued
the first major analysis of local government finance in Great Britain
since before the First World War (*Local Government Finance*,
Cmnd 6453, London: HMSO). This chapter draws heavily on
material in the Report.

PART I

THE SCALE AND SCOPE OF LOCAL GOVERNMENT
EXPENDITURE

It is estimated that in the year 1975–6 total expenditure by local
authorities in England, Wales and Scotland will amount to £13,000
million on the current account and £3,876 million on the capital
account. The last year for which firm figures are available is 1973–4
when total current expenditure was £10,733 million and total capital
expenditure was £4,237 million. Table 10.1 shows an analysis of
current expenditure by service. Two services accounted for the
largest part of the sum. About 36 per cent of the total was spent on
education and another 16 per cent was devoted to housing. Although
social services spent only a little over 8 per cent, that figure was
nearly double what was spent four years before.

Table 10.1   *Actual Local Authority Current Expenditure
by Service in 1973–4*

	England £m.	Wales £m.	Total E & W £m.	Scot- land £m.	Total E, W & S £m.
Education	3,163	194	3,357	353	3,710
Health and personal social services	676	40	716	69	785
Police and fire	624	34	658	68	726
Highways	520	40	560	65	625
Housing (including housing revenue A/C)	1,418	73	1,491	223	1,714
Environmental services	958	53	1,011	71	1,082
Other rate fund services	1,072	61	1,133	88	1,221
Trading services	442	29	471	61	532
Superannuation and special funds	316	19	335	3	338
TOTAL	9,189	543	9,732	1,001	10,733

Table 10.2 shows an analysis of this current expenditure by category, illustrating that about 45 per cent covers wages and salaries. Loan charges, which form 20 per cent of total current expenditure, have been growing as a proportion, and now account for 68 per cent of the amount spent on housing.

Table 10.2   *Actual Local Authority Current Expenditure
by Category 1973–4 in England and Wales only*

	England £m.	Wales £m.	Total E & W £m.
Salaries and wages	4,123	263	4,386
Loan charges	1,743	100	1,843
Other expenditure	3,323	180	3,503
TOTAL	9,189	543	9,732

Table 10.3 analyses total capital expenditure by service, and shows that the largest amount, 44 per cent, was devoted to housing. The nearest service was education, with 12 per cent: roads accounted for 8 per cent.

Table 10.3   *Actual Local Authority Capital Expenditure by Service 1973–4*

	England £m.	Wales £m.	Total E & W £m.	Scot-land £m.	Total E, W & S £m.
Education	448	31	479	58	537
Housing (including housing revenue A/C)	1,796	96	1,892	185	2,077
Highways	307	22	329	44	373
Sewerage	266	20	286	29	315
Environmental services	239	18	257	34	291
Other rate fund services	287	18	305	24	329
Trading services	263	29	292	23	315
TOTAL	3,606	234	3,840	397	4,237

Table 10.4 shows an analysis of this capital expenditure by category. By far the largest element was new construction, about 60 per cent, and half of that was spent on housing.

Table 10.4   *Actual Local Authority Capital Expenditure by Category 1973–4 in England and Wales only*

	England £m.	Wales £m.	Total E & W £m.
New construction	2,067	147	2,214
Land and existing buildings	562	19	581
Other expenditure	977	68	1,045
TOTAL	3,606	234	3,840

Since at least 1890 local authority spending has been growing steadily and at a faster rate than the economy as a whole. Total local government expenditure was just over £50 million in 1890. By 1920 the figure was £130 million and by 1938 £530 million. Between 1949–50 and 1973–4 it rose from £1,300 million to £14,000 million, an eleven-fold increase over a twenty-five-year period. Over the same period local government expenditure on goods and services has taken an increasing share of the gross domestic product, rising from 8·6 per cent in 1949 to 12·4 per cent in 1974, and rising probably to about 13·5 per cent in 1975. If within local government expenditure are included transfers of money largely to the private sector, like student grants and housing subsidies, then total local government expenditure represented about 16½ per cent of gross domestic product in 1974 and probably about 17½ per cent in 1975. Local government expenditure has also been increasing faster than public expenditure generally. In 1950 local authorities spent 23·4 per cent of all public expenditure and their share now is running at about 31 per cent.

CURRENT INCOME

The balance

The sources from which the current expenditure of local government is financed have not changed materially since 1890. There are three. Rates are the only local tax available to local authorities. They are a tax on the occupation of property. Second come fees and charges paid by consumers of some of the services. And third are government grants. Although loans have been raised for capital works they have usually been repaid with interest from revenue sources.

There has been a significant change in the relative importance of each of these sources over the years. In 1949–50 the three sources bore an almost equal burden: rates provided 34 per cent, government grants 34 per cent and fees and charges 32 per cent. By 1973–4 government grants had risen to 45 per cent, rates had fallen to 28 per cent and fees and charges to 27 per cent. This tendency for government grants to increase is of very long standing. In 1913, for instance, they accounted for only 15 per cent. Until very recently they had been increasing very fast. This continuing increase meant that the growth in local government expenditure of recent years had been met more from general taxation and grants than from local sources. A similar picture emerges if the figures are examined in a different way. Not all local government expenditure qualifies for grant support, and that which does is described in official terms as 'relevant expenditure'. Some 66·5 per cent of this amount was paid from grant and 33·5 per cent from rates in 1975–6. In 1966–7 grants had paid 51 per cent and rates 49 per cent.

However, the government in pursuit of its counterinflation policy of restraining public expenditure reduced the grant percentage in 1976–7 to 65·5 per cent and in 1977–8 to 61 per cent, thus forcing local authorities to choose between raising their rates or cutting their expenditure by reducing their standards of provision.

Rates

An important distinction has to be made between domestic and non-domestic rates. Since rates are a tax on the benefit of occupation, in the former they are a tax on the consumption of housing. In the latter they fall mainly on commercial and industrial properties, although there is a varied category of other non-domestic properties, comprising public buildings, like schools, hospitals, town halls and government offices, whose rates are paid from central or local taxation. Table 10.5 shows for 1975–6 the estimated yield of rates from

Table 10.5 *Estimated Yield of Rates 1975–6*

	England & Wales £m.	Wales £m.	Scotland £m.
Domestic	1,515	50	179
Commercial and industrial	1,900	85	150
Other non-domestic	430	20	73
TOTAL	3,845	155	402

its component sources. Commercial and industrial properties contribute the largest share. The yield of non-domestic rates has been increasing faster than that of domestic rates, and faster than that of other taxes borne by industry and commerce. In recent years the government has intervened in the rating system in order to shift increases in rates away from the domestic onto the non-domestic sector by introducing a system of rate rebates for low-income households and a 'domestic element' of the grant in order to lessen increases in rates paid by all householders. The intervention has had two effects. The proportion of personal disposable income paid in rates by domestic ratepayers has remained remarkably constant as an average. From 1966–7 it has stayed at around 2½ per cent to 1973–4, and it is estimated to be similar in 1974–5: this same proportion was taken just before the Second World War too. The second effect of government intervention has been to move the burden to the non-domestic ratepayer. The total rating bill increased between 1966 and 1974 by about 120 per cent, but the domestic ratepayers' bill rose by only 80 per cent compared with a 150 per cent increase for the non-domestic ratepayer.

Miscellaneous income
The decline of income from fees and charges cannot be attributed to deliberate government policy. There is no evidence of any consistent policy on such charges or of any policy about the means used to decide on the levels of charges. Just over half of this miscellaneous income comes from rents and trading income, the latter mainly public transport, and a quarter represents income to the superannuation funds and interest payments. The remaining quarter is

income from sales, fees and charges for services financed from the rates, representing about 6 per cent of expenditure on these services. In 1973-4 local authorities in England and Wales raised about £1,400 million in local fees and charges, equivalent to around 15 per cent of their current expenditure. Housing rents accounted for about £700 million, and trading services for about £140 million, including about £75 million from passenger transport services. Another £540 million was raised from a wide range of items, such as licence fees, residence charges for old people's homes, car parking charges, trade refuse collection, library charges, charges for recreational facilities and sales of school meals and milk.

Grants
Grants paid by the government from general taxation to local authorities first appeared in 1835 with the objective of reimbursing local authorities for that part of their expenditure devoted to national purposes. Grants were generally 'specific' grants, that is, they were paid to support specified services and could be spent only on those services. During the twentieth century the basis on which grants have been paid to local authorities has altered in four important ways. First, since 1948 the government has had as a major objective in distributing grant to make good the differences between the resources of individual local authorities. Grant is used to compensate local authorities with taxable resources below a national standard. Second, the government has sought ever more sophisticated measurements of the factors that determine the expenditure needs of local authorities. The objective is to compensate local authorities for their varying needs to spend, which arise either because different authorities require different volumes of service or because the cost of providing each unit of service differs from one authority to another. Third, since 1958 the number of 'specific' grants has been reduced and the principle of the 'general' or 'block' grant has been predominant. The objective here is to widen the discretion of local authorities and to allow them to use the money more on purposes that they and not the central government thinks best. Fourth, the government has increasingly used the grant as a means of regulating the level of local authorities' own taxation. The government decides on the level of grant after taking a view of what it regards as a desirable level of local expenditure and an acceptable increase in the level of rates. Grant has increased in recent years because the government considered that local rates could not bear a heavier burden in financing the expansion of local government services.

There are three main types of grant: Rate Support Grant, specific grants and supplementary grants. The Rate Support Grant is a 'block' grant. It is paid in respect of rate fund expenditure as a whole and is not earmarked for particular purposes. Of the £7,700 million estimated aggregate Exchequer grant in 1976–7, Rate Support Grant accounts for £6,700 million or 87 per cent. Specific grants are paid in respect of particular services or projects and local authorities are obliged to use them for those purposes. They are commonly, but not necessarily, paid as a percentage of expenditure. They will account for 9 per cent of aggregate Exchequer grant in 1976–7. The largest specific grant is for police, which accounts for nearly two-thirds of the total of specific grants. Supplementary grants are paid in respect of transport services and national parks and are available for a variety of purposes within these services. Their amount is based on a government assessment of the formulation and implementation of policies by local authorities. In 1976–7 they will account for 4 per cent of aggregate Exchequer grant and are almost entirely for transport. Table 10.6 presents the figures.

Table 10.6 *Aggregate Exchequer Grant 1976–7*

	England & Wales £m.	*Scotland* £m.	*Great Britain* £m.
Rate Support Grant	5,921	823	6,744
Specific grants	643	61	704
Supplementary grants	288	—	288
Aggregate Exchequer grant	6,852	884	7,736

The Rate Support Grant is, therefore, the principal grant. It has three elements: resources, needs and domestic. The objective of the first two is to enable local authorities to provide similar levels of service without widely varying burdens of taxation. The aim, therefore, is to compensate local authorities for disparities in their resources, or taxable capacity, and for differences in their needs to spend, which arise either from differences in the volume of a required service, for example differences in numbers of school children or old people, or from differences in the costs of providing a particular unit of service, for example because population is thinly spread over a wide area or concentrated in a small area. Essentially the needs element is designed to compensate for differences between authorities in the amount they need to spend per head of population. The resources element is paid to authorities whose rateable value per head, the present measure of taxable resources, is less than the national standard rateable value set by the government. The needs element is extremely complex. Each authority's entitlement is calculated by reference to a formula, prescribed annually by the government. The formula is based on an analysis of past expenditure and indicators of expenditure needs which appear best to explain variations between authorities in expenditure per head. The analysis seeks to find a statistical explanation of the variation in expenditure between authorities in terms of objective factors, such as population, various categories of school children and population density. The justification for this method is the belief that there is no better measure of spending needs than what local authorities, responding to their views of local needs, have found it necessary to spend. Past expenditure is regarded as a proxy for spending need.

The domestic element has as its objective to cushion the effect on domestic ratepayers of increases in local expenditure. Each authority receives the sums needed to reimburse it for the relief given to domestic ratepayers according to a tax rate laid down annually by the government. This element has grown from 3·6 per cent of average rate bills in England in 1967–8 to 27·5 per cent in 1975–6. Table 10.7 analyses the various elements of the Rate Support Grant.

Table 10.7   *Rate Support Grant 1976–7*

	England & Wales £m.	Scotland £m.	Great Britain £m.
Needs	3,565	624	4,189
Resources	1,716	156	1,872
Domestic	640	43	683
Total Rate Support Grant	5,921	823	6,744

CAPITAL

So far this chapter has been considering current expenditure. Capital expenditure is treated differently. Local authorities raise capital at present in four ways. Government grants produce about 5 per cent, revenue contributes 10 per cent, sales of capital assets yield around 10 per cent and loans produce the remaining 75 per cent. The biggest single source of those loans is the Public Works Loan Board, which contributes some 40 per cent of total borrowing; much of the remaining proportion is raised on the market. The total outstanding loan debt for local government in Great Britain for 1973–4 was £19,641 million and the loan charges payable on it were £2,367 million. By 1975 the estimate of this total debt had reached £25,000 million. In 1963–4 the total outstanding loan debt had been £7,944 million and loan charges £635 million, only 8 per cent compared with 12 per cent for 1973–4. In recent years the volume of debt has grown considerably and rates of interest have risen sharply. Longer-term debt (that held for periods longer than one year) amounted to £20,553 million and was divided between the Public Works Loan Board, (£10,044 million), banks and institutions (£8,063 million), stock issues (£1,477 million) and negotiable bonds (£969 million).

TRENDS

A number of trends of recent years appears significant.

(a) There has been an almost continuous growth in local government expenditure from at least 1890, both in absolute terms and in the share of gross domestic product which it has taken.

(b) Since the Second World War the share which local government takes of public expenditure has been increasing.

(c) Public demand for more services and better services has been growing.

(d) An increasing proportion of total local government expenditure has been provided by the government, rising from 15 per cent in 1913 to 45 per cent in 1973.

(e) While the proportion that ratepayers contribute to local expenditure has been steadily declining the absolute amount has been rising, and in the last few years steeply.

(f) Government intervention has been designed to prevent domestic rates rising faster than was thought desirable, thus concealing from ratepayers the true cost of the additional and better services being provided.

PART II

THE CRISIS AND THE LAYFIELD COMMITTEE

In 1974 there were unprecedented rate increases that provoked howls of protest. The average increase was just under 30 per cent, but some ratepayers faced increases of over 160 per cent. These huge increases stirred up ratepayers' groups and threats of rate strikes. The Conservative Party produced proposals to abolish domestic rates, and the Labour government was defeated in the House of Commons in June 1974 on a Conservative motion for a fundamental reform of the rating system, despite a government promise to set up a Committee of Inquiry. The public outcry against the rates was responsible for stimulating government action. It had no solution at hand, and so followed the traditional practice of setting up a Committee of Inquiry, under the lawyer Frank Layfield. The terms of reference of the Committee were very broad – 'to review the whole system of local government finance' and 'to make recommendations'. The government's motives were probably mixed. It genuinely wanted to find a solution to a baffling problem and it wanted to be able to quieten down public anxiety and escape political embarrassment by being able to point to the Committee busily at work. The report of the Committee was published in May 1976 and it turned out to be a mammoth, thorough and radical review. It ranged over the whole field of local government finance and not just rates.

LAYFIELD'S MAIN THEME

It explained that the crisis that occurred in 1974 was brought to a head by the combination of a number of factors, including the unexpected level of inflation which hit particularly hard local authorities whose activities are very labour intensive and whose main independent source of taxation did not adjust for inflation as most national taxes. There were also the disruption and higher costs caused by local government reorganisation, large changes in grant distribution and the reorganisation of water and sewerage services that all put a great strain on the financial arrangements. Nevertheless, the Committee concluded what the crisis exposed were not simply the weak spots in an otherwise sound system, but a collection of financial arrangements, whose objectives were not clear and which had never been properly related to one another. There was no coherent financial system.

The main weakness which the Committee identified was not extravagance nor corruption but a confusion between the government and local government over responsibility for local spending. Local government expenditure might be said to be out of control since no one was clearly responsible. The government includes local services in its planning of public expenditure, but local authorities have not been involved in this planning process. They feel that the bulk of their expenditure is determined by decisions in which they play no part. The government, on the other hand, has no effective means of ensuring that local spending conforms with its plans. Its control over capital expenditure is direct and can be effective, but over current expenditure it is indirect, mainly through the grant. As a result, neither the government nor local authorities have felt fully responsible for the level of spending that actually occurred. The government has often underestimated the cost of implementing its policies and put conflicting pressures on local authorities, on the one hand to improve their services and on the other to restrain the growth in their expenditure. At the same time, the true cost of expanding local services was not brought home to councils and their electors because of the steady increase in the rate of grant and unpredictable changes in its distribution. The Report's main finding is that there is a lack of accountability for local spending. Responsibility for expenditure should be clarified, so that responsibility for decisions on policy that lead to expenditure should coincide with responsibility for finding the money to pay for it. The public can, therefore, hold accountable those that take the decisions on policy and to tax them. Decisions on policy, expenditure and taxing should be taken together, since expenditure depends on policy.

The Committee detected over the years a growing trend to centralisation, despite the expressed wish of successive governments to strengthen local democracy. The Report states that the drift to central control over local government expenditure, combined with confusion over responsibility for expenditure and taxation, will continue unless a decision is taken to place the main responsibility firmly either with the government or with local authorities. The Committee posed a choice: either to give clear and recognised responsibility to the government to take the main decisions on local government expenditure, or to strengthen local accountability by placing the responsibility for local government expenditure on local authorities.

The Committee explored the possibility of a halfway house that might have been politically attractive. The idea was that the government would pay the full cost of meeting defined minimum standards for each service, leaving local authorities with discretion to pay for higher standards out of local taxation. A similar approach was to distinguish between national services or parts of services to be determined and financed nationally, and local services to be determined and financed locally. But such a halfway house was difficult to build and would in any case lead to the centralist solution. Categories of expenditure that were either totally mandatory or totally discretionary were very few. Most local government expenditure fell between the two, determined neither by central requirement nor by free local choice but by a complex mixture of pressures, such as advice and urging from government departments, inspection, accumulated past practice, nationally accepted standards, professional attitudes, political influences and actions of various pressure groups, both local and national. Where statutes imposed a duty, the obligation was expressed in general terms, leaving scope for local interpretation.

There are major difficulties in devising standards. Such standards have in the past been input standards and related mainly to the quality of physical products such as houses or schools. Even here it has been difficult to specify appropriate minimum standards and to define the current costs of meeting them in different areas. It would be much more difficult to define output standards for education or policing and to measure the cost of achieving them, largely because there is at present no agreed measure of the output of a teacher or a policeman.

After examining the problem of defining national minimum standards, the Committee concluded that to define such standards would mean specifying a required scale of provision in terms that could be related to the cost of achieving it in each area and for all services. Central involvement would, therefore, have to be more specific and detailed than now. Politically it was also unlikely that the government would be prepared to accept national minimum standards that were stable. Pressures would concentrate on the government to raise the standards, and in the process of continually revising standards the scope of local discretion would be eroded by increasing government concern about what should be provided. It would just not rest content with low minimum standards.

The main feature of a system based on central responsibility is that the government would be accountable for the totality of local expenditure. It would determine how much each authority should spend and for what purpose. Each authority's grant would be based on the government's view of what it ought to spend. Oversight of each local authority's expenditure would be a major new administrative task for the government, involving an expansion of civil servants both at headquarters and in the regions. In this central responsibility model the present combination of fees, grants and rates could continue. Grants would be at a high and increasing level, and rating, which the Committee considered was an appropriate local tax, would remain as the single tax for local government.

The essence of a system based on local responsibility is that local authorities would be responsible to their electorates both for the expenditure they incurred and the revenue they raised. Matters reserved for government decision would be defined by statute and confined to essential issues of national policy. In the system based on local responsibility local authorities would require another source of revenue under their own control, so as to reduce their dependence on a single, narrow and inflexible tax, resulting in high and increasing grants that were bound to undermine local responsibility. Only a local income tax, out of the many other taxes reviewed by the Committee, suited its criteria of producing a substantial yield and of promoting accountability. For years a local income tax has been mentioned as a possible new source of local revenue. The Layfield Committee has devised a workable scheme: it has specified its features and has costed the arrangements for both the Inland Revenue who would have the main administrative responsibility and employers who would collect most of it. The scheme is administratively feasible, but costly, and the Committee conclude that these costs would be justified but only if the local income tax were accompanied by the political will to give greater powers of decision to local authorities.

Even with this local responsibility solution substantial grants would still be needed, amounting to at least 40 per cent of relevant expenditure, to compensate for differences in spending needs and in taxable resources. But through the local income tax the dependence of local authorities on government grants would be far less than in the central responsibility model and the capacity of local tax to meet growth in expenditure would be increased. Government control of expenditure would be exercised not in order to influence the development of individual services but only for the purpose of economic management. For this objective the Committee proposed some new ingenious controls, including the regulator through which local authorities would be required to surrender part of their tax revenue in excess of a centrally prescribed norm and the provision for a proportion, again centrally determined, of capital expenditure to be met out of revenue. Such instruments would enable the government to have the necessary control over expenditure for economic management purposes while not infringing the principle of local discretion for both policy and taxation.

LAYFIELD'S INSTITUTIONAL PROPOSALS

Whatever choice is made, the Committee state that there is a need for a new institution to improve the flow of information between the government and local authorities, to ensure that they understand each other's point of view and to monitor the relationship between them. One reason for this proposal is the Committee's feeling that while there are close links between government departments and the directors of local authority services reinforcing pressures to promote their development and therefore expenditure, there is no equivalent point within the government that supports those in local government who are concerned with the best use of resources. The Report recommends the establishment of a joint forum of ministers and local elected representatives chaired by a Treasury minister and with a powerful independent secretariat. If local authorities had the main responsibility for expenditure, the forum would provide the government with information about local authority plans and policies and would communicate to local authorities the government's views on the needs of the economy and priorities for individual services. If the government had the main responsibility, the forum would enable local authorities to be consulted and make their views known.

The value of the independent secretariat is that it would fill a gap in present arrangements. There is no one responsible for taking a disinterested view of what is going on in local government and between local authorities and central government. No one is responsible for looking at trends, seeking out the facts, analysing them and presenting them for discussion. The Director and the staff of the secretariat, being independent of both central and local government, would be able to take an impartial view of events, to help remove differences of interpretation of the situation which can at present cause friction, to assist those both inside and outside local government to reach a better appreciation of developments, to warn of dangerous problems looming ahead, and to ensure more realistic estimates of the cost of introducing new legislation.

The Committee also make suggestions to strengthen the role of the audit service, which is mainly concerned to search out illegal expenditure. It should interpret its role widely and investigate waste, extravagance, inefficient financial administration and poor value for money. The Committee suggest that the audit service should be made completely independent of both central government and local authorities, and have at its head an independent official of a similar high status as the Comptroller and Auditor General who is responsible for auditing the accounts of government departments. He would assign auditors to local authorities, instead of leaving the choice to them, and he should make regular reports on issues of general interest or public concern relating to more than one authority. These reports should focus on comparisons between methods employed by local authorities and results achieved. And he should submit reports to a specially constituted institution, perhaps a committee of the House of Commons, or the new joint forum or a body composed mainly of representatives from local government. This external audit would assist local accountability, since its objective and constructive advice, based on surveys of many local authorities, would make local decision makers, both councillors and voters, more knowledgeable and aware about what was going on inside their local authority. Such an audit service would promote, and not detract from, local responsibility.

On the more strictly financial aspects, the Committee advocates that local authorities shoul· continue to be able to finance capital expenditure from borrowing, and urges that there should be a development of new accounting procedures to identify the full cost of using their capital assets.

On rating, the Committee considered that rates, as a tax on immovable property, were an appropriate tax for local government. Rates are truly local in nature and produce a large and predictable yield. Based on the location of property, they are particularly suitable to be a local tax and they are perceptible and promote accountability. If rating were abolished, the yield of other taxes would have to be increased by £4,000 million. Many of the criticisms often made against rates have been found to be unjustified, for instance the allegation that they are a regressive tax, that is, that they take a bigger share of lower than of higher incomes. Research by the Committee has shown that for households with incomes up to £40 a week rates are progressive, in that the average proportion of income taken by rates increases with income. For households with incomes of £40 to £60 a week rates are roughly proportional to income, and at higher levels rate payments still increase with income but take a decreasing share as income increases. The progressiveness of rates at the lowest income levels arises from the operation of rate rebates and rate payments through supplementary benefits. The regressiveness of rating at the higher levels of income needs to be seen in relation to the progressiveness of income tax at those levels. This point illustrates an important theme that is often neglected. One tax should not be considered in isolation from the total taxation system. It is not necessary for a single tax to have all the desirable characteristics of the total system, but it should not have undesirable characteristics that cannot be corrected or offset elsewhere in the system of taxation or benefits.

The Layfield Committee did not, however, recommend that rating should continue unchanged. It made a number of important proposals. At present rateable value is assessed on the basis of the rent at which property might reasonably be let in a free market. But one consequence of the housing policies of successive governments over many years is that a free market in rented housing is now practically non-existent. The absence of an adequate volume of open market rents makes it impossible to maintain the present basis of valuation for rating. So the Committee concluded that the rating system in the future must be on the basis of capital value for domestic property, that is, the price a property would realise if sold on the open market. Capital value is more comprehensible than rental value; there is more evidence about it and it is now the best measure available of the benefit people derive from the occupation of their houses. In the future, also, regular and frequent revaluations are essential. In the past the postponements of revaluations damaged the rating system. With capital valuation, because of the volatility of the prices of houses and flats, it will be crucial to have frequent revaluations. A maximum period between valuations of five years is suggested, but it is hoped that it could be reduced eventually to three.

Non-domestic rating, the Committee suggested, could continue on a rental basis, but with the introduction of capital values for domestic property the government would need to apply a divisor to them so as to create a common relationship with non-domestic properties. The Committee also saw no grounds for some present exemptions from rates, notably agricultural land and building, and although it was not able to identify any clear principle to justify the favourable treatment of charities, it did not recommend the abolition of their relief from rates, largely because it felt that an outcry would be provoked from the charity lobbies that would kill what was after all not one of the central recommendations.

THE SIGNIFICANCE OF LAYFIELD

The Layfield Report contains many other important proposals on a wide range of financial matters. It also contains an analysis of a variety of other suggestions made to the Committee but which in the end the Committee rejected, for instance, for other new local taxes, for transferring the financial responsibility for some services to the centre, for writing off existing loan debt or for extending capital grants. It points out where further work is needed, for instance, a review of policy and practice in charging for local services, studies to develop output measures for services and research to produce indicators of need. The main Report and the ten companion volumes of evidence and research are a treasure-chest of ideas and information. The Layfield Committee will stimulate a major debate; it has provided the information that different protagonists can draw on, and could set in motion a considerable number of research projects. But the important issue is how the government would react.

The Layfield Report presented a challenge to the government to decide whether to go for the central or the local model of responsibility for expenditure and for the taxation to finance it. To many, the government would try to evade the issue; it would talk about partnership and collaboration, about sharing responsibility, and would try to discover a halfway house. The Layfield Committee provided no intellectual justification for a compromise: if the local responsibility model was not to be adopted, then the government should be explicitly responsible, and should not continue to fix policy and at the same time try to shuffle responsibility for expenditure onto local government. The main message of the Layfield Committee was that responsibility should be clarified. The present crisis in local government finance arose because responsibilities were blurred. The present confusion should not be perpetuated.

As predicted by many the government's response to the Layfield Report in *Local Government Finance* (Cmnd 6813, London: HMSO, May 1977) was to reject the argument that a choice had to be made between more explicit central or more explicit local responsibility. It urged the importance of seeking a middle way through partnership. It denied that a large central grant undermined local discretion over expenditure. As long as the grant was of a block and general form local authorities possessed the freedom to decide their expenditure priorities. Therefore, it saw no need to introduce a local income tax as a substitute for part of grant. Local income tax was also rejected as too expensive and requiring too many additional civil servants. The government affirmed its faith in rating as the sole local tax, and accepted Layfield's advice that assessment should be based on capital not rental values. Spokesmen of local government were generally in favour of this response.

They were not, however, pleased with some other government proposals which they found essentially centralising. The government advocated reforming the Rate Support Grant by means of a new unitary grant involving central judgements of what each local authority would need to spend to provide a standard level of service. It advised more specific, service, grants; central control over capital expenditure, not just over borrowing; and an extension of the national audit service into more comparative and value-for-money investigations. Discussion on these proposals continued into 1978, mainly through a new institution established in 1975, the Consultative Council on Local Government Finance, a weak version of the forum suggested by Layfield. It provides opportunities for central and local government to discuss common problems, but it lacks the independent secretariat that Layfield recommended.

The present financial arrangements are still substantially those in operation during the crisis years of 1974–6. The government was able to control local expenditure then through exhortation, reduction of grant and the introduction of cash limits. In any future crisis the likelihood is that the government will take more direct control. The choice would have been made for more central responsibility. But at the moment the dominant value is partnership, in which the centre is very much the senior partner. More local responsibility looks a lost cause.

Chapter XI

LOCAL GOVERNMENT FINANCE IN FRANCE

Public finance in France has precise boundaries and is quite uniform. The same cannot be said of local financial institutions, whose field of action has grown perceptibly over the years whilst its boundaries have remained less clear cut and its character hybrid. Under the classic scheme of institutions in the nineteenth century, the only real public infra-State bodies were the commune and the *département*.

From being a simple administrative area at the beginning of the century, the commune also acquired, in a few decades, the status of a local, decentralised body. As a result of its deep-seated tradition as a parish of the monarchical regime, and because decentralisation is more advanced there than elsewhere (all the organs – executive and assembly – are elected), the commune appears to be the most authentic and the most stable local community. Since the municipal law of 5 April 1884, still in force but integrated into the communal *Code d'Administration* (decree of 22 May 1957), several reforms of an administrative and financial nature have taken place (statute of 5 January 1959, law of 31 December 1970, law of 16 July 1971, law of 31 December 1973) which, without altering the basic principles of the organisation and functioning of these communities, have responded, through adaptation and accommodation, to the changing needs of society.

The *département* constitutes the second local public body of the classic type. Yet the historical circumstances surrounding its creation (post-revolutionary geographical partitioning, the very centralised administration of the Napoleonic era) undoubtedly stunted the development of departmental decentralisation, which was recognised by law on 10 August 1871, but which never achieved any real significance either on the administrative or financial plane.

Now, since the end of the nineteenth century, the commune and the *département* can no longer be considered as the sole local public bodies in France. Under the panoply of public establishments (*établissements publics*) a new category has in fact appeared, half-way between the classic public establishments and the decentralised authorities: the local public establishments. Born of the inadequacies of the traditional authorities and the demands of modern economic life, these particular public establishments do not threaten the traditional local administration but aid the rationalisation of administrative, technical, economic or financial management in centres of local interest which are generally wider than those which existed previously. The groups of communes with a single purpose (law of 22 March 1890) and those with multiple purposes (statute of 5 January 1959) have been joined by the districts (1959) and the urban communities (law of 31 December 1966).[1] An important milestone in the development of decentralisation has been passed recently with the transformation, by law, of the region from an administrative area to a public establishment (law of 5 July 1972).[2] The problems of finance in the region are far more specific than in the other newly created local establishments. The region possesses not only its own budget but also special resources (tax on driving licences, additional taxes on registration . . .) which broaden the spectrum of local financing.

The financial institutions of local public bodies are strongly marked by the principles of budgetary orthodoxy established for State financing in the first half of the nineteenth century.

The concept of decentralisation and the need for a link with the State system have, however, given rise to a certain number of peculiarities which endow the financial system of local public bodies with a hybrid nature.

In certain respects this system is the reproduction and the transposition of the State system of finance. Traditional budgetary principles are applied in the same way as in the drawing up or adoption of the State Budget. Likewise, the old principles of public accounting, inherited from the decree of 31 May 1862 and restated in that of 29 December 1962, are carried out in the same way at the local level as at State level. The principle of separation of independent auditors from the accountants themselves, in particular demonstrates the existence of two phases: administration and accounting. Moreover, recent transformations in local finance which have given it a new and somewhat original appearance, cannot conceal the essential legal fact that local taxes, of whatever nature, are part of the resources mentioned in Article 34 of the Constitution of 1958. This Article states that: '. . . the law determines the rules governing: – the basis, the extent and the method of gathering taxes of all types . . .'. The outcome of this statement, reinforced by strict legal provisions, is that the legislator, the only authority competent to create State taxes and dues, is also the only authority empowered to decide on the creation of fiscal resources for the local authorities. This competence, unique to Parliament, bestows an unquestionable harmony at the procedural level of the State finance system and that of the secondary communities.

Although it closely resembles the State system of public finance, local fiscal law is not merely a faithful reproduction of it.

In fact, there exists a certain number of features which are unique to local finance. A rapid examination of budgetary procedure reveals, for example, that apart from the two phases of preparation and authorisation of the budget, there exists the phase of approval which responds to the needs of administrative control (very strict at the end of the last century but toned down by the law of 31 December 1970). The accounting phase also represents certain peculiarities due especially to the power of withdrawal of the right of levy from the administrator (the executive authority of the local community) when the accountant feels he has sufficient reason to suspend or refuse payment of expenditure (whilst this right of requisition – important in practice – is given to those State officials who execute the State Budget). Finally, the regulating power of the local authorities has, in fiscal matters, special consequences not only for the fixing of the rate of taxation but also for the use of fiscal resources (the effective collection of optional taxes or, conversely, the waiving of a tax established by law).

We will not embark upon an analysis of the financial systems of the various local public bodies which, in any case, are to a large extent analogous. Rather we shall study the financial system of the commune, both because it serves as a model for other local public bodies and because the crisis in communal financing furnishes an acute example of the financial problems of infra-State communities.

THE LOGIC OF LOCAL FINANCE

Decentralisation is not only felt to be an increasingly pressing need at present, but is also a legal reality with a constitutional basis in France. Paragraph XI, Article 72 of the 1958 Constitution states that: 'the decentralised territorial authorities are freely administered by elected councils . . .'. The financial implications of granting autonomy are not only evident in the implementation of the budgetary rules but also in the renovation of the local fiscal system.

The Budgetary rules
The institutional autonomy possible in a decentralised country is clearly difficult in a more centralised State. However, in budgetary matters a certain balance has always been achieved between State authority and local bodies. Recent moves towards decentralisation have tended to increase the competence of the secondary communities. But, in any case, the rules governing the local budget are fixed according to the extent to which the actors, who are basically the authorities of the local public bodies, are subject to State control.

The actors. The administrators (executive and deliberative) of the local authorities intervene in the budgetary process whilst respecting principles of the division of labour which traditionally prevail at the level of the State budgetary authorities for the planning and adoption of the national budget. It would seem, however, that the roles of the actors at the local level are more evenly divided than at the national level. Whilst a multiplicity of organs is involved on the preparation of the Budget (government, Prime Minister, Minister of Finance, other ministers . . .), at the local level only the executive authority of the public body in question is involved (mayor, prefect, director of the public establishment). The roles are better balanced and, at the local level, there is no infringement of domain comparable to that which exists in State budgetary law which favours the authorities entrusted with elaborating the Budget, and which often takes the form of a real acquisition of power on the part of the executive over the adoption of the Budget. The intervention of the local budgetary authorities takes place under clearer and simpler conditions than at the State level. Whilst one may observe a certain increase in flexibility compared with the classical rules of budgetary unity both at local and at national level and establish parallels, if not close similarities, between the technique of supplementary budgets and laws used for budgetary rectification, it would seem that local budgetary law pays more respect to the original spirit of the principles of budgetary unity than does the State financial system. Indeed, whilst in the course of time the documents and schedules submitted to Parliament have multiplied so alarmingly that the nation's representatives find it increasingly difficult to control them, the communal budget has remained a single document, easy for the local deliberative assembly to examine, and whose volume has, moreover, been reduced following the reform of communal accounting. The draft budget of a commune, which in former times consisted of at least twenty pages, nowadays contains between four pages (for the small communes) and eight pages (for the larger ones).

The adoption of the communal budget takes place in conditions which respect fairly well the freedom of action which the essential actors, the municipal councils, should enjoy. At the local level budgets are broken down into sub-categories and this is much more flexible than at the national level where, since 1958, the technique of the package deal (Article 44 of the Constitution) has been used widely and frequently for the approval of the Finance Bill. The notion of a fixed sitting was abolished by the law of 31 December 1970. Finally, the local assemblies, unlike Parliament (Articles 40–47 of the Constitution), have considerable power to modify the budget proposal which is submitted to them and even to oblige the mayor to present another proposal.

The Sovereign State. Autonomy is not synonymous with independence. Traditionally, the decentralised public bodies are placed under the control of the State in matters concerning both administrative management and budgetary operations.

Historically, the control effected by the power of tutelage (*tutelle*) has been quite strict, both from a point of view of level such as decrees and ministerial orders, and of wide application of its powers of intervention. But, since the Poincaré decrees of 1926, a broad movement towards decentralisation has taken place and has been confirmed recently by the law of 31 December 1970. The effects of this legislative measure are important. In the previous system the approval of the overseeing authority was necessary for budgets in communes of fewer than 9,000 inhabitants when the interest on local debt reached 10 per cent of the average tax receipts and when the level of expenditure exceeded 30,000 centimes. These factors combined made approval of all but about 100 out of around 38,000 communal budgets necessary. Now, as a result of the 1970 law, budgets are executed automatically by law fifteen days after their deposition at the prefecture or the sub-prefecture.

Nevertheless, for a variety of reasons, the State has not renounced all responsibility for supervising the financial activities of the local communities: the current importance of local community expenditure, the national and local character of much communal expenditure, and finally the natural unity which exists between the finances of infra-State bodies and those of the State itself. A minimum of rules have been set down and their observance is controlled and confirmed by the overseeing authority which is gradually assuming the role of arbiter. Here lies the significance of the rule concerning the balanced budget in local affairs. This principle, which contrasts with the possibility of incurring deficit which the State can exercise freely in its financial management, is strict in its interpretation and marks the limits of the budgetary independence of decentralised bodies. Dating from a statute of 5 January 1959, this balance must be realistic and it must also be both a balance of the general account and a balance of each of the sub-sections of expenditure. The overseeing authority intervenes obligatorily when the communal budget has not been balanced.

The arbitrating function of the State which no longer intervenes actively and permanently in the local budgetary process, is manifested essentially in two ways: first, in the form of recommendations and advice addressed annually to the competent authorities of the communes in the form of circulars and directives to aid the drawing up of local budgets: secondly, through sanctions (such as the annulment of illegal measures on the compulsory registration of

local statutory expenditure) in order to counteract exceptionally
serious irregularities.

The renovation of local finances

A historical study of local finance in France might raise doubts as
to its potential for adaptation. The most topical example is furnished
by direct taxation. From the end of the eighteenth century up to
the Caillaux reform of progressive income tax in 1914–17, local
direct taxation, like direct State taxation, was raised on the *quatre
vieilles* levies (taxes on built-up and non-built-up land, taxes on
buildings, and the *patente* (tax paid by businessmen and merchants).
The Caillaux reform suppressed the old State taxes and replaced
them with a system which was both more personalised and more
lucrative, even though a theoretical legal link was maintained
artifically between the taxes of the secondary communities and the
old bases of French taxation (the 'real' base of taxation became
the 'fictitious' base). The obsolescence and the dependence of the
local system of finance could be seen in the invention of additional
taxes (the so-called *centimes additionnels*).

The weaknesses and defects of such a system, so often criticised,
finally led the public authorities to update the local taxation system.
In this context two features are outstanding: the modernisation of
the traditional fiscal system and the appearance of a new type of
resource: local urban taxation.

Modernisation of the traditional fiscal system. Recognised to be both
archaic and iniquitous, local taxation has become the subject, in the
last few years, of important attempts at modernisation which have
affected both direct and indirect taxation in different ways.

The reform of direct taxation has its basis in the statute of 7
January 1959. Subsequently the size and complexity of the general
census for evaluation (about 18 million private dwellings and professional premises, 2·5 million commercial premises and 300,000
industrial establishments) explains the amount of time needed to
accomplish the reform (laws of 2 February 1968 to 31 December
1973, law of 29 July 1975). The law of 31 December 1973, which
is the most important of them, established three new local taxes:
a real estate tax on constructed and non-constructed property, and
inhabited house duty. These taxes, freed from the contrivance of the
'fictitious' base, are established uniformly on the rateable value of
the corresponding buildings (the reference value dates from 1
January 1970) on the basis of the 'real' (presumably market) price of
letting which exists under normal circumstances. A mechanism for
updating rateable value should enable a continual reassessment. The
law of 1973 is also innovative in its reference to the introduction

of personal taxes. In fact, until recently, and in contrast to the evolution of direct taxation at State level, local taxes were only marginally personalised, as they remained dependent on the old Revolutionary conceptions of taxation. Now family allowances and rent subsidies have been standardised in all communes. The law of 29 July 1975 has abolished the old tax paid by merchants and businessmen (*patente*), and has replaced it by the professional tax, the base of which is calculated on salaries paid or receipts collected as well as on the rateable value of the premises used.

The reform of local indirect taxation has been linked with the extension of Value Added Tax (TVA) to the retail trade by a law of 6 January 1966. Until then it was subject to a specific local tax. This new tax had, in the first instance, 85 per cent of its revenues raised from salaries, and after the end of this phase (December 1968) it was replaced by an equivalent payment on the part of the locality from the new taxation system (TVA).

The modernisation of local taxation did not only consist of a modification of existing taxes. Several taxes whose yield was more often than not below the cost of collecting it were abolished (tax on balconies, golf courses and pleasure grounds. Conversely the taxation system was enriched by a newcomer: the local tax on urbanisation.

The creation of a local urbanisation tax. Demographic growth (the population has increased by 25 per cent since the end of the Second World War) and the urban phenomenon (the French urban population increased from 24 million in 1954 to 36 million in 1968 and should reach 45 million by 1985) have necessitated the drawing up of urbanisation programmes and plans for land usage which shape the development of the cities for years to come. At the same time public bodies are to carry out public works programmes (highways, civil engineering programmes) in order to ensure the planned growth of towns. The real estate framework law of 30 December 1967 set up a local development tax to be levied by the commune which issues a construction permit. This tax is based on the value of the whole complex (plots and buildings authorised by the permit). It is a general tax, levied automatically at the normal rate of 1 per cent (it can, in exceptional circumstances, be levied at 3 or 5 per cent) in communes where the plan for land usage has been prescribed, unless the municipal council expressly waives this right.

More recently, the law of 31 December 1975, dealing with real estate policy and urban reform (completed by a decree of 29 May 1976), added a second important element to local urban financing. This is the fine imposed on over-construction (*plafond légal de densité*, or PLD). If a constructor oversteps a certain land-use coefficient he must pay the relevant commune a fine equal to the value of the land he would legally need to utilise to keep within the coefficient, although the effect of this fine is clearly limited by its being restricted to a small number of specific cases (for instance, open spaces, property acquisition destined for State housing).

Finally, it should be noted that the budgetary process and the tax system of the communal authorities have been considerably renovated over the last few years. Although it is changing, the local system of finance is still much criticised and much remains to be done. From 1896, and regularly since 1920, the government has conferred upon reform commissions the task of regulating the question of local finance. But it must be admitted that a problem still exists which will have an important effect on the future and content of decentralisation in France.

THE PROBLEM OF LOCAL FINANCE

The financial difficulties of the towns and rural communes are neither recent (just before the 1789 Revolution the local communities were overburdened with debts) nor peculiar to France, for they are in evidence in even the most prosperous countries (the recent catastrophic situation in New York furnishes an outstanding example of this).

However, this financial crisis takes on a particular significance in France with the demand for greater decentralisation and increased responsibility for secondary public bodies like towns, *départements* and regions. Moreover, there would seem to be additional obstacles to the harmonious functioning of local finance. These are linked to the costs and also to the methods of financing.

The burden of costs
The total expenditure of local public establishments and authorities is increasing more rapidly than that of the State. Whilst between 1967 and 1972 the Finance Bill indicated a 60 per cent increase in expenditure, that of secondary public bodies increased by 82 per cent over the same period.

The fragmentary nature of the communal system, one of the main features of French administrative organisation, contributes largely to the multiplicity of costs and the lack of co-ordination. Out of 37,708 communes, 30,831 have fewer than 1,000 inhabitants. Even more important, 11,000 communes have fewer than 200 inhabitants, the threshold below which a commune would seem not to be financially viable. The situation in the towns, notably the larger ones, is not much better, as was made clear in a White Paper *Les Grandes Villes devant l'Avenir,* published in 1975 by the

Association des Maires des Grandes Villes de France. In twenty years, annual per capita expenditure has quadrupled (325 francs in 1954, 1,289 francs in 1974), whilst average investment costs per town have, in the same period, increased sixfold.

The financial difficulties stemming from expenditure are linked both to their increase and to the question of the sharing of costs between the State and the local authorities.

The development of expenditure. The reasons for increased local expenditure are numerous and inter-related in a modern society. They are due mainly to the demands of urbanisation and economic growth. The raising of the school-leaving age and the diversified growth of the education system have, for example, placed further burdens on the communes.

In other fields the implementation of modern development schemes, either sports facilities (stadiums, gymnasiums, swimming pools) or social services (nurseries, social centres, old people's homes), have had a similar effect on costs. The urbanisation phenomenon has created particular financial costs which will probably increase in the years to come: the creation of urbanisation agencies (law of 30 December 1967); the establishment of land reserves to counteract property speculation, the planning and upkeep of urban highways, the construction of car parks etc. Finally, one other essential area should be noted: the industrial and commercial activities of the local authorities, such as planning of industrial zones and financial concessions to investors. The seventh Plan, like the sixth, makes provision for extensive planning programmes on the part of the local authorities in order to accommodate population movements and the requirements of modernisation. The policy of budgetary orthodoxy which hindered or prevented the realisation of certain national investment programmes had no appreciable effect on local investment programmes which have made considerable progress in the last few years in comparison with similar State investments. In 1967 State capital expenditure and local capital expenditure were respectively 18 billion, 570 million francs and 16 billion, 840 million; in 1972 the situation was reversed: 23 billion, 980 million francs and 30 billion, 630 million. Moreover, it is clear that the growth of investment expenditure cannot be seen in isolation. Apart from autonomous and unavoidable expenses, the implementation of any 'induced' investment involves supplementary working capital. The growth of investment expenditure is thus the main component in the growth of the need for working capital (whether for a cultural centre or a set of traffic lights).

Over and above this natural and automatic increase in local obligations, there are other factors which come into play. Certain economic analysts are of the opinion that the management of the communes, above all the larger ones, has become comparable to the running of a large business, principally because of the diversity and importance of their activities. This comparison may be true in broad terms but does not apply to the management aspect. Indeed, as the Court of Accounts has emphasised, '. . . with the exception of a few large towns, few communes, given the current state of their administrative structure, can claim to have at their disposal adequate facilities for in-depth economic and financial analysis which would aid the correct orientation of their management . . .'.[3] It can be assumed in some cases that inertia, but more often than not a lack of systematic approach, is responsible for the burdensome administrative structure of a large number of communes (due both to the absence of adequate administrative provision and the tendency to rely, too often, on companies not controlled by the local authority). In any case, one must make allowance for the fact that, as the communes are not able to introduce long-term planning into their budgets, they are not encouraged to plan their public works programmes far ahead.

The distribution of expenditure. The local communities are as dissatisfied with the distribution of expenditure between the State and themselves, as they are saddled with the burden placed on them by the increased expenditure. The municipal authorities consider that the State is conferring more and more financial obligations upon them, although many of the services involved are as important at the national as at the local level (e.g. para-educational facilities). Furthermore, the methods by which these burdens are placed upon them are often insidious, in so far as a public works programme is only begun on condition that the local authority fulfils its financial obligations. Such is the case with advances for financing telecommunications projects, financial assistance for the construction of police stations, post offices etc.

The local authorities have also reproached the State with their having to pay value added tax (TVA) (at a rate of 17·6 per cent since 1967) on their public works programmes. This increases costs and reduces the benefits obtained from State aid. In reply to these accusations, civil servants from the Ministries of Finance and Interior state that for some years the State has been involved in 'nationalising' certain local expenditure. Since 1963, for example, it has taken over responsibility for the construction of secondary schools. The towns have been relieved of the costs of the police force, as this has been taken over by the State in communes of more than 10,000 inhabitants. They add that in 1975 a proposal to refund value added tax was made and that this should involve repayments in the order of 5 billion francs by 1979.

The search for a solution, or the possibility of arbitration, on the question of mandatory expenditure would appear to be difficult. It is not possible to establish a permanent distribution of costs, as this would inevitably be to the disadvantage of the local authorities, exposed to an ever-increasing expenditure, as the local representatives attempted to respond to the needs of their constituents. It would be more realistic to establish a policy of periodic review of balance of expenditure between State and commune. This would, of course, need to be flexible, for otherwise it would weaken still further the already dissipated powers of initiative of the local authorities and threaten the move towards decentralisation. Such a policy seems to be the aim of the law of 30 December 1975. This provides for the quinquennial review of the distribution of expenditure between the State and the local communities in certain specific areas: social services and the method of subsidising educational building programmes.

The ineffectiveness of the local system of financing is due not only to the increasing costs but also to the difficulties of financing local expenditure.

The difficulties of financing

Theoretically, the existence of a local tax system, independent of the State, should provide the technical solution for the financing problems of the local authorities. In fact, this income from local taxation is totally inadequate to cover ever-increasing and diversified expenditure. In particular, it is necessary to have recourse to external financing for investment operations. But hand in hand with the inadequacies of the internal system of financing goes the inconvenience of financing from outside the community.

The inadequacies of internal financing. Local taxation has the somewhat remarkable feature of giving satisfaction neither to the local committees because of its inadequate yield, nor to the taxpayer because of the heavy burden which it places upon him. At present the State appropriates 83 per cent of the total tax paid in France, which renders the proportion taken by the local community somewhat insignificant. Moreover, if one considers the income from direct taxation, then between 1970 and 1974 State revenue rose on average by 12 per cent per annum, whilst local authority revenue only rose by 3 per cent and this in spite of the fact that per capita taxation increased considerably at local level; notably in the large towns where per capita revenue increased from 24·85 francs in 1954 to 372·57 in 1974.

The basic reason for this phenomenon stems from the intrinsic nature of the local system of direct taxation. Even after the reform effected by the law of 31 December 1973, property remained the basis of local taxation, and the system has not changed fundamentally since the establishment of the *quatre vieilles* taxes. This system is diametrically opposed to that of the State taxation system which attempts both to make taxation more lucrative by linking it directly to economic activity, such as an increase in the number of people in taxable categories and creation of a company tax, and to link it closer to income. By contrast, local direct taxation has a fairly narrow basis, independent of economic activity, and it utilises techniques which may be classified as lump-sum payments.

There are two main reasons why it is extremely difficult to find a satisfactory method of internal local financing: first, because there is no local means of revenue which could be used as a basis for evaluating tax, and secondly, because the State does not seem prepared to part with a proportion of its revenue from taxation to the local authorities. Different solutions have been proposed in the course of the last few years: a new classification of State and local taxes, the updating of receipts to harmonise with national growth, either by the transfer of a fixed proportion of the State's resources or by the adoption by the local authorities of receipts linked to sales or company profits. Although it is true that no decision has been taken to improve the existing system, it would seem that the best method would be a serious and lasting reform of local taxation which is adapted to the needs of the communes and the abilities of the citizens to contribute.

The inconveniences of external financing. Both because of the inadequacies of the local taxation system and because of the spectacular development of investment expenditure, the local authorities are obliged to have recourse to outside methods of funding. In 1972 the local receipts from investment were constituted as follows: 61·33 per cent from borrowing and 15·60 per cent from subsidies. These two methods of financing which allow a certain number of investments nevertheless present some inconveniences for the local authorities.

It is well known, for example, that the mechanism of dues payable on a subsidy hardly renders this either a gratuitous or a disinterested aid. The control of the State is evident first in the range of subsidy rates (the decree of 10 March 1972 classed the various development projects which might be subsidised and fixed subsidy rates from 10 to 85 per cent according to the type of investment which might be one of five categories); furthermore, a project can only qualify

for subsidy if it has already been included in an investment programme related to nationally organised land-use planning. Finally,
the subsidy is only granted for projects which conform to certain
technical characteristics. In order to avoid the difficulties presented
by specific subsidies, a global subsidy, made available to the local
authorities, was instituted in 1972. But since this date the sum
available has either been blocked or has been so derisory that its
effects have been nil. Besides, generally speaking, the financial aid
granted by the State in the form of subsidies has formed an ever-
decreasing percentage of the local authorities' receipts from investment (27·9 per cent in 1962, 21·2 per cent in 1968 and 15·6 per
cent in 1972). These authorities are, therefore, forced to rely on
borrowing of disturbing and often spectacular proportions: in real
francs the total sum of annual repayments per capita, in large
towns, has multiplied by eighteen in twenty years (rising from 11·5
francs in 1954 to 193·6 francs in 1974). The borrowing system of the
local authorities is rendered relatively complex by the existence of a
'subsidy-borrowing' link: subsidisable projects benefit from most
favourable loan terms from public and para-public funds (notably
those provided by the *Caisse des Dépôts et Consignations*). The
general recourse to borrowing has grave consequences: as a result
of this outside financing the local authorities' control of investment
becomes somewhat theoretical. On the other hand, and most
important of all, for the last twelve years or so the local authorities
have had to use an ever-increasing percentage of their new loans
to repay old debts. A study made by the financial section of the
Economic and Social Council, published in 1973 and entitled *The
possibilities offered to the local authorities of external financing,*
states that '. . . almost three-quarters of the new loans negotiated
by the local authorities were devoted to the repayment of previous
loans . . .'. It is to be hoped that the local debt will not become too
great in years to come, for this would certainly have a lasting effect
on the local system of finance.

Even if it is clear that there are still problems to be solved and
contradictions to overcome in the local system of finance, it is
nevertheless true that a number of interesting initiatives have
recently been taken. In the traditional scheme of French administrative organisation the relations between the State and the local
authorities were regulated exclusively according to the mechanism
of 'tutelage' which ensured an extremely strict separation between
the areas of intervention of these authorities and an intrinsic
inequality between public bodies. Since 1970 a new type of relationship between the State and the local authorities, based on co-
operation in the planning of investment operations and the methods
of financing, seems to have improved upon traditional procedures.

The most typical example of this evolution is the 'contract'. Since the decree of 23 December 1970 planning contracts regulate relations between the State and the urban communities,[4] and to these have been added development contracts for medium-sized towns and, since 1976, contracts which play an important part in the planning and development of rural areas.

This normalisation of financial relations between the State and the local authorities, which takes into account the natural solidarity which exists between the communities as regards development and economic planning, was completed by the creation, in 1975, of a 'Fonds d'Equipement' for the local authorities. Thus a new stage has been reached in the search for a solution to the financial problems of the infra-State authorities.

NOTES

1 See the chapter by Thoenig.
2 See the chapter by Croisat and Souchon.
3 Report of the Cour des Comptes, 1971, pp. 87*ff*.
4 See above, pp. 84, 87.

SHORT BIBLIOGRAPHY

1. *Books*

Bauchard, D. and Guerrier, P., *Economie financière des collectivités locales* (Paris: Colin, 1972).
Cathelineau, J.. *Le Contrôle des finances communales en France* (Paris: Librairie générale de droit et de jurisprudence, 1963).
Savigny, J. de, *L'Etat contre les communes* (Paris: Le Seuil, 1971).

2. *Documents*

Livre blanc sur les finances locales: *Les Grandes Villes devant l'Avenir*, 1975, p. 115.
Les Comptes des collectivités locales et établissements publics locaux jusqu'en 1972 (Service de l'Information du Ministère de l'Economie et des Finances, July 1975).
Reports of the Cour des Comptes.
Etude présentée par la Section des Finances du Conseil Economique et Social: *Les Possibilités offertes aux collectivités locales en matière de ressources financières externes*, Avis et Rapports du Conseil Economique et Social, JP, 31 July 1973, pp. 528–81.

━━━◆━━━

Chapter XII

THE BRITISH DEBATE ON
REGIONALISM AND DEVOLUTION

It is a curious fact that the debate on regionalism and devolution, now nearly a hundred years old, burst upon the British political scene in dramatic fashion in early 1974, and within a few months produced a new pattern of politics in Westminster, after being on the fringe of public argument since the end of the First World War. It has involved the rise to prominence of previously obscure political parties, splits within the major parties and brought about a period of weak majority or minority government. From very humble beginnings in by-election and local election gains in 1967–9 by the nationalist parties it has turned out to be a more significant political issue than that of membership of the European Economic Community. The author, writing in 1978, believes that it is impossible to predict whether the present phase of multi-parties in Parliament will become a permanent feature of the British political system; that which the United Kingdom electorate has created it can as easily destroy.

This essay looks first at the background to the present debate – in terms of an analysis of 'regionalism', 'devolution', 'nationalism' – then at the institutional arrangements that have evolved in Scotland and Wales in the twentieth century, and finally at the various current proposals that are the subject of argument at the national level.

'REGIONALISM' AND 'DEVOLUTION'

In Britain the debate over regionalism has been one about an alleged missing dimension of government[1] – a level of public administration in size of area between the centre and the localities – and the demands for devolution are in part strands within this debate. Systems of government typically operate through a complicated *system* of decentralisation, the elements of which are administrative and political bodies of many different kinds;[2] as developed structures mix up these in characteristic ways, assigning distinct roles and different 'weights' to each,[3] there is considerable scope for schemes of administrative and political reform. *Regionalism* is the demand that this perceived 'gap' be filled by governmental institutions created specifically for this purpose.

The demand for *devolution* is a demand that a special type of region be created. It is distinguished from other forms of regional government by the direct election, rather than appointment, of the regional authority, and by the grant of a wide range of public services, which may be changed as public policy dictates.[4] Some examples of devolution occur within a *special status areas* policy – whereby institutions are established specifically for one area and adapted to its needs – whilst others are created within a policy of *uniformity* – whereby the total area of the country is divided into regions of the same legal status.[5]

The debate over regionalism in the United Kingdom began with the home rule controversy in the last decades of the nineteenth century, but with the partition of Ireland and the independence of its southern part after 1920 the basis for demanding new dimensions of government changed. Political demands for greater self-government for the constituent 'nations' of the United Kingdom tended to be replaced by demands for other forms of regionalism, justified in terms of administrative efficiency and effectiveness in service provision.[6] New dimensions of government were proposed as a means of local government reform, as a means of reducing congestion in the centre and as ways of improving specific public services.

Administrative regionalism has had a curious history in the twentieth century. At the level of ideas regionalism has waxed and waned several times in both popular and academic discussion of governmental reform,[7] whilst in practice there has been an erratic growth of regional administrative institutions since 1918. Occasionally there have been regressions, as in the early 1950s, but by the mid-1970s a regional level was well established in many central departmental organisations, in gas, electricity and water supply industries and in the personal health services, and in a related way, the size of local authorities had been increased.

Though most of the elaborate proposals for regional government include an authority that is elected, directly or indirectly, their supporting arguments must be clearly distinguished from the political demands for home rule, devolution and separation. The basic reasoning behind administrative regionalism is that certain services can only be effectively provided at a regional level; if they are the responsibility of the centre, they must be removed from London, if of local government, then local authorities must be increased in size, if all areas are unsuitable, new ones must be created. Town planners have been particularly attracted to the latter, though their regions generally do not resemble the provinces favoured by economists for economic development. Though nationalists and other thorough-going devolutionists often deploy service provision arguments, the latter are for the most part hostile to home rule. Reasons of technical efficiency sometimes indicate that the Principality and the Kingdom are too small and sometimes too large; in many cases both ought to be dismembered. For instance, from the point of view of economic planning North Wales ought not to be linked with the South but with Merseyside, and a new Severnside ought to join together both sides of the national border. The present debate over devolution must be approached through an analysis of nationalism, rather than of administrative efficiency.

NATIONALISM

Nationalism as a force in United Kingdom politics has also waxed and waned in an irregular fashion. There was a brief flourish of both Welsh and Scottish nationalism in the 1880s and 1890s, when radical schemes of devolution for the whole archipelago were popular, and home rule continued to attract some support until the mid-1920s,[8] but once Ireland was removed from the Great Britain political arena, the nationalist movements became part of the British political fringe. They remained barely above the threshold of political visibility, only occasionally receiving a brief accession of support which made central politicians take notice of them for a period. All this changed in 1966. Both nationalist parties grew in popular support more substantially than for several decades; when this began to recede in 1969 and 1970 they did not fall back to previous subliminal levels and in 1973 began to increase in political strength again. Both Plaid Cymru and the Scottish National Party are now established as important forces in the British political system. But what sort of phenomena are they?

Both nationalist movements belong to the general category of 'unsatisfied' or 'emergent' nationalisms – a category now well represented throughout the world, as most countries have at least one region whose people claim to be sufficiently distinct to deserve their own special political institutions.[9] Each consists of at least three wings – a cultural movement, a political party and a violent sector. The cultural and violent wings are more in evidence in Wales, but the Scottish National Party has been considerably more success-ful in organisational and electoral terms.[10]

Within the United Kingdom context Wales and Scotland are peripheral areas, or rather groups of peripheral areas, suffering social and economic disadvantages compared with many parts of England. Economically they are areas of high unemployment, low income and wealth per head, particularly vulnerable to the 'downs' of the trade cycle. Socially they suffer from an inferior housing stock, lack of opportunities for use of educational attainments and from a declining public transport system. Their marginal nature used to be reflected in high emigration rates, which also had severe social effects.

There are, however, some important differences between them. Wales has a language still spoken by over 20 per cent of its population, whilst Gaelic is claimed by only $1\frac{1}{2}$ per cent of the Scottish people, most living in the Highlands and Islands. Scottish culture is much more a variant of English than is Welsh.[11] However, Scotland has its own traditional institutions which date from pre-union times – in education, the law and religion – and its own political institutions in Whitehall and Westminster[12] which, though not so old, are now well established. Comparable institutions in Wales either do not exist – there are no special religious and legal institutions – or are imitations of the Scottish ones, in some cases dating from the last quarter of the nineteenth century but in the case of the Welsh Office only created in 1964.[13]

More significantly, though each has a border with England that has remained unchanged for centuries, they have been treated differently by socio-geographical developments. The Scottish–English border runs through relatively unpopulated country and any lack of homogeneity in the Kingdom derives from internal divisons. The Welsh–English border is socially meaningless because many parts of Wales have much closer connections with a part of England than they do with the rest of Wales. The feasibility of separation is thus less for Wales.

THE SECRETARY-OF-STATE SYSTEM

The twentieth century has seen the growth of recognition of the special problems of the two 'national' areas in Great Britain, which has only indirectly been connected with nationalist sentiment, and the concrete manifestation of this recognition has been the creation of the *secretary-of-state system*, first in Scotland and then in Wales. In formal terms the debate over devolution is an argument whether elected assemblies with a wide range of functions and considerable autonomy would be more adequate in dealing with the problems of the two countries than the present system.

The *secretary-of-state system* is created by the use of the principle of *specialisation by place* within the central government, including both Whitehall and Westminster. By the 1970s it was possible to describe in simple terms the basic organisational model of which the Scottish and Welsh Offices are interpretations. This is done by the diagram on page 209 and the examples are set out systematically in Table 12.2, without the complications of the differing legislative arrangements.[14]

The basic point to note about the institutions described in this table is that the system is more than the person of the secretary of state. It consists of a *political directorate,* headed by a cabinet minister aided by various junior ministers, a *central liaison staff* in London, a *set of departments* located in the capital city of the area, and a *set of satellite bodies* with varying degrees of attachment to one of the above three. The political directorate is an integral part of the United Kingdom executive, the central office part of the highest levels of the civil service, the departments are the service-providing agencies and the satellites play the sort of roles that non-departmental organisations generally play in the British system.[15]

The difficulty with the debate about devolution is that the advantages of the secretary-of-state system from the point of view of the centre are its disadvantages from the point of view of the nationalists. It gives the area a direct voice at the centre of the United Kingdom political system, by guaranteeing the presence of a 'representative' in the cabinet and enabling its political leadership to play a part in the cabinet committee system, thus bringing Welsh and Scottish considerations to bear on decisions at the most important stages. The price of influence in the centre is, however, subordination to all the forces of executive domination of British government, to party discipline and to the doctrine of collective responsibility. It provides for greater territorial integration as the affairs of the areas are always considered in conjunction with the problems of the whole State, but it gives rise to demands for uniformity of policy, legislation and administration which reduce the capacity of the system to adapt to their special features. It provides automatically through the consolidated fund for the diversion of public money from England to the areas, so that public expenditure per head is markedly higher, but in doing so determines the composition and level of public activities with little reference to national sentiment.

There are other problems, such as those of modifying legislative procedures and arrangements, recruiting politicians to the directorates and civil servants to the departments, and dividing services into groups with different geographical scope, but these are in effect consequences of a more fundamental point. The system provides for responsiveness of the area government to the centre, but there is virtually no accountability to opinion in the areas themselves. In all systems of decentralisation there is a tension between the two types of public accountability; the secretary-of-state system tilts the balance very much in favour of central control and influence and against local control of political leaders.[16]

It is not hard to see why this pattern of treatment for special problem areas recommends itself to the centre, for it guarantees that the area's own institutions will not cause too much trouble by deviating too far from central policy. Centralist politicians and civil servants can rightly point to many of the specific gains that Scotland and Wales have made under existing arrangements, but equally the nationalists and devolutionists can point to the lack of public accountability *within* the regions themselves. Though the present system is usually criticised in terms of specific policy and administrative 'failures' it is better to regard *accountability* not as something which improves or damages individual named decisions but as a general property of all governmental actions. A decision may be entirely laudable in itself but it will always lack something if it is not made *within* an accountable system. Accountability is a basic political value, not only an end to other things.

DEVOLUTION

This point helps to explain why the debate between centralisers and devolutionists is so disjointed. No number of specific instances of benefits will compensate the nationalist for lack of area accountability; the latter is a *good* that the centralist values little – and might even count as a *bad*. But despite its basic orientation towards a responsive system the centre has been pushed by political forces into accepting devolution as the proper development for the British governmental system in the 1980s. Realistic political leaders in Westminster have come to the view that a measure of self-government for the Kingdom and the Principality must be introduced. Though some thought that the nationalist tide could be outwaited, and others were premature in heralding its demise,[17] the 1974 elections established the two parties as forces to be taken into account for a decade at least. Because of its reliance on Welsh and Scottish seats the Labour leadership was forced to undergo a dramatic change of view and almost overnight became devolutionists.

When the penultimate draft of this chapter was written the debate on devolution was in a state of suspended animation, overshadowed by signs of economic recovery and predictions of a forthcoming general election. The first attempt by the Labour government to apply their manifesto promise foundered in the House of Commons – see below for an outline of developments – but in summer 1977 it was stated that when the proposed legislation was reintroduced there would be separate bills for Wales and Scotland. It seemed unlikely that any significant new contributions would emerge when the debate resumed because all parties and groups had made their position quite clear and their internal tensions drastically reduce their ability to innovate. The major focus of debate has continued to be the Labour government's legislative proposals and these will be described briefly after the main features of the pattern of political forces has been outlined for the period 1975–7.

ATTITUDES TO DEVOLUTION[18]

The publication of the Labour government's proposals in 1975, followed by the Scotland and Wales Bill in late November 1976, created internal difficulties for all political parties except the Scottish Nationalists. As they are striving for independence within the Commonwealth and European Economic Community they were able to support the government in Parliament, whilst criticising it for not granting enough freedom to the Kingdom. A Scottish assembly of this sort they felt, however, could easily lead to separation soon after their party won a majority in it.

Formally the Welsh Nationalists could take the same line as their Scottish counterparts, but geographically and economically separation from England poses many very difficult problems for the Principality. Plaid Cymru therefore supported the government but its attitudes seemed to be more ambiguous about the long term. In addition once the real potentialities of devolution came to be more widely appreciated there was something of a backlash, particularly because of fears that a policy of bilingualism might be adopted by a Welsh assembly for the public service. Members of Parliament from the major parties in Wales were able to show more opposition to the bill, and when the government decided that referenda should be held in each area before the changes were actually implemented many commentators predicted that, though Scotland would vote for devolution, the Welsh would not.

The Liberals, as the successors to Gladstone and Lloyd George, were able to support the government whilst criticising the proposals on major and minor grounds. They had long stood for greater freedom for the two areas as well as democratic regionalism for the provinces of England, but to some extent they found themselves overtaken by the growth in support for the Nationalists and by the sudden conversion of the Labour leadership.

The most difficult situation was encountered by the Conservative Party, which for many years had called itself the 'Unionist' party, a title retained by some local associations long after Home Rule had ceased to be a live issue. As a result of events in the late 1960s and early 1970s the party had become an English party – it had never been strong in Wales, it was no longer possible to regard the Ulster Unionists as simply a special form of Conservative, and the rise of the Nationalists hastened a process of long-term decline in Scottish support. Rifts appeared between English and Scottish Conservatives as the former expressed strong hostility to nationalism and did not appear to appreciate the problems that the latter faced when confronted by expressions of national sentiment. There were also splits within Scottish Conservatism between those who preferred to fight the Scottish National Party head-on and those who believed that support for devolution was necessary if the party was to survive in Scotland at all. Thus a few voted for the Labour government, a greater number abstained, but the majority supported its leadership's proposals for a non-executive assembly – the best compromise that the party could evolve.[19]

The Labour Party also suffered internal divisions as a result of its leadership's conversion to devolution. Though there had been originally a devolutionary strand within the party, this had been submerged in the 1930s, and the centralist tradition is now so strong that many English backbench members have strongly opposed the greater autonomy that is offered to Wales and Scotland because they believe that it implies preferential treatment, as against, say, the north-east and the north-west. Welsh Labour members are also strongly centralist and several fought hard to ensure that there would be a referendum before any changes were made in the Principality.

Some Labour members, however, felt that the proposals did not go far enough and a break-away Scottish Labour Party was formed by two backbench members. The tensions felt within the Conservative Party between England and Scotland over the best policy to ward off the Nationalist threat were also experienced within the Labour Party, but in the short run the official policy had the benefit for the government that it ensured considerable nationalist support. Ultimately, however, the inability of the leadership to push its legislative proposals quickly through the committee stages led to the temporary abandonment of the bill and the loss of that support, thus necessitating the present Labour–Liberal alliance.

THE LABOUR GOVERNMENT'S PROPOSALS, 1975–7

The specific legislative proposals first published by the Labour government in 1975 and modified in 1976 and 1977 naturally occupied the centre of the stage; unlike those of other parties they had and still have some chance of being enacted. They were first announced in a White Paper *Our Changing Democracy: Devolution to Scotland and Wales* (Cmnd 6348, November 1975), modified by *Devolution to Scotland and Wales: Supplementary Statement* (Cmnd 6585, August 1976) and laid before Parliament in legislative form on 29 November 1976, as the *Scotland and Wales Bill*. There is no space here to deal with the details of the latter, still less the changes that were made at various stages. Naturally the bill contained provisions for a transitional period and for institutional arrangements that are not strictly part of devolution; these will not be discussed here but attention will be focused on those features that are essential to any scheme for a working system of regionalism – the nature of the area authority, the allocation of functions between levels, finance, and procedures for asserting responsiveness to the centre.

The main features of the proposed legislation are summarised in the Appendix. The important features that the reader should pick out as being of strategic significance were as follows:

First, Scotland and Wales were treated differently in one basic respect; Scotland was given a version of cabinet government whilst the Welsh system was modelled on local authority organisation. That is, in Scotland there was to be an executive body headed by a chief executive and responsible to the assembly, whilst in Wales executive powers were to be dispersed throughout a committee system, with an executive grafted on, its members being drawn from the leaders of individual committees.

Secondly, responsibility for a wide range of public services was to be given to each assembly (the list was very similar for both) but the nature of the powers differed. The Welsh Assembly was to take over Westminster legislation after it had received the Royal Assent and fulfil the role played by ministers and civil servants in the enacting of subordinate legislation, that is, it was to make statutory instruments relating to Wales only. In the case of Scotland, however, the Assembly itself was to pass legislation and there were to be United Kingdom processes for monitoring this and seeing that it remained within the framework of constitutional law.

Thirdly, the devolved services were to be financed by a bloc grant voted by Parliament, fixed by reference to local needs and general considerations of equality, after consultation with the area's leaders, to be paid at regular intervals and distributed amongst the various services by the authority within the area. Capital finance was to be operated through a separate fund. There were to be no significant regional taxes; Scottish and Welsh citizens were to pay United Kingdom taxes in the usual way. There was to be the usual public expenditure control system.

Fourthly, and this is the key to the way the system will work if implemented, there was a new role provided for the secretaries of state. The powers of the central government, and the legislative provisions that accompany them, were intended to introduce a degree of responsiveness into the system, but in doing so the extent of area accountability was reduced. The question to be asked of the clauses that concern United Kingdom powers is: do they balance accountability and responsiveness in a workable manner, given the possible political demands that may be generated within each area?

The debate over devolution for Scotland and Wales will be resolved in the next three years, with the balance of probability in favour of those who want a limited degree of autonomy on the lines proposed by the Labour government. After that the future will depend on the results of the assembly elections; will the system settle down as an integral part of a new political structure in the United Kingdom or will Scotland eventually become independent? I believe that only the Scottish electorate can answer that question. In respect of Wales the Welsh electorate will play a similar role though its scope is necessarily more limited because of the social geography of the Principality.

THE PROBLEM OF ENGLAND

If devolution comes to Scotland and Wales, what of England?[20] Should England be regionalised and each region given its own assembly on the lines of the Welsh model? Pressure for this will undoubtedly grow, but as the demand appears to start from such a low level it is unlikely to be successful. Political support for regionalism in England has always been weakened by the fact that the boundaries offered are not obvious, indeed they are usually nonsensical, on traditional, cultural or socio-geographical grounds – drawing them is an exercise in fictional construction. It is perhaps a sense of this weakness in the political basis for demands for English regionalism that led the government to publish a consultative document – *Devolution: The English Dimension* (December 1976) – of a non-committal and indecisive nature. This lists alternatives, with possible advantages and disadvantages, and ends by posing a series of questions to which the public are invited to give their own answers. These include 'Do the people of England have a sense of regional identity strong enough to support regional units of government?' and 'Would the development of regional institutions solve or reduce any national problems? If so, which?'. It would be a brave, or rather foolhardy, person who would answer these in the positive. In the absence of an upsurge of English regional 'patriotism' the government is unlikely to press towards any significant changes in the administration of the larger of the two Kingdoms.

CONCLUSION

In the short space of this chapter it has not been possible to discuss the problems that devolution will create within the British system of government. These arise because devolutionary systems, like full-blown local government and federations, are necessarily more complicated than simple unitary ones. They are expensive in terms of time, money and personnel; they create 'black boxes' between the separate authorities; they promote inequality and reduce accountability in general. But such arguments have little impact in the present debate on those to whom national, regional and local freedoms are basic 'goods', and such beliefs, rather than precise calculations of cost and benefit, are the source of political demands for regionalism and devolution.

Table 12.1   *Seats and Votes for Nationalist Parties**

Year	Plaid Cymru			Scottish National Party		
	A	B	C	A	B	C
1929	1	1·6		2	5·2	
1931	2	16·1		5	12·3	
1935	1	6·9		8	12·2	
1945	7	9·1		8	9·1	
1950	7	6·8		3	7·4	
1951	4	6·1		2	10·0	
1955	11	11·3		2	14·8	
1959	20	10·3		5	11·3	
1964	23	8·4		15	10·6	
1966	20	8·7		23	14·1	
1970	36	12·4		65	12·8	1
1974 (February)	36	11·7	2	70	22·7	7
1974 (October)	36	11·6	3	71	30·6	11

Note: A = number of seats contested, B = average % of vote received in contested seats, C = number of seats won.
Source: F. W. S. Craig, *Minor Parties at British Parliamentary Elections* (London: Macmillan, 1975), pp. 123 and 124.
*The figures given here are for general elections only; the nationalists also contested many by-elections, Plaid Cymru winning one (1966) and the Scottish National Party three (1945, 1967, 1973).

Table 12.2   *The Secretary-of-State System*

The traditional areas of the United Kingdom (other than England) are governed in a special manner, through a set of political institutions within the executive. Each has its own secretary of state, but this office is only part of the governmental system.

	Scotland (1885)	*Wales (1964)*	*Northern Ireland (1972)*

The Political Directorate

The political directorate consists of a 'team' of members of the executive, headed by the secretary of state, and each having some functional responsibilities within the overall jurisdiction of the Office.

Scotland (1885)	*Wales (1964)*	*Northern Ireland (1972)*
Secretary of state	Secretary of state	Secretary of state
2 ministers of state		2 ministers of state
1 parliamentary under-secretary	2 parliamentary under-secretaries	2 parliamentary under-secretaries

Central Liaison Staff

The central liaison staff have offices both in the territory and in Whitehall; their function is to deal with the rest of central government and with parliamentary business, such as legislation, and to provide common services to the operational departments and divisions.

Scotland (1885)	*Wales (1964)*	*Northern Ireland (1972)*
Scottish Office (Dover House, Whitehall, and St Andrews House, Edinburgh)	Welsh Office (Gwydyr House, Whitehall, and Crown Buildings, Cardiff)	Northern Ireland Office (Great George St, London, and Stormont Castle and Dundonald House, Belfast)

Operational Units

Services are actually provided, and functions performed, through operational units, called variously 'departments', 'offices', 'divisions' and 'groups', all located in the territory itself.

Scotland (1885)	*Wales (1964)*	*Northern Ireland (1972)*
9 major groups of services, some further subdivided in 21 divisions, e.g. Scottish Development Department, Scottish Economic Planning Department and Social Work Department, Scottish Education Department, Scottish Home and Health Department, Department of Agriculture and Fisheries for Scotland	e.g. Welsh Education Office, Health and Social Work Department, Highways Group	8 Northern Ireland Departments inherited from the Stormont system some of the divisions of the Northern Ireland Office in Belfast

Figure 1 *The Secretary-of-State System:*
the basic organisational model[a]

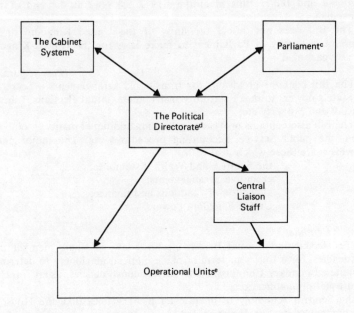

Notes: (a) For more details see the references in notes 8, 12, 13, 14. Note also that the arrows joining the elements of the model indicate only inter-action and not necessarily control.

(b) 'The Cabinet System' refers to the cabinet committee system as well as the cabinet meeting itself.

(c) The sort of special parliamentary adaptions are not described here as they vary from area to area, but they can include special institutional arrange-ments, such as committees, special procedures, for instance for legislating, and special occasions, such as a general debate on the affairs of the area.

(d) The division of functions within the political directorate is a matter for the individuals concerned.

(e) Operational units include departments, divisions, boards, commissions, agencies and corporations.

APPENDIX

Scotland and Wales Bill (as originally presented to Parliament in November 1976; for brief mention of the changes made for the separate *Scotland* and *Wales* Bills in autumn 1977 see note at the end of this appendix).

The Bill does not 'affect the unity of the United Kingdom or the supreme authority of Parliament to make laws for the United Kingdom or any part of it'

(Part I, para. 1)

The Bill contains provisions for transitional arrangements – Secretary of State's powers to make statutory instruments, initial elections, transfer of staff and property etc.

The Bill also contains provisions governing additional matters – ombudsmen, the public service, accounting procedures etc. The major parts, however, are those which deal with:

> the Scottish and Welsh Assemblies;
> executive arrangements;
> allocation of functions and finance;
> United Kingdom powers.

The Assemblies

to be elected under usual British electoral law, in single member constituencies, for a four year term of office, judicial machinery to determine disputes, Boundary Commissions to review constituencies, usual franchise and usual disqualifications

the Scottish Assembly to operate on plenary lines (like the House of Commons) whilst the Welsh Assembly to operate on committee system lines (like a local authority); both have powers to make own standing orders, but subject to conditions and to appoint staff of the assembly

both assemblies have to appoint committees, but in Scotland they are to scrutinise and advise, whilst in Wales they are to be executive

Executive Arrangements

Scotland is to have cabinet government through a Scottish Executive, consisting of a Chief Executive and other members; the former to be appointed by Secretary of State being someone with the confidence of the Assembly, and the latter on the advice of the former

the Welsh Assembly is a body corporate and acts either collectively or through committees to whom powers have been delegated; it must, however, appoint an Executive Committee, consisting of the leaders of other committees and others, and Chairman of this Committee shall be called the Chief Executive; this Committee will have a supervisory and controlling role within the Assembly

provision is made for the execution of statutory instruments and orders by the Scottish Executive and the Welsh Assembly, and their scrutiny by a committee of each assembly

*Allocation of Functions**

the Scottish Assembly has powers relating to education, health, social welfare, water etc, local government, ancient monuments etc, registration, local matters, local finance, the environment, agricultural land and fisheries, deer, dwellings, fire services, transport, inland waterways, forestry, tourism, pollution, salmon and fresh water fisheries, public holidays, charities, private law, crime, legal profession and legal aid, courts etc, tribunals etc.

there are also some powers within the competence of the Scottish Executive but not the Assembly; also most of the present local authority powers are reserved to local government

the Welsh Assembly has powers relating to education, health and social services, water and land drainage, local government, ancient monuments etc, local matters, rating and valuation, tribunals etc, environment, agricultural land and fisheries, housing, tourism, forestry, registration, roads and bridges, transport, road traffic, fire services, the countryside, superannuation.

present local authority powers are reserved to local government

Finance

each area will have two funds; a Consolidated Fund and a Loans Fund. Payments into and out of these will be strictly controlled by accounting and auditing procedures modelled on Parliament's; the initiative for expenditure must come from the Scottish Executive and the Welsh Executive Committee, but must be scrutinised by the Assemblies and agreed

payments into both consolidated funds to be made pursuant on a Parliamentary order, accompanied by reasons, prepared by the Secretary of State; payments into the loans funds to be made from the National Loans Fund under several conditions; short term borrowing also provided for

each area shall have a Comptroller and Auditor General, annual accounts and a scrutiny committee of the Assembly.

United Kingdom Powers

powers to make agency arrangements, require reports and returns

power of Secretary of State to reserve Scottish legislation for Parliamentary approval in certain circumstances

power to give directions about proposed actions, subject to Parliamentary approval; also to revoke statutory instruments in same way

powers to issue guidelines in respect of certain services and other bodies

power in relation to conditions of service of certain persons

see also financial roles and roles in relation to Scottish Executive

*The exact scope of the powers devolved is determined by the specification of the Part of the United Kingdom statute in the Schedules to the bill. In many cases they are only a small part of what is meant by those words.

Note: The main features of the above were retained by the government in autumn 1977 when separate bills for Scotland and Wales were introduced. The changes that were made included a reduction in powers in the hands of the secretary of state and a strengthening of the role of the Privy Council, more freedom for the assemblies to determine their procedures and organisation and new arrangements for administering the bloc fund system of finance.

The bill for Scotland has received very rough treatment from the House of Commons, particularly in committee, but there is little point in detailing changes made as the government will probably try to reverse some of them and there is still the House of Lords to come.

NOTES

1 See B. C. Smith, *Regionalism in England 2: Its Nature and Purpose, 1905–65* (London: Acton Society Trust, 1965).

2 The analysis of decentralisation is discussed in B. C. Smith and J. Stanyer, *Administering Britain*, Fontana Studies in Public Administration (London: Collins, 1976), pp. 58–65, 88–133.

3 Britain and France combine field administration and local government differently, and both countries have been under pressure to modify their traditional system in various ways, some of which are described in other chapters of this book. Here attention is focused on the alleged 'gap'.

4 In local government they would be called *omnibus* authorities.

5 Northern Ireland under the Stormont system was an example of a special status type of devolution, whilst the proposals of Foot and Steel on the Kilbrandon Commission (Cmnd 5460, 1973) were for uniform devolution.

6 An early example of this was found with the Fabians in 1905. See Smith, *Regionalism in England 2*, p. 7. Other examples may also be found in this book.

7 Some of the changes of opinion are described briefly in H. V. Wiseman, 'Regional government in the United Kingdom', *Parliamentary Affairs*, vol. 19, no. 1 (1965–6).

8 See J. N. Wolfe (ed.), *Government and Nationalism in Scotland* (Edinburgh: Edinburgh University Press, 1969), ch. 1.

9 Some of the 'unsatisfied nationalisms' are described in H. Seton-Watson, 'Unsatisfied nationalisms', *Journal of Contemporary History*, vol. 6, no. 1 (1971).

10 See Table 12.1 and also *The Times* and *The Economist* for the period 1967 to the present.

11 In 1967 there was considerable tension within Plaid Cymru between the culturalists and the economists – see E. H. Davies, 'Welsh nationalism', *Political Quarterly*, vol. 39, no. 3 (1968).

12 See J. G. Kellas, *The Scottish Political System*, chs 3 and 5.

13 See E. Rowlands, 'The politics of regional administration: the establishment of the Welsh Office', *Public Administration*, vol. 50 (Autumn 1972).

14 Parliamentary arrangements are described in Kellas, *The Scottish Political System*, ch. 5, and R. L. Borthwick, 'The Welsh Grand Committee', *Parliamentary Affairs*, vol. 21, no. 3 (1967–8).

15 For a discussion of these bodies in general see articles by D. Kelling and P. Self in *Public Administration*, vol. 54 (Summer 1976) entitled 'Beyond ministerial departments: mapping the administrative terrain'.

16 For a discussion of public accountability within decentralised systems see J. Stanyer, 'Divided responsibilities: accountability in decentralised government', *Public Administration Bulletin*, no. 17 (December 1974).

17 The appointment of the Crowther (later Kilbrandon) Commission in 1969 was an example of the former; I. Maclean. 'The rise and fall of the

Scottish National Party', *Political Studies*, vol. 18, no. 3 (1970), an example of the latter.

18 This brief summary of the major attitudes displayed towards the Labour government's proposals is based on the Second Reading debate and reports and letters in *The Times* for the succeeding months. It does not do justice to the variety of opinions held *within* each party.

19 The government had a majority of forty-five at the end of the Second Reading debate, including the Liberals, the Scottish Labour Party, five Conservatives, two Ulster Unionists and Gerry Fitt; ten Labour members voted with the Conservatives, as did eight Ulster Unionists. Twenty-nine Labour and thirty-two Conservative members abstained.

20 See B. C. Smith, 'Confusions in regionalism', *Political Quarterly*, vol. 48, no. 1 (January–March 1977).

Chapter XIII

REGIONALISATION IN FRANCE

Regionalisation in France is not an official response to criticism which casts doubt upon centralisation as either a simple mode of government or as a cultural model characteristic of French society.

The type of regionalisation contained in the reforms already carried out or in the process of realisation is one method of resolving the crisis in the French administration characterised by its incapacity to accomplish its ever-increasing number of tasks and of ensuring the satisfactory running of a constantly evolving society.

Regionalisation in France can be defined as a complex and hybrid set of proposals, comprising a set of values, institutions and administrative practices which are conservative rather than innovative and which have not, therefore, responded to the grievance of regional minorities.

THE DEBATE ON THE REGIONS

There exists in France a long regionalist or decentralist tradition in the sense of an ongoing struggle for the recognition of local, communal, regional and provincial autonomy. This struggle has been motivated by diverse and often opposing ideological perspectives, such as the counter-revolutionary tradition which inspired the national revolution of the Vichy government and the socialist current which developed out of the thought of Proudhon and which inspired, in part, the ideology behind the Paris Commune of 1871 and even the Marxist or Leftist thinking of contemporary autonomists.

None of these traditions has, however, influenced the authors of the regional reform which is more pragmatic and voluntarist in its conception of the region.

The region – an expression of political decentralisation

From the beginning of the century, when this term came to enrich French political vocabulary, the region has been at the centre of doctrinal argument.[1]

Under the Third Republic, decentralisation was one of the constant themes of traditional Right-wing opposition to the Republican

State. It was also a major preoccupation of the, mainly Republican, members of the French regionalist movement.

Action Française was, without doubt, the movement on the Right which fought hardest for decentralisation. Maurras and his followers employed the term province rather than region to describe a clearly defined economic area circumscribed by natural frontiers, and within which there existed a community of intellectual and moral interests which would benefit from real administrative autonomy in the same way that the provinces, regions and towns of the *ancien régime* had benefited from protected freedom and franchise.

As a result of decentralisation a new political division of labour would emerge; communal affairs would be the concern of the commune, provincial affairs that of the provinces, and questions of national destiny that of the higher organs of State. In his constant struggle against parliamentary democracy Maurras' argument in favour of decentralisation occupied an important position: it castigated the levelling out of cultural differences through Jacobin centralisation, the arbitrary manner in which the *départements* had been created, the behaviour of the Deputies and the ministers who used the administration to reward electoral faithfulness, and the stifling incompetence of the bureaucratic administration.

According to Maurras a Republican government could not decentralise because 'all great public offices are elective. Therefore, any government, in order to be re-elected, has an interest in maintaining control over as many public administrators as possible, in other words in centralising . . . the natural term for a Republic is, in fact, democratic State socialism: a masterpiece of centralisation.'[2] Only the traditional, hereditary anti-parliamentary monarchy could decentralise and realise the Maurrassian ideal: authority above and the Republic below.

The logic of this thinking, which attempted to differentiate between a monarchist type of structure at the base and the Republican system at national level, provoked a reaction in the form of Republican unity to defend all the revolutionary gains . . . including Jacobin centralisation.[3]

The sociologist Durkheim defended a system which freed men from local constraints and officials and made the material and intellectual advance of the French people easier. Clémenceau also denounced those who 'wish to decentralise not freedom but reaction, who wish by setting up roman enclaves to protect themselves against the liberating forces of the French Republic! '[4]

The *Mouvement Régionaliste Français* was a pole of action throughout the course of this period. Founded at the end of the nineteenth century, the *Mouvement* was a sort of club uniting diverse personalities, politicians (Boncour, Tardieu), men of letters

(Barrès, Mistral) and academics (Vidal de la Blache, Brun), who felt they were acting to reconcile national unity and regional differences within the framework of the Republican State. Influenced by liberalism but also by the thought of Proudhon, the movement militated for a regionalism which should be:

- realistic: capable of harmonising the ethnic, historical and cultural diversity of a French society which looked to the future without denying its past;
- empirical: reform should come from below, from local initiatives, from a regional renaissance encouraged by the State;
- balanced: reconciling the authority of the State with local freedom, tradition with progress, the individual with the nation as a whole.

In spite of a programme of reform which was both complete and realistic, the *Mouvement Régionaliste Français*, like *Action Française*, never enjoyed sufficient popular support to call into question the bases or the functioning of the traditional administration. And yet, regionalism was a theme of the national revolution, and the Maurrassians and the leaders of the *Mouvement Régionaliste Français* (in spite of the ideological difference which separated them) were associated in the work of the *Commission du Conseil National*, which was entrusted with the task of administrative reorganisation. In fact, the government of Vichy which appointed regional prefects as a result of circumstances arising out of the Occupation and problems of food control, was incapable of carrying out the proposal of the *Conseil National* which was essentially decentralist in inspiration and involved the creation of seventeen provinces, each with their own institutions and precise powers. The constraints of the French State tradition were such that even 'the most traditionalist regime of our recent political history did not dare to permit the establishment of a regional power which enjoyed real autonomy in decision-making'.[5]

Thus, throughout the Third Republic, the Vichy régime and the first years of the Fourth Republic, no far-reaching reform threatened the permanence and continuity of the traditional local administration. During that period the administration was able to cope with the problems of a society characterised by a Malthusian economy, weak social mobility and an increasingly ageing population. In other respects, within the context of relative socio-economic stability, local and departmental interests benefited from effective protection by the national political authorities.

The traditional local authorities, in fact, enjoyed representation and considerable influence through the medium of the Senate, the

Conseil de la République which assumed (as the upper chamber of Parliament) the parliamentary representation of those authorities according to the letter and the spirit of the constitutional texts of 1875 and 1946 and also through the extremely conservative *Association des Maires de France*.[6] The traditional administration was, furthermore, protected by the accumulation of offices at municipal, departmental and national level and by the existence of identical administrative and electoral boundaries which lead to 'the evaluation of all local administrative reform in terms of its political impact'.[7]

The region as envisaged in the texts of the various administrative reforms

New conceptions of the region developed during the 1950s. They found expression both inside and outside the State apparatus and favoured the implementation of reforms and new administrative practices.

The first notions on the region were to be found within the framework of general doctrines – Maurrassianism, liberalism, Proudhonism – which, through lack of popular support, never progressed beyond discussions on general principles. At the beginning of the 1960s, however, a new conception of regionalism developed out of the voluntarist school and took shape within the context of regional planning and development in response to the new demands of the French economy.[8]

The expansion and concentration of economic forces within France, stimulated by foreign competition which became even more threatening with the establishment of the Common Market, modified the bases of the local economy. There were crises in certain sectors (steel, textile, shipbuilding industries) which upset the economic life of entire regions, medium and small firms ran into difficulties because local prices were non-competitive and agricultural land was requisitioned to satisfy the needs of the European tourist industry, and rural migration accelerated.

To the traditional disparity between 'Paris and the French desert' was added yet another: that between the regions benefiting from the industrial boom due to their natural resources or to their role as privileged areas of exchange and trade, and the poorer agricultural areas condemned to stagnation and an ageing population.

Had the State not intervened to control this development a serious social crisis would no doubt have occurred. The entrenchment of extreme Right-wing Poujadist opposition in the *départements* which were the victims of this expansion, the re-emergence, though still slight, of autonomist movements, the creation of economic expansion committees on the initiative of the local chambers of commerce in response to the professional and administrative structures' inability to adapt to the changing situation, were all indicative in their several ways of a malaise within regional society.

To 'reduce uncertainties', the regional planners defined a strategy which, whilst it preserved the ascendancy of the Jacobin State, favoured a more balanced development throughout the country as a whole.

The splitting up of the country into twenty-two regions in 1956 was a response, in the first instance, to the demand of Gravier and the French geographers in 1947 for a narrowing of the gap between 'Paris and the provincial desert'. The *département* was considered too narrow a unit for decentralisation or for a more equitable redistribution of wealth. The division into regions, each representing a certain economic and geographical unit, would give a solid framework to the politics of land-use planning because:

– the region was a homogenous economic area within which to implement a policy of industrial decentralisation and redistribution of public investment;
– inter-regional comparison facilitated the local distribution of the fruits of national policy without threatening the principles and the rationale to which it lay claim.

After the decree of 30 June 1955 the regional action programme allowed the government to adopt all measures favouring the development of those regions suffering from underemployment or from inadequate economic development especially by facilitating agricultural reconversion, the establishment of new industries, the expansion of tourism and, at the same time, the regulation of growth in the more economically favoured regions. So, the efforts of the land-use planners were primarily devoted to the problems of redistribution and better use of land in order to ensure a more satisfactory demographic and socio-economic balance between the regions which made up the national land mass.

Dating from the Fifth Plan, a broadening of these perspectives took place with the establishment of regional planning with a local perspective.

In the course of the planning process, the function of the regions may be analysed in the following manner:

(1) The regional division of 1956 served as a basis for studies on public works planning.
(2) It permitted re-orientation of investment once the importance of the politics of regional development had been defined in rela-

tion to national politics and once the required type of inter-regional balance had been decided upon.

(3) The local aspect of the national plans dealt with the localisation of public investment and the priorities and the method of financing the work to be carried out.

In order to improve the forecasts of the planners, but also to reduce the social and political effects of government policy, by disciplining and canalising local initiatives, the region was included in the formation and execution of the Plan. The establishment from 1964 onwards of regional institutions with strictly limited terms of reference and channels for consultation created a new form of participation at regional level, and a national policy for the economic development of the regions which should favour the emergence of a regional consciousness expressing itself within the framework of action defined by the government.

This regionalisation from above does not question the basic principles of the traditional administrative system. Regionalisation, such as it is, is defined and organised as much by the decrees of 1964 and the law of 1972 as by the proposal which was rejected in the referendum of 1969.[9] It is more a deconcentration than a decentralisation process, more the regionalisation of State power[10] than the encouraging of regional regeneration and autonomy. This is shown by a study of the institutional machinery.

THE INSTITUTIONAL STRUCTURES OF THE REGION

The regional preoccupations of the last twenty years have their roots in problems of economic development.

The emergence of institutional structures

The modern region is the child of interventionism, planning and land-use planning. This 'blood relationship' has left its mark on regional institutional structures. It was in the sphere of local economics that the first regional organs saw the light of day before they received the institutional blessing of the public authorities and, more especially, an administrative structure.

Gradually, through usage, and under the protective cloak of the administration, a certain number of institutions emerged over a period of about ten years. They were finally confirmed by the administrative reform of 1964.

The first institutions in question were the Economic Expansion Committees. These were private legal associations recognised to be of benefit to the public and composed of professionals and elected representatives in each *département*. In 1954, the public authorities specified their organisational structure and established the method of their regional co-ordination: the Committee for Regional Economic Expansion (CREE). Their role, though official, was mainly consultative. They were the cog in a permanent dialogue between the administration and the regional economic bodies.

Another stage was reached in 1955 with the formation of the Economic Regions or the *Régions de Programme*. The establishment of regional action programmes (decree of 30 June 1955) aided the co-ordination of regional economic development. It was as a result of these programmes that it was decided to split the country into twenty-two regions (decree of 28 November 1956). These regions served as a framework for the drawing up of the regional land-use plans. The *Inspecteurs Généraux de l'Administration en Mission Extraordinaire* (IGAME) were responsible for the general co-ordination of the measures prescribed in the programmes of regional action within the economic regions thus created. From then on, both administrative and economic matters were centred around these areas.

The blueprint for the framework of a French regional institutional structure was thus drawn up. The details were to be more clearly defined by the decrees of 7 January 1959 and 2 June 1960 which set up the regional action area (*circonscription d'action régionale*) which was the name of this regional framework until 1972.

These decrees created institutions which were to become permanent, but which would evolve and develop into the institutions which exist today. These institutions comprise on the one hand the administration and on the other, the representatives of local society: at first these were only representatives of the socio-economic world, but these were later joined by elected representatives.

Each area of regional action was given a co-ordinating prefect who called together the departmental prefects concerned into an Interdepartmental Conference. The co-ordinating prefect was assisted by the Regional Economic Expansion Committee.

This institutional apparatus was to evolve rapidly, for the experiences and practice of the designated economic areas gave increasing substance to the regional phenomenon. The need for a framework better equipped to participate and act led to the administrative reforms of 1964.

The regional institutions of 1964: the region, the administrative area of regional action

The reforms of March 1964 gave the region, now officially recognised, a regional prefect, assisted by a regional mission and regional administrative conference. Moreover, it also set up the Commissions for Regional Economic Development (CODER). Economic development was the primary task of this new structure whose secondary, but explicit, objective was better administrative co-ordination. At the level of institutions the decrees of 1964 responded to two requirements: they confirmed the existence of the economic region, but equally they responded to the need to improve administrative management. This reform allowed regionalisation to take a big step forward. It created a permanent and uniform organisation as far as administration and regional representation were concerned.

The administration. The regional prefect. Administrative action was instituted at the level of the regional prefect, as the representative of central authority. He replaces the co-ordinating prefect in the area of regional action. He is the departmental prefect in the main town of the area, but is no longer merely the *primus inter pares* as was the co-ordinating prefect. He has far greater autonomy because, under the terms of Article 2 of the decree of 1964,

'the regional prefect has, as his responsibility, the execution of government policy regarding economic development and land-use planning in his area. He stimulates and controls the activities of the departmental prefects within his region, as well as those of administrative heads of field services and the chairmen or directors of public companies or mixed economy enterprises whose field of activity may embrace several *départements* within the area and which do not have a national character. He is, furthermore, required to control and co-ordinate the administrative activity of the civil service and public establishments whose field of activity embraces several *départements* within his area. Finally he may also be invested with special functions by decree of the *Conseil d'Etat*. He receives his orders from the Prime Minister and from other ministers in matters pertaining to their competence.'

The regional administrative conference. Under the presidency of the regional prefect, this conference gathers together the departmental prefects, the paymaster-general of the region, the national economic inspector appointed within the area and, in matters pertaining to their competence, the regional representatives of the ministries. It deals with the problems created by public investment and its effects on the economic and social life of the region. Its real functioning depends on the attitude adopted towards it by the regional prefect and the personal reactions of the departmental prefects.

The reform of 1964 confined it to a purely consultative role. And although the regional prefect is obliged to consult it, he can, by law, ignore its opinions.

The regional mission. In the exercise of his functions, the regional prefect has at his disposal 'a mission whose members are chosen from among administrative and technical officials and who are appointed by Prime Ministerial decree'. The regional prefect may have recourse to a brains trust, composed mainly of former students of the *Ecole Nationale d'Administration*, members of the *grands corps*, sub-prefects and civil administrators.

The composition and the role of the regional missions are more important than the text of the law suggests. The staff of the regional prefect comprises between four and eight young officials of high rank, some seconded full-time, others part-time. With the prefectoral members attached to the mission, the brains trust of the regional prefect is comprised of a permanent organisation of some ten to fifteen persons.

Administrative reorganisation. Around the regional prefect are organised the regional services of the different State administrations, and his power over them has been reinforced. Indeed, the regional prefect is the holder of all the powers exercised up till then by the heads of the civil service in the region, with the exception of education, tax and work inspectorate. Thus, ministers can only delegate via the prefect who may then proceed to sub-delegate an administrative head. He presides over all the commissions whose competence extends beyond the *département*. He centralises all the posts of the regional services and reports on the quality of the regional field services.

Regional representation. Regional representation was institutionalised in the CODER. Its main feature was that it was essentially consultative. Its composition was tripartite: half its members were the representatives of the socio-economic sector, one-quarter were locally elected and one-quarter were qualified people appointed by the government. It was appointed for five years. This composition was the result of a compromise. In fact, at the time of the creation of the CODER two theses were advanced: one proposed the transformation in each region of the Economic Expansion Committee into a Regional Economic and Social Council, thus giving responsibility to the socio-economic forces. Another proposed the participation of elected representatives, departmental councils and municipal councils.

Each *département* had a number of representatives commensurate with the economic balance of the region. The CODERs were composed of between twenty and fifty members, depending on the size of the region. They were presided over by the regional prefect and were consulted uniquely on the initiative of public authorities.

Therefore, it was clear that the administration was both omnipotent and omnipresent within the heart of the regional institutions. Of course the CODER was qualified to enter into discussions with the regional prefect and the regional administrative conference, but it was the regional prefect who fixed the agenda, determined the dates of the sittings and was responsible for the commission's secretariat as well as for the preliminary instructions in matters which were submitted to him.

Functions of the regional institutions. They were essentially of an economic nature. When the Plan for economic and social development was being prepared each minister sent his instructions to the regional prefect informing him of the amount of credit budgeted by his ministry for the region during the five years of the Plan's duration. After consultation at departmental level a regional plan was drawn up and submitted to the CODER before being sent to the Inter-ministerial Committee set up to study all the regional plans.

The CODER intervened in the three stages of the Plan: preparation, decision, execution. The participation of the CODER could be complete and efficacious at the level of execution as well as at the preparatory stage. The problems occurred at the level of decision making: it was at this stage that the CODER's work might be undermined.

Clearly, at the level of preparation, even if the CODER refused to accept the report of the regional prefect, this report could be dispatched to the central administration although the judgement of the Commission was unfavourable. That could have formed a basis for many tensions and conflicts in the regions, but in practice it rarely, almost never, came to this point, thanks to the diplomacy of the regional prefect.

The classical prefectoral tendency to identify with regional rather than national interests played a role in this. At the decision-making level the regional prefect discussed with Paris, to see which of the different requests made by the region were possible and feasible, taking into account national policy and internal balance.

These 'regional slices' of the Plan, established with the help of this dialogue between Paris and the region, were then administered by the region which monitored and controlled the execution of the Plan.

The statutes of the region. Both the regional administrative structures and the representational structures of the region revealed a desire to create a regional consciousness whilst, at the same time, conserving the essentials of power in the hands of the representatives of central authority. This was strengthened by the statutes of the region, the administrative area of regional action. The reform of 1964 revealed the eternal preoccupation with not creating any new authorities and with not touching the existing administrative structures. There was, therefore, no regional budget any more than there was a regional administration. Most of those who participated at regional level, whether State personnel or members of the CODER, had and preserved an office or a local function.

Whatever its imperfections, the reform of 1964 permitted a certain number of local actors to work together: members of the administration and representatives of the economic world. It also aided the creation of a collective consciousness at regional level. In short, the reform of 1964 set the stage for a further and necessary development of the regional phenomenon. 'For four years, regionalists of all shades of opinion, autonomists, European federalists, clubs, technocrats or the merely sentimental, enumerated the evils of Jacobin centralism and prepared the ground for a further, essential stage of "regionalisation" in statements, debates and articles which helped to create a regional consciousness. The call for regionalism had been made, who was to answer the call?'[11]

Recent institutional solutions
In a speech delivered at Lyons on 25 March 1968, General de Gaulle stated:

'The general process of evolution is carrying our country towards a new type of balance. The multisecular effort towards centralisation which was, for a long time, necessary to bring about and maintain unity, in spite of dissension in the provinces which were successively drawn back to the fold, is no longer imperative today. On the contrary, it is regional activity which now appears to be the mainspring of future economic power.'

A first project for reform was proposed in 1969, but it failed. A second one was brought out in 1972 and this contained the French regional institutions which are currently in operation.

Recent regional institutions are all characterised by the pride of place given to the participation of the active regional forces which have asserted themselves more and more in their dealings with the administration.

The idea of participation, which the events of May 1968 had inspired in General de Gaulle, was at the basis of his reform project of 1969. This idea was also present in the reform of 1972 which established the current French regional organisation.

The region as a territorial authority: the rejected project of 1969. In April 1969 General de Gaulle offered the French people, in a referendum, a reform both of the Senate and the regions: the heading of the text submitted for referendum was as follows: 'Bill relating to the creation of regions and the reform of the Senate.' The failure of the referendum of 27 April 1969 led to the departure of General de Gaulle and put off this project for a combination of reasons which had little to do with the basic regional problem.

(a) Although it failed, this project is an important milestone in the evolution of the region in France because it envisaged the region as a territorial authority.

Within the existing geographical framework of twenty-one areas of action a real territorial authority was to be created similar to the *départements* and the communes. This was a remarkable innovation, for the region, raised to the level of a *territorial authority*, possessed a moral character, its own resources and above all a broadly defined domain covering public works programmes such as housing and urban developments which implied a corresponding diminution or disappearance of State intervention in these fields.

But the remit of the region comprised only development and planning. Its competence was always defined in advance and resided in the economic, social and cultural spheres.

(b) The organs of the 1969 region reflect an inconsistency which was not ironed out by the draft bill. Of course, a territorial authority was created, but the administrative area still remained. In fact, as with the *département* and the commune, the region possessed the double quality of administrative area and territorial authority. The 1969 organisation of the region rested, therefore, on two organs which reflected its legal duality: the regional prefect, an essentially devolved organ, and the regional council representing the territorial authority.

The regional prefect. He was to be the successor to and resembled the regional prefect of the reform of 1964. He was still the departmental prefect of the main town of the *département* and the plurality of his two functions continued. He, too, was supported by the regional administrative conference and the regional mission.

Delegated by the government, he was in charge of the administration of the region. His mission was not limited to the economic development and planning of the region, as was that of the regional prefect of 1964. The draft bill of 1969 established a process of evolution with the institution of a co-ordinating prefect, which tended to submit the departmental prefects to the authority of a 'super-prefect'.

An agent of the State, the regional prefect was also the executive of the regional council. Article 5 of the draft bill stipulated: 'the

Regional Prefect is responsible for preliminary instruction on matters submitted to the Regional Council as well as for the execution of the decisions of this latter body'.

The regional council. The composition of the regional council was tripartite. It was composed of Deputies elected in the region, regional territorial councillors elected by the departmental and municipal councils, and socio-professional regional councillors appointed by the representative organs.

It had consultative and deliberative competence. It possessed the consultative powers of the CODER in regard to the regional aspects of the National Plan. But, whilst the CODER had only a consultative role in the matter, the regional council voted on that portion of the Plan which related to public funding of a regional and departmental nature. Finally, the most essential power of the council was, undeniably, its vote on the regional budget.

These were the basic lines of the draft bill of 1969.

The rejection of this proposal by the referendum did not, however, close the file on regionalism. Pompidou returned to the subject at Lyons on 30 October 1970 and the question of the regions found an outlet once again in the law of 5 July 1972.

The law of 5 July 1972: the region as a public establishment, or the current regional institution. From Article 1 onwards, this law clearly established the legal position of the region as it exists today in France. 'In each area of regional activity, called a "region", a public establishment will be set up which will be called by the same name.'

There is no longer any question of a territorial authority. The region satisfies both national unity and departmental autonomy. And yet, with its establishment, a real decentralising regionalisation began to take shape in France.

The regional prefect. He remains the executive of the region and he combines this function with that of head of the State administration in the regional area. He examines matters submitted to the regional council and carries out its decisions. His is the task of preparing and administering the budget of the region, of being responsible for expenditure and of signing the order to pay.

The prefect is both an agent of the State and of the region.

As far as his role as agent of the State is concerned, the administration and the relations between the regional prefect and the regional administration, the terms of the 1964 reform are maintained.

The regional assemblies. The law of 5 July 1972 endows the region with a bicameral system based on the co-existence of a 'political' assembly – the regional council – and an 'economic' assembly – the economic and social committee.

The law attempts to make a compromise between the various possibilities and degrees of participation at regional level, on the one hand maintaining socio-economic participation whilst opening its deliberations to the elected representatives of the populations of the region, and on the other hand, giving decision-making powers to the region whilst maintaining its consultative role.

The regional council. It is composed of Deputies and Senators of the region and of the representatives of local authorities elected by the departmental councils, the municipal councils and the urban district councils.

The composition of the regional council reflects the notion of co-operation and harmony between the State and the different public authorities at a lower level.

It was not intended in this assembly to create a new breed of elected members but rather 'to encourage national, departmental and municipal representatives, elected either by direct or indirect suffrage, to work together at different levels'.[12]

The presence of Members of Parliament did not go unquestioned. Indeed, it is quite true that whilst they may guarantee cohesion between the choices of the State and those of the region, over and above this technical justification, the only reason for their being present in the council is that they maintain national unity.

The rather complex method of representation of locally elected members ensures that their number is equal to that of the Senators and Deputies of the region. Each *département* has a number of seats proportional to its population. The representatives of the local authorities are elected by each departmental council and should account for 30 per cent at least of the membership of the regional council. The representatives of the departmental councils are, moreover, equal to half the total number of regional councillors elected by the departmental assemblies. A specific number of mayors of communes not represented as agglomerations are included. Finally, the representation of agglomerations is worked out by a rather complex system taking into account both legal and demographic factors.

The composition and the mode of appointment of the regional councils are the result of somewhat complex mechanisms. Thus, certain delegates of urban communities are elected indirectly. The regional council appears more as a juxtaposition of delegations than as an assembly called to translate the regional interest into action.

Each regional council decides upon its rules of procedure and sets up its own organs: standing committees, technical commissions and, of course, a 'permanent' commission whose composition is renewed each year. Each regional council elects its chairman annually.

As far as powers are concerned, whilst the regional council may have a consultative role in certain domains, it holds the monopoly on decision making within the region. Its decision-making power is exercised mainly in the budgetary and fiscal domain. This is an important innovation in the regional constitutional history of France.

The regional council expresses its views (*avis*) during the whole process of preparation and execution of the national Plan. Articles 8, 9 and 10 of the 1972 law stipulate: 'The Regional Council deliberates and expresses an opinion on the problems of development and land-use planning in the region, subjects upon which it must be obligatorily consulted. It takes part in studies on regional land-use planning in the preparation and execution of the Plan in its different phases, notably by the preparation of reports on general aspects.' It 'expresses its views at least once a year on the conditions relating to the use of State funds allocated for investment in regional or departmental projects'.

A consultative body, but above all a deliberating body, the regional council, created by the law of 1972, preserves an innovating character: for the first time in France an elected assembly deals with regional problems. The participation of regional actors from the economic sphere is of no small importance. Although their role is exclusively consultative, their activities furnish the main function of the second regional assembly.

The economic and social committee. This is the successor of the CODER of 1964. Its powers, like those of the CODER, are purely consultative. It advises both the regional prefect and the regional council. Its composition aims to ensure the participation of socio-professional groups in regional activity. According to Article 14 of the 1972 law, the economic and social committee 'is composed of representatives of organisations and activities of an economic, social, professional, family, educational, scientific, cultural and sporting nature within the region'.

As soon as an organisation exists it nominates its representatives. This is the case with the unions. In the case of non-organised activity it is the responsibility of the public authorities to decide upon the nature of its representation. Thus the notion of 'qualified persons', which existed in the CODER, can also be found here.

Like the regional council, the economic and social committee decides upon its rules of procedure, elects a chairman, a standing committee and commissions.

Article 14 of the 1972 law defines the powers of the economic and social committee: it is consulted on 'matters which are within the competence of the region, matters submitted to the regional council'. These consultations 'are prior to the deliberations or opinion given by the Regional Council'.

Finally, if the regional council cannot follow the advice of the economic and social committee, the latter can order its *Rapporteur* to publish its opinion before the relevant commission of the council which cannot refuse to hear it. The law is, moreover, extremely detailed concerning the relationship between the two assemblies. These relations are permanent, and provision is made for the two assemblies to work together. Most of the time, moreover, the various commissions of both bodies are the same.

Regional resources. The great innovation of the 1972 law is the creation of a corporate body, provided with its own budget and with the power to vote taxes. The creation of a regional budget fed by direct taxation completes the regionalisation of the budget and of State investment.

The law fixes the financial resources of the region. Certain of them do not come from taxation. They come, in fact, from the transfer of funds from the State and the local authorities and, more especially, from funds acquired by borrowing or from State subsidies. Borrowing must be confirmed by the central administration and the policy adopted by the regions in this matter has varied considerably: certain regions have recourse to borrowing and incur large debts, others refuse to borrow almost as a matter of principle.

The fiscal resources are of two kinds. There is the standard rate on driving licences, a tax transferred from the State to the region. The region also acquires some of its income from taxes which it has the right to impose: it cannot create new taxes but may add supplements to some State or local tax. It may, for example, charge an additional sum on the State road tax, or on local property taxes. But the text of 1972 places a ceiling: the fiscal revenue of the region should not be more than 25 [now 45] francs per capita. The resources which the regions are allowed to levy are very modest and the regional budgets are equally modest. If they are inflated in certain regions this is because these regions have borrowed considerably.

The functioning of the 1972 regional institutions. As soon as the new regional institutions were set up and began to function, opposition to them emerged. This opposition is of two varieties – what may be called opposition of principle and opposition from within the institutions themselves.

When the regional institutions were set up in 1974, there was a certain opposition of principle and a refusal to participate. Indeed, in some regions certain socio-professional categories refused to sit on the economic and social committee. Some trades unions, the CFDT, the CGT and the FEN, refrained from taking their seats in certain regions. Their reasons were ideological: 'the reform is a capitalist attempt to adapt the political and economic structures so that they correspond to its own process of development'.[13] A second argument turned on the powers of the region. According to the unions, who refuse to accept the type of region created by the law of 1972, the reform does not give it any real power. The three unions also consider themselves to be humiliated by the place allotted to them on the economic and social committee in which they feel they are under-represented. This under-representation is further aggravated, according to the unions, by 'the presence on the Committees of representatives of pseudo-union organisations which are not independent' (here they refer to the representatives of the small Right-wing CFT and the CGST who participate in the committees of several regions).[14]

Finally, we must also examine the cases of certain professional organisations which have also refused to take their seats. An example is the *Conférence Régionale des Métiers Rhône-Alpes* which decided not to nominate candidates to the local economic and social committee, for it considered its representation inadequate and refused to accept an assembly whose function involved the raising of taxes.

Another type of opposition, less open and within the new institutions themselves, also exists. Here it is a question of conflicts within the regional machines, a transference of departmental and geographical rivalries, antagonisms between the towns and between urban and rural communities. This is reflected by a balance or imbalance in the composition of the organs of the regional assemblies: standing committees, commissions, vice-presidencies etc. Thus, in some regions certain *départements* are not represented in the standing committees of the economic and social committee, or one *département* has several vice-presidencies. Or even, as in the case of the standing committee of the regional council of the Rhône-Alpes, whilst all the *départements* were represented, not one of the three large towns, Lyons, Grenoble and Saint-Etienne, was represented.

The local and departmental solidarity factor, like geographical rivalries, are no less present in the institutions of 1972 than they were in those of 1964.

The composition of the regional assemblies comprises a certain number of characteristics unique to the institutions of 1972. In particular there are three problems which are directly linked to the new institutions. First, the accumulation of offices, for, given the terms of the law of 1972, over and above his mandate to the regional assembly, each councillor holds at least one and up to three other offices. Secondly, the presence of Members of Parliament which overshadows certain local preoccupations, or at least does not always allow for the adequate expression of local representatives' views on certain problems.[15] Finally, the role of the chairmen of the regional councils who represent a power with which central government has to reckon.[16]

The French politico-administrative system was still largely inspired by the Jacobin tradition in the establishment of these institutions: neither the values, nor the decision-making powers can escape from the control of the central State or its representatives. As to the consultative institutions of 1964 and the more 'decisional' institutions of 1972, although they have become progressively more open to local participation, they none the less remain under the control of a system in which 'the regional level once more reflects the traditional relationship with Paris without contributing anything new. In many ways the regionalisation of the Plan, behind the novelty and the modernity of the language employed, is only one more bureaucratic procedure.'[17]

REGIONAL BEHAVIOUR

One of the objectives of regional reform, to encourage a regional consciousness by instituting common action over regional development, implies new types of behaviour on the part of the actors: the locally elected representatives, representatives of professional groups and trades unions, and the local administrations.

To what extent have the changes made between 1964 and 1972 helped to overcome the traditional grievances concerning the power relationship between the administration and local society? Have the priority given to the *département* and the inter-relationships between authority, representation and influence been changed?

The practice in the regional institutions indicates the persistence of traditional behaviour patterns in spite of the emergence of more radical behaviour which is, however, situated outside the area of governmental projects and their realisation.

The persistence of traditional behaviour
A sociological study made in 1966 indicates the relative failure of the reform, a conclusion which more recent events have confirmed.[18] In the two regions under study – Champagne and Aquitaine – all the regional actors remained closely attached to their *département*, and relegated the region to the function of an intermediary between the State and the *départements* for the allocation of public funds. Attachment to the *département* was reinforced by the value placed on the prefect – its natural defender – on the autonomy of the *département* within the region and on the institution of negotiations between *départements* within the regional conferences. The reasons given for this by interested parties were based on the superiority of the departmental organisation in the exercise of functions such as administrative action, dialogue with the citizens and the mobilisation of local energies.

This satisfaction with the traditional institutions on the part of the regional actors should not be allowed to camouflage the deeper reasons which are at the root of their convictions. For the locally elected representatives, their field of action and their horizon are dependent on the departmental framework within which they have woven a solid network of influence and have acquired political weight. The departmental administration and the field services of the ministries, in spite of their differences, regard with mistrust new institutions like the regional mission, which could threaten their privileged relationship with local society or with the central Parisian ministries. As for the representatives of the employers' and union organisations, their attitudes are more ambiguous in so far as they are dependent on their own organisation and strategic constraints.

Under these conditions, regional reform is powerless to modify consciousness and behaviour: the regional prefect is acceptable simply because he has no powers over the *départements* and he exercises the one function which the region is recognised to possess: that of pressure on the central administration to the benefit of the local authorities. It appears, furthermore, that the values of the Jacobin model have been sufficiently internalised by the regional actors for them to prefer a deconcentration of State functions to a federalist reform or administrative decentralisation.

This is all the more so as the representatives of weak *départements* fear that regional autonomy would weaken the role of the central State, that protector of the weak and guarantor of national balance.

The timidity of the reforms undertaken explains these results, P. Grémion writes: 'the regionalisation of the Fifth Plan was the reproduction at a higher level of the relationships institutionalised within the departmental framework between the State bureaucracy and the representatives of local society'[19] and the regional assembly – the CODER – only furnished minimal co-ordination between departmental programmes.

Other evidence confirms these conclusions. For example, regional consultation was arranged from August 1968 onwards by the public authorities to gather opinions and suggestions on the general direction of the 1964 reform from all the organisations or persons who hoped to play a role in the region.[20] This consultation, largely improvised as regards its timing and directives and suspect in the manner of its information gathering, brought to light a certain number of widely held opinions: the communes and the *départements* with their current powers should be maintained, the regional prefect should be clearly distinguished from the departmental prefects in order to fulfil his role as co-ordinator and arbiter. The reform was also perceived as a means of ending an abusive and inefficient concentration of powers rather than as a means by which the regions might affirm their own personality. Finally, regional consciousness appeared relatively weak, and only really as a counterweight to the authority of Paris.

Did the reform of 1972 afford a better opportunity for the emergence of a regional consciousness and the establishment of a different behaviour pattern? It is too early to have objective data from which to draw a conclusion. However, it appears that the modifications introduced in the composition of the regional assembly, especially the place of nationally elected members, favour a regrouping of a bi-polar nature according to national allegiances between majority and opposition. The appointment of chairmen, the formation of groups, the composition of the commissions correspond in many regions to the parliamentary pattern: parties supporting candidates, deals, alliances and power games in the wings.[21] Should one, therefore, deduce that the regional assemblies are tribunes of opposition when the parties of the Left have a majority and that they are in a struggle against the regional prefect, the State's representative, in the same way as they are in struggle against the government in the Palais Bourbon? This would be an exaggerated conclusion to draw, particularly as local and regional constraints and the diversity of situations makes any kind of generalisation impossible.

Thus, changes in the power relationships are insufficient to bring about a new form of participation which breaks with secular habits and is accompanied by new behaviour patterns . . . which are, nevertheless, evident outside the institutions newly created, but for different reasons.

The emergence of new regional behaviour patterns
For some years, in fact, new attitudes and behaviour patterns have been developing outside the regional institutions. There has been a tendency to bypass the legal political and administrative authorities. This behaviour is particularly forceful when it is the expression of autonomist claims within the framework of the historical region with a linguistic and cultural basis, and without reference to the territorial boundaries of 1956. This is especially the case in Brittany, Occitania,[22] Corsica and, naturally, the Basque Country and French Catalonia.

In spite of the unique character of each one of these regions there do exist a number of common features:

(1) They belong to those regions which did not benefit from the economic expansion of the preceding period: their products – wine and meat – do not benefit, in Brussels, from a Community income as favourable as that allotted to the more favoured

regions producing wheat and beet. Under-industrialised, they are the victims of both national and Community political restraints, of industrial concentration and of the search for the profitability which results from it. As they suffer from high unemployment, they are more often than not mere labour reserves for the expanding industrial towns and regions, and/or holiday areas, in which external capital in search of substantial profit from the exploitation of the tourist industry is invested, without any permanent benefit to the local community.

(2) These unfavourable economic conditions destroy social balance and contribute to the development of a feeling of insecurity as a result of the disappearance of the old society which consisted of family farms and a certain number of local traditional activities which are no longer profitable.

(3) The population of these regions is painfully aware of the loss of its linguistic and cultural identity. It is true that it has always been the victim of a centralised and uniform education system which fought against local dialects and 'outdated' cultural practices.

The combination of relative economic underdevelopment and the progressive decay of cultural differences has favoured a new awareness and autonomist behaviour which has extended even to physical violence. Three types of behaviour can be distinguished:

(1) The cultural behaviour of the Breton bards and the Occitanian *felibres*[23] who fight for the preservation of the language and literature of a minority culture. Certain of them do not question the legal political and administrative organisation; others, conversely, fight for an 'ethnic' and regional Europe which would do away with the national bodies which suffocate the life of ethnic minorities.[24]

(2) The political behaviour of notables agitating as a pressure group to obtain favourable measures from the political authorities. Thus CELIB, the co-ordinating committee for the study of Breton interests, has for years adopted the policy of political and parliamentary pressure in order to defend the economic interests of the Breton *départements*.

(3) Recent behaviour resulting from regionalism of a revolutionary nature, like that of the Front for the Liberation of Brittany, Action for the Recognition of Corsica, and other less well-known organisations which analyse the current situation – in spite of the theoretical and strategic differences which separate these organisations – in terms of imperialism, by analogy with the freedom movements of the Third World:[25] the national

minorities of France are internal colonies and the analysis of the colonial phenomenon can be applied to them; economic imperialism is linked to French cultural imperialism; both class struggle and the liberation of national minorities must be demanded.

Intellectuals attempt to elaborate a theory which reconciles autonomist aspirations with Marxist-inspired socialism.[26] Without adequate popular support, these movements are condemned to play a fringe role and will either return to retrospective and nostalgic positions (the culturalist organisations) or be swallowed up by the extreme Left (the revolutionary organisations) and thus descend into logomachy and sectarianism.

To whom do these organisations, and notably the revolutionary ones, appeal? To very few, no doubt, in comparison with the traditional organisations (parties, trades unions and professional groups) which have superior means and a much larger potential for mobilisation. And yet they have a sufficiently fertile soil, within the context of current social movements (strikes, demonstrations by peasants and winegrowers), to express autonomist grievances in speeches and symbols (slogans, flags) as though many of the demonstrators were attempting to find an ethnic identity in defending their economic and professional interests. They may also serve to crystallise more radical attitudes. This is the case in Brittany, where the FLB, estimating the situation to be pre-revolutionary, has launched itself into an armed struggle and claims responsibility for a certain number of assassination attempts. It is also true in Occitania where 'the activists can take advantage of the current disarray in the wine industry by cunningly mingling Occitanian claims from the Left with Poujadism of a most reactionary and violent nature, and by embracing Proudhonian and ecological ideas . . .'[27] The dramatic events in Aleria, in Corsica, in August 1975 and in the region of Narbonne at the beginning of 1976 show that the discontent is sufficiently deep for this new regional behaviour to be taken seriously.

In general, it seems that this behaviour is part of the latent and yet manifest unrest which has existed since May 1968,[28] part of the questioning of the centralised and bureaucratic organisation of the French State, part of the search for basic communities built on interpersonal links, part of a solidarity based on deep human rapports.

Under these conditions, is it possible to reduce the problem of regionalisation to one of deconcentration,[29] or to one of decentralisation within the broader framework of European integration?[30]

Figure 2   *Plan of Regional and Departmental Organisation*

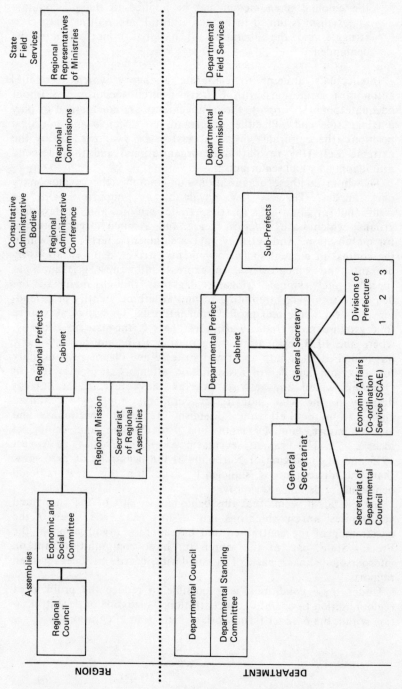

Figure 3 *The French Regions*

CONCLUSION

The regional reforms were born of a need to employ economic space in a new way. Defined and applied by an administration which remains the off-shoot of a long historical tradition of centralisation, these reforms have had only a limited capacity for innovation.

In legal terms they do not go beyond the stage of a form of decentralisation which is expressed through control of the machinery of co-ordination and through constant recourse to central authority through the intermediary of the regional prefect in order to decide, act, obtain a decision of a general nature.

Doubtless, this state of affairs is in conformity with the French model of society, in keeping with the French taste for distant and diffuse authority, for impersonal rules which ensure, in principle, the independence of all, whilst protecting each from the arbitrariness of these same authorities.[31] But is this model not in the process of changing under the influence of new constraints and protest movements which are affecting much of the public sector – law, army, university? Are these not the signs of a deeper change?

NOTES

1 According to the texts used by T. Flory, the origin of the term can be attributed to a Provençal poet, M. de Berluc-Perussis (1874), or to Barrès in 1899. T. Flory, *Le Mouvement régional français* (Paris: PUF, 1966).

2 C. Maurras, *Mes Idées politiques* (Paris: Fayard, 1968), pp. 220–1.

3 Doubtless Maurras had read Tocqueville's work *L'Ancien Régime et la Révolution* correctly. This work provides overwhelming proof for Maurrassian logic: the Revolution and the Empire only continued the centralising of the French monarchy.

4 Quotation taken from Flory, *Le Mouvement régional français*.

5 P. Barral, 'Idéal et pratique du régionalisme dans le régime de Vichy', *Revue française de sciences politiques*, vol. 24, no. 5 (October, 1974), pp. 911–40.

6 The opposition of the Senators and the local notables was supposedly one of the causes of the failure of the referendum of 27 April 1969. *Cahiers de l'Institut d'Etudes politiques de Grenoble* (Paris: Cujas, 1970), p. 500.

7 Ch. Roig, 'L'administration locale et les changements sociaux', *Administration Traditionnelle et Planification Régionale*, Cahiers de la FNSP (Paris: Colin, 1964), p. 14.

8 J. L. Quermonne, 'Vers un régionalisme fonctionnel?', *Revue française de science politique*, vol. 13, no. 4 (December 1963). pp. 849–76.

9 See the chapter by Thoenig, pp. 81–2 above.

10 C. de Vos, 'La région à la recherche d'un sens', *Urbanisation, Développement régional et pouvoirs politiques*, Annales de la Faculté des Lettres et Sciences humaines de Nice (Laboratoire de Sociologie), Nice, 1975, pp. 141–2.

11 P. Camous, 'La genèse du projet gouvernemental', *La Réforme régionale et le référendum du 27 Avril 1969* (Paris: Cujas, 1970), p. 31.

12 Debate in the National Assembly, *Journal Officiel*, 27 April 1972, p. 1106.

13 *Dauphiné Libéré*, 16 January 1974.

14 ibid.

15 During the sittings, the parliamentarians have appeared far more at ease than the departmental councillors or the municipal councillors who have only had experience at local level. The locally elected representatives, departmental councillors or representatives of the municipal councils, have felt themselves to be cast in the shade. Sometimes they have even been relegated to the role of observers in a contest whose rules were alien to them! The desire to give the regional council a more 'localist' image has been expressed by many representatives of departmental or municipal assemblies. And the frustration of certain locally elected members is evident when they complain of this supremacy: 'the guiding principle which I would like to see dominate in this assembly, and I say it in the name of a certain number of councillors, would be that we try not to devote too much time to matters of parliamentary interest but rather concern ourselves with what is happening at the local level' (Regional Council of Rhône-Alpes, 15 January 1974, roneo verbatim report, p. 15).

A Member of Parliament also denounced this tendency: 'as a Member of Parliament I have felt, and share the concern of a considerable number of councillors who are not parliamentarians, that it is regrettable that the work necessary to the smooth running of our assembly should be essentially carried out by parliamentarians' (Regional Council of Rhône-Alpes, ibid., p. 12).

16 See the chapter by Birnbaum, pp. 114–26 above.

17 P. Grémion, 'La théorie de l'apprentissage institutionnel et la régionalisation du cinquième Plan', *Revue française de sciences politiques*, vol. 22, no. 2 (April, 1973), pp. 308–9.

18 P. Grémion and J. P. Worms, *Les Institutions régionales et la société locale* (Paris: CNRS, Groupe de sociologie des organisations, 1968).

19 Grémion, 'La théorie de l'apprentissage institutionnel', pp. 305–21.

20 J. L. Bodiguel, 'La consultation régionale', *La Réforme régionale et le référendum du 27 Avril 1969*, op. cit., pp. 93–4.

21 A. Sorbara, 'Mise en place des utilisations régionales dans Midi-Pyrénées'; M.-F. Souchon, 'Mise en place des institutions régionales dans Rhône-Alpes': Communications aux Journées d'Etudes de la section languedocienne de l'Institut Français des Sciences Administratives, Rapport et communications, Montpellier, 2–3 December 1974, Université de Montpellier 1 et Université des Sciences Sociales de Toulouse.

22 The territorial limits of Occitania are an unending source of controversy. In spite of common historical, cultural and linguistic bases, there are deep differences between the different components of Occitania, even between Languedoc-Roussillon and Provence.

23 *Felibres* is the term applied to a member of the 'felebrige' – a society of poets and prose writers formed in 1854 with the object of preserving the Provencal dialect (Translator's note).

24 For example, G. Heraud, *L'Europe des ethnies* (Paris: Presses d'Europe, 1963).

25 Revolutionary regionalism developed after the upheavals of the Algerian war. The best-known and the oldest work on this subject is: R. Lafont, *La Révolution régionaliste* (Paris: Gallimard, 1967).

26 A reading of some numbers of *Les Temps Modernes* dedicated to national minorities – August–September 1973, 553 pages – reveals the ambitions and defects of current analyses. In fact:

'(a) how can the aspirations of minorities be articulated within the context of a theory which considers men as the abstract member of a universal society?

(b) by limiting French nationalism to the ideological expression of the interests of the bourgeoisie, one fails to grasp the importance of cultural factors which are at the basis of a feeling of national 'belonging' of which history offers many examples;

(c) how can the struggle of these nationalities be articulated, given the heterogeneity of the so-called revolutionary social classes which go to make up each one of these nationalities in France?'

27 G. Bazalgues, 'Les organisations occitanes', *Les Temps Modernes*, op. cit., p. 158.

28 H. Marcuse incorporates the regional dispute into his analysis of May 1968: 'The first revolt which aimed at radical transmutation of values, a qualitative transformation of the way of life . . . the graffiti of the "angry youth" linked Karl Marx to André Breton: the slogan "all power to the imagination" corresponds to "committees everywhere": a pianist played jazz at the barricades, and the red flag did not spoil the beauty of the statue to the author of *Les Misérables*: the students on strike in Toulouse demanded the renaissance of the language of the troubadours and the albigeois.' *Vers la libération* (Paris: Minuit, 1969), p. 36.

29 According to the authors of various reforms undertaken since 1964.

30 According to the theory of regional power so dear to Servan-Schreiber and the Reformist Movement.

31 M. Crozier, *Le Phénomène bureaucratique* (Paris: Le Seuil, 1963).

INDEX